DALHOUSIE UNIVERSITY
SCHOOL OF LIBRARY AND INFORMATION STUDIES SERIES

Hot, Hotter, Hottest

THE BEST OF THE YA HOTLINE

EDITED BY VIVIAN HOWARD

Dalhousie University School of Library and Information Studies Series, No. 3

THE SCARECROW PRESS, INC.
Lanham, Maryland • London
2002

SCARECROW PRESS, INC.

Published in the United States of America
by Scarecrow Press, Inc.
4720 Boston Way, Lanham, Maryland 20706
www.scarecrowpress.com

4 Pleydell Gardens, Folkestone
Kent CT20 2DN, England

British Library Cataloguing in Publication Information Available

Library of Congress Cataloging-in-Publication Data, Available

Available ISBN 0-8108-4240-8 (alk. paper)

♾™ The paper used in this publication meets the minimum requirements of American National Standard for Information Sciences—Permanence of Paper for Printed Library Materials, ANSI/NISO Z39.48-1992. Manufactured in the United States of America.

This book is dedicated to
David, Anna, and Geoffrey.

Contents

Foreword

YA Hotline: 24 YEARS AND COUNTING

Toward the end of the '70s, when *YA Hotline (YAHL)* began publication, there was a growing movement to establish a separate identity for young adult studies. Children's literature, with its long, distinguished history, was incorporated into the curricula of most library schools and schools of education. Young adult courses were less common, and the idea of such a specialization was somewhat controversial. Many veteran children's librarians saw no distinction between service to children and service to adolescents, and they were reluctant to cede a portion of their domain.

The courses offered at the time were usually entitled "Young Adult Literature." However, this was a bit of a misnomer, perhaps even an oxymoron! The adolescent user group prefers comic books, graphic novels, magazines, newspapers, and nonfiction for their reading pleasure rather than anything that might be identified as "literature." In addition, the fiction that many teens enjoy has frequently been attacked and disparaged by critics and professors as subliterature in the form of "problem novels." Lovers of children's literature, with their motto of "Only the best is good enough," found YA literature hard to swallow.

However, it was clear to those working with adolescents that the traditional concern with quality literature found in children's literature courses needed to be broadened in a YA course to embrace material addressing the developmental needs, concerns, and preferences of teenagers. The debate surrounding these issues was led by such influential advocates as Dorothy Broderick and Mary Kay Chelton.

Not only was (and is) there a great difference between serving children and responding to the needs of adolescents, it was also evident, early on, that the personalities of the librarians working with the two distinct groups often differed. At my first ALA Annual Conference, I walked into a meeting of the Children's Services Division (as it was then called) and found a quiet, reasonable, polite discussion taking place concerning themes in classic children's literature. Some of the members knitted while they talked and listened.

The Young Adult Service Division meeting, which I went to next, was quite different in tone and content. A great roar of debate and disagreement surrounding topics such as sex education, drug use, delinquency, and protest spilled out into the corridor. Tables were pounded (and sometimes stood upon) and voices were raised by young librarians who looked and acted more like their clients than like the sedate group of children's librarians down the hall.

Out of this ferment came a clear understanding that any attempt to teach a conventional literature course, with a focus on comparative themes, symbolic references, and character analysis, was largely irrelevant; worse, it let down adolescents with the following needs:

* Learning to read
* Learning to enjoy reading
* Finding themselves in what they read
* Reading current, accurate, well-chosen material dealing with issues important to them and which could be applied to their lives

Beyond this, students in a young adult services course—that is, those who aspire to serve teens in school or public libraries or in the classroom—need to learn about adolescents: their ambitions, fears and needs, in order to construct services appropriate for them.

A California publication of the time, the *Young Adult Alternative Newsletter (YAAN)* pointed the way toward a new model for youth service. Produced by a band of radical northern Californian YA librarians and edited by Carol Starr, the yellow-colored, long-format newsletter was packed with descriptions of exemplary and original YA programs, tips for practicing librarians, and avant-garde advocacy for teens. *YAAN* was outspoken, hard-hitting, and com-

mitted. It was practically the only publication available in the field at the time, and it was eagerly read by subscribers across North America.

YAAN provided the model for the newsletter I created when I began to teach the YA course at the University of Toronto in 1976. I decided to ask the students in the course to produce a similar sort of newsletter with a Canadian emphasis. Production of the newsletter constituted the major assignment for the course. I took the idea and the title with me when I moved to Dalhousie University in 1977.

The pedagogical aims of the *YAHL* assignment were clear from the outset:

* To provide a means for the students to move outside the books and the classroom and to meet, talk with, interview, question, and listen to young adults
* To meet and exchange information with professional youth workers, librarians, and others
* To obtain experience in carrying out surveys and data collection
* To learn to write, edit, layout, publish, and promote a newsletter
* To learn to compose for publication
* To learn to work as part of a team with fellow students
* To explore in-depth a theme of importance to adolescents
* To gain a measure of recognition as a published writer

With no computers or word processing, the early issues were fairly rough and ready. Copy was typewritten. Illustrations were hand drawn and often tipped in unevenly.

The December 1977 issue, however, demonstrated the true potential for such a journal. The YA class produced a carefully researched issue on human relations and sexuality. The core of the issue was what was termed (tongue placed firmly in cheek) "A modest bookshelf on human relations and sexuality." The bookshelf represented an attempt to select a basic collection of excellent sex education materials suitable for every high school, junior high, and public library. The students in the YA class examined and reviewed everything available.

The issue also included a bibliography of reviewing tools and a list of suggested criteria for evaluating such materials for collections. Examples of rejected titles were also included to illustrate the point. Benjamin Spock's *A Teenager's Guide to Life and Love*, for example, was rejected as out-of-date, misleading, and paternalistic. (The student reviewer noted that homosexuality was buried between sections on Sexual Deviance and Sadism and Masochism.)

YAHL gained considerable attention for that issue. Orders were received from around the world, and a bulk order was placed by the Family Planning Division of the Department of Health and Welfare.

Over the years the subscription list grew to 300, with readers in the United Kingdom, Australia, the United States, and nationally across Canada.

Themes for issues are chosen by the students in the course. Topics are discussed and students self-select themselves into topic teams. This informed and youthful approach means that *YAHL* has frequently anticipated trends and covered topics not treated in the rest of the professional media. As early as 1978, for example, Issue #3 examined the "fractured family" and the impact of divorce on the lives of teenagers. Other prescient issues were #5, "Write On," in which high school students were interviewed about their hopes to write and get published. *YAHL* supplied some useful suggestions and a bibliography of publishing tools. For Issue #9, government statis-

tics and personal interviews were used to examine youth employment. "Women and SF," Issue #17, listed the large number of female science fiction writers (sometimes writing under a male alias), discussed sexism in the literature and especially in the magazine covers, and published, for the first time, many beautiful illustrations drawn by aspiring teenaged artists.

The double issue #19/20 gave a definitive annotated listing of Canadian YA titles. Students working on Issue #24, "Nuclear War," were taken aback to discover during their extensive interviewing, just how deeply this little discussed topic was on the minds of adolescents. Popular literature was covered in Issue #25/26, "Murder Mysteries," and Issue #33, "Romance Reading." The earlier issue on sexuality was brought up to date in Issue #29/30, "Sex Ed Materials." In the early '90s, *YAHL* produced a very useful issue on AIDS. "Women and Violence" was the topic of Issue #41. Team members came away shaken by the accounts they received concerning date rape and other assaults. In the late '90s a "green" issue was produced, taking up environmental concerns. *YAHL* continues to tackle topics of interest to teens and those who serve them.

It is encouraging to see, now that I have retired and left Dalhousie University, that *YAHL*, one of the longest running YA journals in the world, continues to provide both a useful assignment for students in the YA course and a useful professional journal for the subscribing practitioners. *YAHL* has come a long way from the first paste-up editions to what is now—a slickly produced and attractive production. The goal, however, remains the same: to bring adolescents, YA service students, and practitioners together for the good of all.

Larry Amey
Albuquerque, New Mexico

Introduction

It is one of the great pleasures of my current role as instructor of the Young Adult Literature and Media Interests class to oversee students as they collaborate to produce an issue of the *YA Hotline*. Since I stepped into the shoes left vacant by the departure of Larry Amey, I have been continually impressed by the creativity, originality, and commitment of students as they prepare their newsletters.

When the idea of compiling a "best of the *YA Hotline*" volume was first suggested, I was enthusiastic about the opportunity to find a wider readership for some of the excellent work that has gone into the *Hotline* over the past two and a half decades. However, selecting the specific articles to appear in this publication was no easy task. First of all, I strove to achieve a representative range and balance of topics. I also tried to include articles of most immediate value to those teachers and librarians and others who work directly with teens. Second, I wanted to make sure that the information still had relevance and appeal to a twenty-first-cen-

tury readership. This involved verifying all the URLs mentioned in this volume. The URLs for the various Web sites were current as of May 2001. Third, I needed to contact the original authors to obtain permission to reproduce their work.

The final requirement proved to be the most challenging. It was relatively easy to track down the contributors to the most recent issues, but it was much more difficult to locate individuals who had produced issues of the *YA Hotline* in the 1980s and 1970s. As a result, this volume is weighted more heavily toward the past decade. I would have loved to have included articles from the very earliest days of the *Hotline*, but too many of the original authors had long since lost contact with the School of Library and Information Studies at Dalhousie University.

Nonetheless, this volume does contain a fascinating sampling of some of the issues that the *YA Hotline* has explored over the years. The articles often deal with material that was, at the time, newsbreaking. Eating disorders were just beginning to gain media attention in the 1980s, and the *YA Hotline* devoted Issues 44 and 58 to a probing discussion of the topic of body image and young adults. The Internet was just emerging as a source of teen fascination in the mid-1990s, and the *Hotline* was there to analyze both sides of this double-edged sword in Issue 57. Issue 59 explores teens' ongoing love affair with the car. Issues 53 and 61 tackle the popularity of horror, the occult, and witchcraft in young adult media, while Issue 55 examines the rise of the graphic novel, from underground phenomenon to mainstream respectability. Two very recent issues analyze the appeal of the biography to young adults (Issue 62) and the importance of multicultural literature for teens (Issue 64). The topics included in this volume are of high interest and relevance both for young adults themselves and for those who work with them.

The *YA Hotline*, as Larry Amey has already pointed out, is a publication in which process and product merge. Many of the individuals who have worked on the *YA Hotline* over the years have gone on to work with young adults as youth services librarians or teachers. Others have chosen different paths and work in professional settings in which their contact with teens is minimal. Whatever the ultimate professional path, however, everyone who has worked on the *YA Hotline* has learned an incalculable amount from the experience. I am delighted that their work can now be celebrated in this volume.

Several people have contributed their time and energy to this project. I would like to thank all the students over the years who have worked on the *YA Hotline*, whether or not their work is included in this volume. Your energy, creativity, and enthusiasm has been the driving force behind the success of this publication. Thanks also go to Dr. Norman Horrocks, former director of the School of Library and Information Studies at Dalhousie University, for first suggesting the idea for this volume and for his help in the editing process, and to Dr. Bertrum MacDonald, current director, for providing the necessary institutional support. I also owe a huge thank-you to Shanna Balogh, Linda Dehmel, and Rae-Lynne Patterson for their typing, proofreading, and overall good humour throughout this project. My gratitude to you all.

Vivian Howard
Halifax, Nova Scotia
Canada

Eating Disorders

YA Hotline, Issue No. 44, 1989

DENISE SOMERS, RUBY B. WEINSHENKER, AND MURIEL M. ZIMMER

DEFINING OUR TERMS

Anorexia nervosa and bulimia are eating disorders that pose an increasing threat to young adults. According to the *Diagnostic and Statistical Manual of Mental Disorders*, the most widely accepted standard for diagnosing mental problems, "anorexia nervosa requires evidence of the following in a patient: an intense fear of becoming obese that does not diminish as weight loss progresses; disturbance of body image, e.g., claiming to 'feel fat' even when emaciated; loss of at least 25 percent of original body weight; and refusal to maintain normal body weight. Bulimia is characterized by secret, episodic binge eating and termination of such eating episodes by abdominal pain, sleep, or self-induced vomiting; frequent weight fluctuations of more than 10 pounds due to alternating binges and fasts; awareness that the eating pattern is abnormal and fear of not being able to stop eating voluntarily; and depressed mood and self-deprecating thoughts following the eating binges."

The focus of this issue of the *YA Hotline* is on the existing problem. This is a feminist issue. Personal and societal expectations and family pressures predispose young girls to eating disorders. To compile information that would be of use to those who work with young adults, we interviewed people who are involved in diagnosing anorexia and bulimia. Then we compiled our information. We discussed some of the issues and questioned young adults. We concluded by discussing the importance of public awareness of eating disorders and personal responsibility for recovery.

IDENTIFYING ANOREXIA AND BULIMIA

Symptoms common to both:

* extreme concern about appearances
* social withdrawal
* low self-esteem
* secretive vomiting

- moodiness
- guilt about eating
- food preoccupation
- feeling fat without reason
- frequent weighing
- hoarding food
- use of laxatives, diuretics, purgatives, and emetics
- inflexibility
- perfectionism
- intolerance
- oversensitivity

Symptoms of anorexia:

- significant weight loss without any reason
- reduction of eating, denying hunger
- dieting without a reason
- unusual eating habits and preoccupation with diet
- amenorrhea in women
- signs of starvation, hair thinning and loss, fine hair (lanugo) on body, bloated feeling, yellowed appearance of palms and soles of the feet

Symptoms of bulimia:

- unusual dental problems
- swelling of the glands under the jaw
- habitual overeating when stressed
- weight fluctuations of ten pounds or more
- evidence of purging by vomiting/laxative/diuretic use
- evidence of binging

RISKS OF ANOREXIA AND BULIMIA

- Malnutrition
- Dental problems

- Severe dehydration
- Rupturing of internal membranes
- Ruptured stomach and esophagus
- Gastritis
- Ulcers
- Vagal-nerve block
- Irritable-bowel syndrome
- Bowel tumors
- Megacolon
- Intestinal infection
- Ruptured facial blood vessels
- "Insulin Dump" (from sugar binges)
- Hypoglycemia
- Chronic sinusitis
- Kidney damage
- Bleeding and infection of the throat
- Endocrine problems
- Abnormal metabolism
- Electrolyte imbalances which can lead to various neuromuscular problems, including muscle spasms, cardiac arrest and death

COPING WITH EATING DISORDERS

The anorexic or bulimic person wants to have control and will resent it if someone tries to take this away. Since this is a food obsession it is not good to dwell on food-related discussions. It is better to encourage involvement in non-food related activities. Blame reinforces the person's feelings of failure, and comments on the person's weight or appearance will not be helpful, as people who suffer from eating disorders have a low sense of esteem at this time. Denial is usually the first reaction of the person with eating disorders, and patience is necessary in dealing with this long-term illness. Professional help is essential for the anorexic or bulimic person. Counseling those who have to cope with people who have eating disorders will help to prevent the problem from interfering with the normal functioning of the family. Knowledge about eating disorders is important because understanding is the key to coping.

A BULIMIC'S STORY

E. asked that she not be identified by name. She is seventeen years old, and a Grade 10 student at a local Halifax high school. She works part-time in a library, after school and on weekends, shelving library materials. In the remaining time, she writes poetry and listens to music. She most enjoys spending time with her boyfriend, taking walks and going to movies together. E. has blue eyes, auburn hair and . . . bulimia.

She remembers the first time she thought that there was something wrong with her body. At thirteen years, she was teased at school by being called ugly. Although she was of normal weight, she was more developed physically than the other girls her age, and this was a source of embarrassment for her. She was afraid of developing further. At that time, she was enrolled in dance classes where her dance instructor encouraged a lithe, thin body. To appear thinner when dancing, she would tightly wrap cloth around her chest. A perfectionist, and wanting to be liked, she began a series of diets. When dieting left her extremely hungry, she began to binge, eating large quantities of food at one sitting. When the binge was over, she would be uncomfortable and guilt-ridden. Unable to bear those feelings, she would put her fingers or a spoon down her throat to cause vomiting. She felt at that time that it made sense to do it. Purging made her feel more relaxed.

At first, the purging behaviour was carried out only after the binge eating episodes. Soon, however, E. began to purge after anything was eaten. At her worst point, she purged five times per day. She recalls being very secretive. She was living with her parents then and did not want them to discover her behaviour. So while she vomited, she would turn the bathroom shower on. Or, she would go to her "secret place" in a field beyond her house to purge. Her eating habits, she believes, caused her to experience constipation, and she relied heavily on laxatives. Between bouts of bulimic activity E. would eat very little for extended periods of time, and during a four month period, her weight dropped from 115 lbs. to 75 lbs. Smiling at the irony, she recalls that while she was starving and bingeing, she took a daily vitamin pill.

Soon, others began to notice that something was wrong. A friend discovered E.'s behaviour, and approached the school's guidance counsellor. E. remembers pleading with the counsellor that her parents not be told of her disorder. However, her parents were already aware that something was wrong. E.'s mother had found her diary, which contained the details of the eating disorder. When confronted by her parents, E. denied she had a problem and told them that she purged only once in a while. E. attempted to convince her friends that what she was doing was harmless. She still feels ashamed of her attempts to be "convincing." It is interesting to note, that when E. watched *The Karen Carpenter Story* (1989) on television, she did not identify with

Karen Carpenter. She viewed their behaviour as dissimilar. E. felt that Karen was crazy, and had a worse problem than she did.

E. began seeing a number of counsellors. First there was a series of visits with a psychologist. The visits proved unsuccessful E. admits, because she was not yet ready to confront her problem. Sessions with a psychiatrist followed, and eventually she was hospitalized for depression. Finally, E. felt the time was right to deal with her behaviour. She was tired of scheduling her life around binging and purging. There were changes, new things in her life that needed attention: a new job, a new boyfriend, new demands at school. And, E. just felt too ill to continue the destructive behaviour. Soon, she began meeting with a counsellor with whom she felt comfortable. E. began to forgive herself about her past and to work and concentrate on the future.

Today E. experiences various health problems that she believes originated with her bulimic activities, and this worries her. Although she has gained some weight, she still remains 10 lbs. below what is recommended. However, during the past months, E. has made great strides, and believes that her bulimia is under control. And, she is looking forward to her future, to attending university, being a social worker, marrying, having children. But for the moment, she continues to heal.

THE CHANGING IMAGE OF FEMALE BEAUTY

One of the precious few things in life that we can depend upon is change. The image of what is beautiful in women changes according to the particular time frame under discussion and its social and cultural surroundings. This article traces viewpoints on female beauty in order to place our present views on beauty within an historical context. Unfortunately, our present views of female beauty, which are influenced considerably by the media, encourage females to aspire towards a universally thin image. The problem with today's present value of thin, female beauty is that many women try to attain this thinness at all costs and in dangerous ways.

Historical research proves that plump women are beautiful. A fat woman is a sure sign of a good provider, that is, she can sustain childbirth and disease with bodily resources to spare. The ampleness of women in paintings by Botticelli and Rubens verify that "plump is beautiful."

Plumpness is still considered beautiful in some parts of the world today. In India, where many people are still unable to meet daily survival needs, plump women are considered beautiful because this is a sign of wealth. Plump women can afford to eat more than enough. This wealth of food is seen as beautiful.

Female thinness is considered beautiful throughout most of North America today. This is unfortunate because only a small percentage of humans are naturally lean, or ectomorphs, while others are naturally muscular, or mesomorphs, and still others are naturally chubby, or endomorphs.

Humans are social creatures; we live in groups. We depend on feedback from our friends, family, and those around us at school or at work to comment on how we look and dress. This personal feedback influences our behaviour. The media gives us feedback and influences our behaviour as well. The media sends us subtle messages about how we should look and dress. Difficulty arises when people fail to distinguish between the version of reality presented in the media and the real world.

Watching any amount of television can lead us to the false belief that all females are generally attractive, if not gorgeous; all females wear makeup; all females are able bodied; all females, except for a tiny minority, are under the age of 35; all women enjoy polishing furniture and cooking; all women hold down white collar jobs; and all females, except for a tiny minority, are thin. The media presents these images of females as stereotypical.

In reality many females are plain looking, many females do not wear makeup, many females are disabled, many females are over 35, many women detest housework, many women hold down clerical or blue collar jobs, and many females are not thin. The sad part about the media's stereotyping is that many females buy this image. We've been had. This acceptance of the media's image of us leaves us unhappy for many of us do not fit this image. This all leads to the unhealthy attitude that if we are not thin we are most certainly not beautiful.

Some women are overly influenced by media images of very thin beautiful females. Dr. Neelma Dhar, of the Eating Disorder Clinic at the Victoria General Hospital, Halifax, says that many women flirt with eating disorders in their quest for thinness. An overzealous approach to thinness gives us eating disorders, weight control centers, and diets, diets, diets to lose those extra pounds. But how thin is thin? Twiggy, the famous British model, was certainly too thin. Even Jane Fonda admits to bulimic bouts. What price is glory in this battle for thinness?

We need to realize that female ideals of beauty can be perverse at times. Examples of female beauty practices from the present and past that are questionable, if not dangerous, include:

* Ballerinas that look beautiful *en pointe*, but in reality have horrible looking feet because the body is not designed to withstand balancing all its weight on the points of its toes for extended periods of time. Ballerinas' feet are bruised and bleed regularly from this abuse.
* To some degree, high heels damage women. Most North American women consider high heels as the only proper foot attire for formal occasions. High heels change a body's alignment, put undue strain on a person's back and legs, and can create back problems if they are worn excessively.
* The women of the Ubangi tribe were once encouraged to put large wooden disks in their lower lips; this was culturally accepted as beautiful. This unnatural practice hindered these women's ability to eat and talk.
* One Asian tribe used to decorate women's necks and lower legs with brass rings. The rings were permanently fitted in place. The more rings you wore, the more beautiful you appeared in this culture. Collarbones were distorted and crushed into the body in order to accomplish this. These women could not move around or feed themselves easily.
* The Chinese used to bind wealthy women's feet so that they would appear smaller and more beautiful. The arch was physically distorted and some of the foot was cut back in order to accomplish this. Women with bound feet could not walk by themselves; they needed their servant to support them.

With these examples of perverted beauty practices in mind, it doesn't seem such a large step to perverting eating patterns in order to attain a proper degree of fashionable thinness. Once again females are being sold a poor bill of goods. It is not necessary to be thin to be beautiful anymore than it is necessary to wear wooden disks in our lower lips to be beautiful.

Recommendations

It is time to listen to the reports of such groups as Media Watch, a national women's organization that analyzes the images of women in the media. Martha Muzychka, a representative of Media Watch, ranks media in the top three influences on children. As well, Ann Bell, the president of the Advisory Council on the Status of Women in Newfoundland, blames the education system for failing to show young women what the outside world will be like for them.

It is time to ask questions. We must question our culture's portrayal of female beauty. We must question our own perceptions of female beauty. Heather Ferguson, a counsellor at Saint Mary's University in Halifax who designs Body/Image workshops, suggests asking yourself the following questions to determine if you are at home with your own body. Do you:

* Avoid or hate looking at yourself in the mirror when you get out of the bath or shower?
* At such times, find yourself zeroing in on your "flaws" (e.g., hips or stomach) and ignoring your "assets" (shapely arms, small waist . . .)?

* Find it difficult to accept your basic body shape and type, whether square or muscular, pear-shaped, or short and curvy?
* Hate clothes shopping because you think nothing suits you?
* Constantly compare yourself to friends and envy them their bodies, or certain aspects of their bodies?
* Compare yourself to models and actors/actresses—and get very depressed when you do not match up?
* Think that if you were thinner or better proportioned you would be happier at school/work or in your relationship?
* Find yourself arguing with your partner/lover/friends about your body? (They say you look fine, and you insist they are lying.)
* Worry that he/she finds you undesirable because you are badly proportioned or fear that you are being compared with others?

If you answer yes to many of these questions, you are not willing to accept your body just as it really is. You are not willing to accept yourself. Chances are that if you long for a more svelte form than your mirror reflects, this svelte image you hold within your mind's eye is greatly influenced by the media. See this media influence for what it is, a $40 billion, big business hype.

CONCLUSION

Young women need to be informed about reality, and the media is certainly not doing this. It is up to the educators to impress on young women that media images are fairy tales, and not to be taken seriously.

We must encourage young women to further their education. Tracey Jones, the head librarian at the Halifax North Branch Public Library, tells young females to put their heart and soul into their education. Without an education they can look forward to perpetuating the cycle of women earning 65 cents for every dollar that men earn. It is up to us, as educators, to empower young women and provide them with accurate information about reality. The reality is that we must be vigilant and carefully examine the images of beauty presented to us. It is up to us to see that some examples of female beauty are anything but beautiful.

FICTION REVIEWS

Greenberg, Jan. *The Pig Out Blues.* **New York: Dell, 1982. ISBN 0-374-35937-7**

A dramatic account of a 15 year old's struggle for self-identity and happiness, this book will appeal to young, female teenagers. Jodie has a very troubled relationship with her mother, a single parent. Jodie finds release in the school's drama club, and in food binges. Jodie's mother, a fashion buyer, is insistent that Jodie control her weight. Jodie's world falls apart when she fails in the drama club, fainting at tryouts due to the stress of excessive dieting. Two friendships, one with a nearby family, the other with her boss, help Jodie through her hard times. The story is believable, and encourages the reader to accept that problems can be worked out. Written by the author of *I Never Promised You a Rose Garden.*

Harris, Dorothy Joan. *Even If It Kills Me.* **Richard Hill, ONT: Scholastic, 1987. 197 p. ISBN 0-590-71763-4**

Melanie Burton is the classic anorexic. She is a compulsive perfectionist, an A student, the quiet daughter. She wants to be noticed, and after her father's chance remark about puppy fat she begins to mimic her mother's dieting in the belief that thinness will make her popular.

She carries the disease to the point where she must be hospitalized, and after a confrontation with an even more severely afflicted anorexic, begins her slow recovery with a doctor's help.

Harris has thoroughly researched her subject. The book is a realistic chronicle of the disease from its roots in a lack of family communication, media influences, and teenage insecurity to its manifestation in compulsive arrangement of foods in patterns, mental lapses due to malnutrition, hair growth on the arms, vomiting, and death due to malnutrition. It is an interesting yet terrifying novel.

Hautzig, Deborah. *Second Star to the Right.* **New York: Greenwillow Books, 1981. 151 p. ISBN 0-688-00498-9**

Leslie Hiller is a fourteen-year-old who is hospitalized because of an eating disorder. Told in the first person voice, Leslie's purpose in the narrative is "to try to figure out how things turned out the way they did." Leslie is described as she gradually becomes anorexic. At first, Leslie appears as a happy, healthy teenager, until a preoccupation with her weight appears, with an all too common belief that if she were thin, life would be perfect. Standard dieting leads to self-starvation, and too weak to function, Leslie is hospitalized. Remarkably, the reader is allowed glimpses into Leslie's psyche through an internal dialogue: the actual erratic, hysteric thoughts which motivate the bizarre actions characteristic of the disorder. This internal dialogue lends understanding and compassion towards Leslie, and an emotional power to the narrative. The complex causes of the problem are alluded to throughout, and are "blame mom" in tone. A realistic ending is provided, not happy, but hopeful. The novel was nominated for the American Book Award in the children's fiction category in 1982. It is appropriate for ages 12 and up.

Hudlow, Emily Ellison. *Alabaster Chambers*. New York: St. Martin's Press, 1979. 215 p. ISBN 0-312-01702-2

Alabaster Chambers is a compelling narrative which places diagnosis and treatment of anorexia and bulimic behaviour within the context of complex inter-personal relationships. Telia loses her perspective on every aspect of her life because of her food obsession. Her preoccupation with control over her body prevents her from dealing with failed personal relationships and academic problems.

When Dr. Carolyn Stepler agrees to accept Telia as a patient her affair with Michael comes to an abrupt halt, but the consequences of this relationship jeopardizes Telia's recovery. This novel raises the question of whether an extra-marital fling can be justified and tests the boundaries of professional-client relationships. *Alabaster Chambers* emphasizes the preventative role of honest communication and the importance of obtaining psychiatric help to correct destructive habits of the mind and the need for medical care to arrest physical deterioration. This novel will be read with interest by anyone of high school age or older.

Josephs, Rebecca. *Early Disorder*. New York: Farrar Strauss Giroux, 1980. 186 p. ISBN 0-374-14579-Z

Willa Mahv is "an A student, an achiever, a favourite child, a promising young pianist, impressive to grown-ups." So why is she slowly starving herself to death? A dreadfully unhappy member of a successful, well adjusted family she feels smothered, and food is her method of gaining control.

Eventually a psychiatrist and her quiet French teacher help her conquer her fears and inadequacies; her dread of being female, growing up and going out on her own.

Josephs gives an intriguing look at anorexia through the eyes of a tortured victim. The equally tortured family; her revulsion of food; manipulation of others; the panic of the victim; and her attempt at recovery are rivetingly portrayed by the author.

Kafka, Franz. "The Hunger Artist," *Selected Stories of Franz Kafka*. New York: The Modern Library, 1952. ISBN 0-394-60422-9

A sensitive and symbolic work, Kafka's story will appeal to mature teens. The setting is last century Europe where a street performer works as a hunger artist. This performer regularly starves himself sitting inside a cage for 40 days, an attraction that mesmerizes the crowds. Some fans buy season tickets for the event, but the crowd finally tires of his show. Kafka is didactic. He points out how society feasts on depravity and he parodies the obsessive quality of artists. He insists that there must be limits or our world falls apart and goes mad. The wasted artist is replaced by a wild animal, and the jaded crowd awakens to this new amusement, the shocking spectacle of vibrant nature forced behind bars.

Levenkron, Steven. *The Best Little Girl in the World*. New York: Warner Books, 1981. ISBN 0-446-32278-4

In his compelling, insightful novel, Steven Levenkron follows 15 year old Francesca, an excellent student, model daughter, and aspiring ballerina, as she kills her "fat" self to become the "slim" and in control Kessa. Although a work of fiction, Levenkron accurately describes the world of anorexia nervosa, one in which he works professionally. He focuses on the key issues: the need for control, the complex causes which are seldom related to food, the destructiveness of the disorder, and the need for professional treatment. This book offers valuable information and support in the fight against eating disorders.

Levenkron, Steven. *Kessa*. New York: Warner Books, 1986. 247 p. ISBN 0-445-20175-4

One of America's foremost experts on anorexia nervosa, Steven Levenkron, reveals his deep and thorough understanding of this disease in the telling of Kessa's story. He compassionately details her struggles, fears, obsessions, and efforts to accept herself and her limitations. Rich intuitive descriptions provide a gripping and fascinating story that readers will remember long after the book is read. Although hard for some of us to understand, it is real life in a story. Of interest to all, this book will be of special interest to educators, to friends and families of those burdened with the disease, to the patients themselves, and to health professionals.

Miner, Jane Claypool. *Jeanne Up and Down*. New York: Scholastic, 1987. ISBN 0-590-40053-3

Jeanne Lee has three wishes: to be thin, to be blonde, and to be beautiful. Never mind that she is tall, big-boned, and has dark hair. She wants to lose 50 pounds in an attempt to reach this "ideal." Fifteen year old Jeanne comes from a middle-class family; she is struggling with her self-image, her acting ambitions, falling in love, a broken family, and changing friendships. Jane Claypool Miner, in a fast-paced, easy-to-read style, uses Jeanne's problems to highlight the turbulent times faced by all young adults as they attempt to learn about themselves. The novel is valuable in that it repeatedly points out

the importance of loving and accepting yourself as you are and not according to someone's "ideal."

Ney, John. *Ox Under Pressure*. Philadelphia: Lippincott, 1976. ISBN 0-397-31653-4

The third novel in John Ney's Ox Olmstead trilogy tells of Ox's sojourn in Long Island, New York, where he has travelled with his wealthy Palm Beach father. While there Ox becomes involved with Arabella Marlborough, the daughter of his father's old school mate.

The only child of an upper-middle-class family, Arabella suffered from anorexia and still is not fully recovered. Her father, an overbearing bully who wants to control Arabella's life and that of her over-tranquilized mother, constantly reminds her how much her treatment has cost him.

Arabella tells Ox that the disease occurs because, "One is starved for affection. It's a way of demonstrating that lack. It's a cry for help, a form of petulance, a kind of emotional sickness." Her disease forms an interesting contrast to Ox's obsessive overeating which seems to stem from the same lack of emotional sustenance.

Although Arabella is a secondary character, her disease is an important aspect of the plot and of her character, that of the fragile girl who buckles under the world's pressures. It is a useful introduction to the disease for many readers who may not be interested in reading a novel with a female protagonist.

Richman, Ivy. *The Hunger Scream*. New York: Walker & Co., 1983. 188 p. ISBN 0-8027-6514-9

Powerless within her family, Lily assumes control over one aspect of her life, her body. Through dieting, she can be slim like her mother; and by preventing herself from maturing normally, she can challenge her five-year-old sister Juju for her father's affection. Daniel, the black boy she loves, and Erica, her plump popular friend, notice that she has a problem. Daniel's grandmother and Ms. Snell at school also notice that something is seriously wrong, but Lily is not convinced. She prides herself on her self control and resents their involvement. She feels that her parents are trying to force her to eat as part of their effort to control her whole life. In silent desperation she runs and hides. When she returns she is ready to listen to Dr. Coburn's psychiatric analysis.

This is a useful book for those who work with young adults because the many factors that contribute to the anorexic condition are assessed, and hospital treatment and family therapy are discussed. A poignant story of one seventeen-year-old's struggle with anorexia, this novel has relevance for all young girls who feel that they are unable to free themselves from parental domination and for all parents who may be the unwitting cause of eating disorders.

Stren, Patti. *I Was a Fifteen Year Old Blimp.* Toronto: Irwin, 1985. 185 p. ISBN 0-7725-1538-7

Gabby Finklestein feels she is in control of her situation when she is in control of her weight. Then she develops bulimia nervosa. Subsequent events, a family who love her, a caring girlfriend, a camp counsellor, and a strong-willed boyfriend expedite her realization that talking about her problems will help. In addition she comes to the self-realization that being thin is not the answer to all of life's complications, and in the process she gains self-esteem. Patti Stren presents a moving portrait of young women and their sometimes drastic methods of weight control. As a young adult, Stren, herself, had a weight problem. Perhaps this experience helped her to develop these genuine characters and the intuitive story. Sometimes funny and sometimes sad, this account of Gabby's maturation is always quick paced, interesting, and entertaining. The book is of special interest to young adults and those interested in bulimia.

Willey, Margaret. *The Bigger Book of Lydia.* New York: Harper & Row, 1983. 215 p. ISBN 0-06-026485-3

At ten years, Lydia Bitte is very self-conscious about her small size. When her equally small father is killed in an accident, Lydia associates smallness with vulnerability, and becomes obsessed with growing. She begins "The Bigger Book," a notebook in which she records information about size, growth, danger, and death. At fifteen years, Lydia and her family welcome a house guest, Michelle, who at the same age as Lydia, boards with the family to be nearer the clinic where she is being treated for anorexia. A close friendship develops between Lydia and Michelle, and through their friendship, they acquire the strength to face their various problems. Although anorexia is not the dominant theme, its treatment within the novel is not serious, and Michelle as an anorexic is neither convincing nor believable; the notion of body size obsession and the meanings attributed to sizes, however, are addressed well. Most worthwhile is the friendship between the two interesting young women. This first novel is appropriate for ages 12 and up.

NONFICTION REVIEWS

Abraham, Suzanne and Derek Llewellyn-Jones. *Eating Disorders: The Facts.* **New York: Oxford University Press, 1987. 162 p. Index. ISBN 0-19-261699-4**

The physical, psychological, and social aspects, the precipitants and the possible cures for anorexia nervosa, bulimia and obesity are explained in straight forward, factual language. Case histories add a human dimension, and demonstrate the variety of individual problems these people encounter. Those afflicted, their families, friends and those wishing to gain a general understanding of these disorders will find this book useful.

Eagles, Douglas A. *Nutritional Diseases.* **New York: Franklin Watts, 1987. ISBN 0-531-10391-9**

In this book, Douglas Eagles has presented various aspects of nutritional diseases, such as starvation, diabetes and protein deficiency. Chapter 10 deals with eating disorders such as anorexia and bulimia. In 5 pages, Eagles clearly defines the disorders and highlights the complexities. This would be a very good reference book for a high school library. It provides a solid, basic knowledge as well as suggestions for further reading.

Kolodny, Nancy J. *When Food's a Foe: How to Confront and Conquer Eating Disorders.* **Toronto: Little, Brown, 1987. 143 p. ISBN 0-316-50167-0**

Written in an up-beat and conversational style, the purpose of the book is to help teenagers to recognize the symptoms of anorexia and bulimia, acknowledge the problem, and learn specific strategies to help. Part 1 deals with predisposing factors such as body-image, self-image, self-esteem, and habits. Anorexia and bulimia are defined with their characteristics, and emotional, physical, and social effects. Part 2 offers sound advice on confronting the disorder and what to expect, on seeking additional help, and helping others with eating disorders. Designed as a "hands-on" book, a variety of formats are presented: questionnaires, checklists, exercises, diagrams, and charts. Interspersed are scenarios, cartoons, and quotes from teenagers who have experienced eating disorders. The author is the Executive Director of the Behavioral Medicine Institute in Connecticut, where she is head of the Eating Disorders Program. The book is appropriate for ages 12 to 17.

Liu, Aimee. *Solitaire.* **New York: Harper & Row, 1979. 215 p. ISBN 0-06-012652-3**

Aimee Liu tells her own story. Rejected by her peers and disturbed by her parents' constant quarrelling and her mother's domination, Aimee finds a way to be pure, strong and in control, yet remain a child. Starvation is the goal of her adolescence.

Anorexia and bulimia are both aspects of her eating behaviour as she alternately starves herself and binges. Childhood rape and subsequent unpleasant sexual encounters have left her with a fear of sex, and she welcomes amenorrhea which prolongs her childhood. Unlike several of her acquaintances, her eating disorder is suspected but never diagnosed. The breakthrough in her condition comes with personal realization and a desire to change. After three months of living with Ken, a boy with anorexic tendencies, she suddenly realizes that her mother is right: limiting herself socially during her first year of university is unwise. Her period of rebellion is at an end and she is free to revise all her former attitudes. The strength of purpose that enabled her to maintain a thin body can now be channeled into the development of a healthy lifestyle.

This biography may be read with interest by those who deal with young adults and by both boys and girls of 14 and up.

National Eating Disorder Information Centre. *An Introduction to Eating Disorders: The Facts on Anorexia Nervosa and Bulimia.* Toronto: National Eating Disorder Information Centre.

This 12-page pamphlet provides the general public and professional community with the history of the Centre, its aims, and its funding. It includes concise information on anorexia nervosa and bulimia: their incidences, definitions, shared symptoms, physical problems related to weight loss, physical problems related to binge eating, vomiting and purgative abuse, effects of weight loss, warning signs, factors which lead to eating disorders (sociocultural, emotional, family), treatment (hospitalization, counselling, support groups, medication, dietician), coping with an anorexic or bulimic person, and recommended reading.

O'Neill, Cherry Boone. *Starving for Attention.* New York: Dell, 1982. ISBN 0-440-17620-4

Cherry Boone O'Neill narrates this frightening documentary of her life and death battle with eating disorders. Her adolescent perfectionism controls her life and leads to: hidden abuse of her mother's diet pills, self-induced vomiting to skip high school classes, excessive exercise programs, crash diets, and culminates in the traumatic death of her best friend.

Cherry then goes on a self-imposed exile from her friends. Her mother finally sees how thin Cherry is and sends her to a doctor. He threatens her with hospitalization. Years of conflict ensue. She finally begins to be honest with her future husband. Cherry swings between progress and relapse and is hospitalized once at 80 lbs. Her life does turn around after psychiatric counselling and a change in lifestyle. A collection of personal letters and Cherry's willingness to be brutally honest with her readers succeeds in giving her story strong impact.

Rumney, Avis. *Dying to Please: Anorexia Nervosa and Its Cure.* London: McFarland, 1983. ISBN 0-89950-083-8

Avis Rumney speaks from 17 years of personal experience as an anorexic and from her professional position as a family, marriage, and child counsellor. She outlines the problems that anticipate anorexia: perfectionism, competition, unresolved grief, distortion of body image, and sexual dysfunction. Rumney's criteria for curing anorexia include a person's ability to change to accurate body image, eat normally, develop consistent self identity, achieve a sense of competence, adjust socially, and develop close and intimate relationships with other people. The book concludes with different approaches to cure anorexia and highlights the author's treatment at Cathexis Institute. Rumney's appeal stems from her ability to speak about anorexia with her personal voice as well as with her professional counsellor's objectivity.

Wolhart, Dayna. *The Facts about Anorexia Nervosa and Bulimia.* **Mankato, Minn.: Crestwood House, 1988. 48 p. ISBN 0-89686-416-2**

A factual, easy to read explanation of anorexia and bulimia. The text deals with symptoms, causes and treatments of these eating disorders. Large print, coloured up-to-date photos, and relevant information makes this useful reading aimed at male and female readers who may carry dieting too far. Useful for school and YA collections in public libraries.

Is Earthwoman Doomed?

YA Hotline, Issue No. 46, 1992

DAVID HANSEN, ELIZABETH JONES, KATHLEEN MACLEOD PRENTISS, AND WENDY RICHARDSON

ENVIRONMENTAL LITERATURE FOR YAS

The intent of environmental literature is to change your everyday life—to convince you to think differently. You should not be able to "enjoy" an environmental book in the relaxed way you enjoy other good reads! We can get depressed and despair when faced with the irreversible destruction that has already been wreaked on our world—it often seems that it is already too late. If adults are scared by the gloomy predictions, consider the nightmares it brings to young people for whom the future is everything. Knowledge is vital for an informed citizenry—a future generation who will care about the environment, but young adults should be presented with some real sense of how the environmental problems can be met successfully.

There is now a flood of environmental literature; in fact, books about the environment are themselves a cause of destruction—trees must be destroyed and chemicals used to produce them. Careful choices should be made when selecting environmental books for YAs.

Some characteristics to look for include:

* honesty and factual accuracy.
* love of the earth, not "scare tactics."
* readability: reading levels appropriate to the intended YA group.
* emphasis on the beauty of what we have to lose, not on the depressing destruction.
* avoiding boring and preachy books with a "message."

✳ selecting those with a practical approach: "This is what you can do!"

There are three categories of environmental books:

1. The first category includes books which explain specific issues in picture format with accompanying text. For example: *Portraits of the Rainforest* by Adrian Forsyth. Firefly Books, 1990. ISBN 0-921820-13-5, and *Save the Birds* by A. W. Diamond, R. Bateman, R. L. Schreiber. Breakwater Books, 1989. ISBN 0-92091108101.

2. The second category includes the practical guides which show what individuals can do, such as *The Canadian Green Consumer Guide* by Pollution Probe Foundation. McClelland & Stewart, 1989. ISBN 0-07710-71620-0 and *The Daily Planet: A Hands-on Guide to a Greener Environment* by Paul Griss. Key Porter, 1990. ISBN 1-55013-216-4.

3. Books in the third category take a philosophical approach to environmental issues. Some examples are *The Eco Wars: A Layman's Guide to the Ecology Movement* by David Day. Harrap, 1989. ISBN 0-245-54723-1 and *Global Warming* by Stephen H. Schneider. Sierra, 1989. ISBN 0-87156-693-1. Since the reading levels of these books are generally high, they are most useful for teachers, teacher-librarians, and YA librarians and sophisticated young adult readers. For younger YAs, try *The Kids' Environment Handbook: What's Awry and Why* by Anne Pedersen. John Muir, 1991. ISBN 0-945465-75-2, 192 p.

Environmental literature for YAs should be honest but optimistic; as individuals, YAs must be convinced that his or her contributions do matter; we are all partners in protecting and polluting our environment. Environmental protection offers financial savings, a profound cosmetic effect on the natural surroundings, improved health, and a future outlook that is bright and productive, but first, we must understand that individual responsibility and integrity are keynotes.

IN THE SPIRIT: HAS ACTIVISM BEEN REVIVED?

In the sixties, young adults prided themselves on the divergence between their lifestyle and what was commonly labeled "the establishment." Protests were in vogue and surfaced in many unconventional guises. There were marches and sit-ins, bra-burnings and bed-ins (will we ever forget John and Yoko bantering with the press from their honeymoon suite?). It was the Age of Aquarius, the summer of love, everyone was feelin' groovy.

While many of their elders ridiculed their behaviour and felt that much was carried to the extreme, the youth movement continued to rally for peace, human rights, and fair treatment from government and big business. Women acknowledged the heightening achievements of the peace movement and adopted writers like Germaine Greer and Betty Friedan as beacons of their liberation effort. It was an exhilarating time which has lost relatively little when viewed with the benefit and reasoning of hindsight. Indeed, recent forays into social history in various media have looked back favourably on the 1960s as somewhat of a Golden Age.

Of course, this sentiment is not universal and sixties fervour, tangible or implied, has as many detractors as it does advocates. What is fascinating, however, is that this revival seems to be most evident among the present generation of young adults. It's not simply the fond remembrance of things past, but a genuine rekindling of that same spirit of challenge, which was the exceptional quality of the 1960s generation. Perhaps it is a reaction to the new conservatism of the 1980s or the greed of the so-called "me" generation which worshipped the icons of MBA and BMW. Take a look around, it's enough to stir the blood of a sixties survivor, they're growing their hair longer, wearing tie-died shirts, and listening to music which bears more than just a fleeting resemblance to its message-laden, folk-rock prototype.

It is this sort of sentiment which fuels the current preoccupation with the environment. Young adults are cognizant of the problem, they recognize its immediacy and should be encouraged in their efforts to address these and other significant issues. Adults who work with youth are in a unique position to reward enthusiastic enterprise. By becoming more aware ourselves, we will only serve to strengthen their resolve in seeking a remedy to an affliction which affects us all.

ST. PATRICK'S GREEN BRIGADE

Sara Tillett and Greg Harnish are grade twelve students at Saint Patrick's High School, one of the largest inner-city high schools in Halifax, Nova Scotia. They became interested in forming a school-centred environment club after Sara was approached by the class president with the idea that such a group might attract some favourable attention from both students at St. Pat's and other nearby metropolitan schools. After some initial meetings, it became clear that in order to establish some direction and achieve certain goals, inter-school cooperation would have to be abandoned and St. Pat's would have to go it alone. Sara and Greg called for another

meeting and S.P.E.C., the official St. Pat's High Environment Club was established in the spring of 1990.

The initial meeting drew approximately thirty eager students, although Greg allows that attendance has now reached a solid plateau of about fifteen to twenty regulars with some sporadic highs and lows. Other activities, such as exams or music festivals, definitely affect participation. Four goals were instituted at the initial meeting, the first and foremost being education for club members as well as the entire student body. Both Sara and Greg concede that ignorance is their worst enemy and that obliterating apathy and raising levels of environmental awareness are the club's primary objectives.

More practical targets identified at the founding session (aside from the educational goals) were the institution of an in-house recycling program, organization of a "Rally for the Earth," and the elimination of disposable styrofoam tableware from the school's cafeteria. To date, the club has met a respectable three of those original objectives. Only the latter has eluded their determined efforts, due mainly to the difficulty of convincing the cafeteria management to change their ways. Sara and Greg depict this hurdle with barely concealed cynicism. It is difficult for enthusiastic and diligent young adults to fathom the intransigence of adult decision-makers.

Lack of support from the cafeteria operators is not reflective of school administration in general. Sara and Greg are lavish in their praise for their principal and several teachers as well. The significance of administration as friend and advocate is a noteworthy complement to the endeavours of these young crusaders. The principal of St. Pat's, with the aid of the school board, has provided expertise and funding in the securing of guest lecturers, admission to workshops and local course offerings, as well as assistance in organizing the initiation of the paper and aluminum recycling programs. While this assistance was gratefully received, the club itself continues to do all the legwork and must persevere in raising funds for the maintenance of the programs.

Other club operations involve fund-raising projects. Bake sales, raffles, and a donation tin at school dances are regular endeavours. An "Environment Info" bulletin board has been established in the corridor directly outside the school library and is "recycled" every three weeks. Special events are also sponsored. One recent example was a Mr. St. Pat's Pageant which, while lampooning certain controversial female-oriented occasions, had the added advantage of charging a fifty-cent admission on behalf of S.P.E.C. Later in the school year, an Environmental Week is in the works. This event will host a junk art contest (with material gleaned from the school yard), a papermaking workshop, a tricycle race (designed to encourage cycling rather than automobile use), a logo contest, a beach clean-up/picnic combo, and the rather ambitious production of an environmental play. In addition, at the end of the year, some of the money raised by the club will be used to buy trees in a rainforest in the name of the graduating class of 1991—a suitable legacy for the efforts of one small group of concerned young adults.

Sara and Greg and the rest of the members of S.P.E.C. are proving that individuals can make a difference—that the place to start cleaning up the environment is right in one's own back yard. As Sara said at the end of our interview, "We do not inherit the Earth from our ancestors, we borrow it from our children."

Sara and Greg recommended the following books for further information and useful tips:

Earth Works Project. *Fifty Simple Things You Can Do to Save the Earth*. Berkeley, CA: Earthworks Press/Greenleaf Publications, 1990. ISBN 0-929634-06-3.

Hummel, Monte. *Endangered Spaces: The Future for Canada's Wilderness*. Toronto: Key Porter, 1989. ISBN 1-55013-101-X.

Lamb, Marjorie. *Two Minutes a Day for a Greener Planet: Quick and Simple Things Americans Can Do to Save the Earth*. New York: Harper & Row, 1990. ISBN 0-06-250507-6.

Pollution Probe Foundation. *The Canadian Green Consumer Guide*. Toronto: McClelland and Stewart, 1990. ISBN 0-7710-7162-0.

ECOLOGICAL ROCK: POP MUSIC'S NEW SOCIAL CONSCIENCE

If a tree falls in the forest, does anybody hear?
Anybody hear the forest fall?

With these lyrics, Bruce Cockburn, Canada's pre-eminent rock crusader, launches his latest assault in a long battle against social and political ignorance. Cockburn's candid, hard-hitting lyrics have been aimed at many targets over the years, often delivered with conspicuous cynicism. One of his best-known songs, written in reaction to the plight of Guatemalan refugees, voices the refrain, "If I had a rocket launcher, some son of a bitch would die . . ."

Of late, however, Cockburn and many other socially conscious members of rock music's elite have begun to address a new and vital issue which touches all citizens of the global village—our common environment.

Since Bob Dylan first alerted us to the changin' times and warned parents that their sons and daughters were beyond their command, rock music has proven to be a catalyst for social change and a powerful medium for reaching youth. Over the years, since rock and roll hit its stride in the 1960s, pop musicians have delivered moral messages to adolescent audiences in a palatable format. Indeed, were it not for that particular medium, the message might not otherwise be heard.

Popular music has helped to crystallize current sentiment in the last three decades with unprecedented fervour and regularity. Sixties artists protested the war in Vietnam, the Kent State killings, and human rights violation. In the seventies, after a brief fling with the nonentity know as disco, rockers turned their attention to the anti-nuclear movement, culminating in the massive MUSE Concerts for a non-nuclear future (No Nukes) at Madison Square Garden. The eighties witnessed a regrouping around political issues and the popular forum for delivery was the mega-benefit concert. Artists rallied against apartheid (Sun City), called for freedom for political prisoners (notably Nelson Mandela), championed the achievements of Amnesty International, sang for African famine relief (Band-Aid and Live Aid), and even directed some attention toward the plight of North American farmers (Farm Aid).

In June of 1989, however, the mega-concert dubbed "Our Common Future" directed its efforts toward a different enemy, the threat of global annihilation through environmental destruction. The event was broadcast to an audience estimated at one billion in over one hundred countries. Unlike its predecessors, the concert was not designed to raise money, but rather, awareness of an assortment of environmental issues which touch us all—from acid rain to the depletion of the ozone layer. Among the performers were some of rock music's legendary talents: Elton John, Diana Ross, Herbie Hancock, Stevie Wonder, and Sting, an unrelenting spokesman for a variety of worthwhile causes. Sting has written songs about dispossessed coal miners (*We Work the Black Seam*) and the mothers, wives, and daughters of the Disappeared (*They Dance Alone*). Sting's latest challenge is the demise of the Brazilian rain forest and he is willing to spend the currency of fame in order to reap the benefits of publicity for the cause.

The pop star has toured extensively throughout Brazil and has taken his private appeal on the road. Accompanied by representatives of the Kayapo Indian tribe, whose existence is threatened by further erosion of the Brazilian rain forest, Sting taped appeals in a variety of languages and solicited support from heads of state. Sting's odyssey is documented in a glossy book entitled *Jungle Stories: The Fight for the Amazon* (Little, Brown, 1989. 128 p.). The book features 100 colour photographs by the Belgian filmmaker, Jean-Pierre Dutilleux, and has been produced as a fund-raiser for the Rainforest Foundation, an organization established by Sting and Dutilleux.

June of 1989 also witnessed the release of *Spirit of the Forest*, a pro-ecology fund-raising song which features more than sixty popular performers. Among these artists are Joni Mitchell, Ringo Starr, and Iggy Pop. Another recording, released in the same year by the Greenpeace organization, was entitled *Rainbow Warriors* and includes performances by U2, Sting, Peter Gabriel, the Eurythmics, and Bryan Adams. Also in 1989, obviously a banner year for environmental concern, Yoko Ono announced the launch of her latest project in memory of her husband, John Lennon. Designated *Greening of the World*, the enterprise will raise money through concerts and sales of books, films, and recordings.

Clearly, rock music is a significant medium for galvanizing youth and extends a major avenue of access for individuals who work with and for adolescents. By maintaining our own awareness of events in the field of contemporary music, we are afforded a splendid opportunity for communicating with today's young adults about issues which are important to us all. And, by the way, don't tell them it's good for them.

Selected Discography of Ecological Rock

Browne, Jackson. *World in Motion*. Elektra Records, 1989.

Cockburn, Bruce. *Big Circumstance*. True North Records, 1989. (features "If a Tree Falls" and "Radium Rain")

Gabriel, Peter. *So*. Geffen Records, 1986. (features "Red Rain")

Hope Chest. Elektra/Asylum, 1990.

Midnight Oil. *Diesel and Dust*. Columbia, 1988.
Blue Sky Mining. Columbia, 1990.

Mitchell, Joni. *Chalk Mark in a Rainstorm*. Geffen Records, 1988. (features "Lakota" and a revision of "Cool Water" from an ecological perspective)

Raffi. *Evergreen/Everblue*. Troubadour/MCA, 1990. (in a departure from performance solely for children)

Rainbow Warriors. Greenpeace International/Geffen Records, 1989.

R.E.M. *Out of Time*. Warner Brothers, 1991.

Segato, Lorraine. *Phoenix*. Red Rock/WEA, 1990.

Simon, Paul. *The Rhythm of the Saints*. Warner Brothers, 1990. (features "Can't Run But")

Sting. *The Soul Cages*. A&M Records, 1991.

Talking Heads. *Naked*. Sire Records, 1988. (features "(Nothing but) Flowers")

10,000 Maniacs. *Blindman's Zoo*. Elektra/Asylum, 1989.

World Party. *Goodbye Jumbo*. Chrysalis Records, 1990.

ENVIRONMENTAL GUILT: WHAT TO DO ABOUT IT?

Nobody can deny that for those of us who want to hear it, there is no lack of information available concerning the state of the environment. A very recent example of a headline was "Environmental Sins Tackled."

We are constantly reminded of these problems, and the long-term local and global effects, ranging from our own drinking water to the general warming of the climate and disappearance of the essential elements of the air we breathe, such as the ozone layer. We can personally witness the way that the earth is deteriorating due to human exploitation. How should we react, and how should our young adults prepare themselves to fight the battle?

The media, environmental organizations, and even our collective conscience, supply us with plenty of answers. We are told, for example, to reuse, recycle, renew; to store all recyclables until they can be deposited at the closest center for recycling; to fight supermarket packaging and not to over package ourselves (right down to juicepacks and plastic party glasses).

Individual efforts may seem insignificant in the face of the larger aspect of environmental abuse. This is the pervasive, enormous disregard for the environment by huge industries which billow smoke, pollute the water supply, and decimate forests which have been in existence for millennia. This behaviour, which is perfectly obvious to all of us, also raises a question in our mind: What difference can we possibly make if these industries are polluting and destroying the earth in such massive proportions to our personal behaviour?

Again, the answer is not difficult to find. The same argument that charity begins at home must also be made for environmental consciousness and appropriate behavior. Still—as some people regard their growing collection of used plastic containers and other material for which it may be difficult to find a further use—it's natural to wonder if we are making a difference, and if the effort is worth it.

The only other choice is to disregard the problem, carry on as if there were an infinite number of tomorrows, and compound the problem ourselves. This surely cannot be the appropriate way to join the global fight to preserve our earth. Fighting the good battle, on a personal, organizational, and corporate level does make a difference, and often, though not always, applying political pressure works.

And what about guilt? Putting it to productive use by personal and group involvement in these efforts serves the double purpose of getting rid of it, as well as to help alleviate our environment of its problems. Let's join together in this effort—"It's a small world." It's also our only one.

PROFILE OF DAVID SUZUKI

In Canada, we see him on television, listen to him on the radio, read his columns in the newspapers, and read his books found in bookstores and libraries. He is Canada's foremost advocate for the environment—David Suzuki.

It is not only Canada that Suzuki is concerned about—it is the world ecosystem. For him, as it should be for all of us, the global perspective encompasses every detail of abuse or care which all countries bestow upon their environments.

It is clear from Suzuki's autobiography, *Metamorphosis: Stages in a Life* (Toronto: Stoddart, 1987), that several factors in his background continue to be influential in his work, even today. A first-generation Canadian, he and his family were interned along with thousands of other Japanese-Canadians after Pearl Harbor. After the war the family relocated to Ontario. Eventually Suzuki attended Amherst College in Massachusetts, and the University of Chicago, where he received his Ph.D. in 1961. His work as a geneticist involved the genetics of fruit flies, and heat sensitivity. He taught and conducted research at the University of British Columbia beginning in 1963; today he still maintains ties with the university, although at present he does not teach there. Suzuki's career took a turn towards the public with his first Canadian Broadcasting Corporation television production,

"Suzuki on Science," in 1972. Other CBC productions in which he has played a major role are "Quirks and Quarks," "Science Magazine," and "A Planet for the Taking."

At this time, perhaps Suzuki's largest audience is found in the readership of his newspaper column. A selection of some of these articles has been published in *Inventing the Future: Reflections on Science, Technology and Nature* (Toronto: Stoddart, 1989). His byline for his Southam Syndicate weekly column "Reflections" describes him as "a writer, radio host and geneticist. " His concern with the environment of the earth is strongly expressed in this informative, sometimes controversial, column. In fact, as this article goes to press for the *YA Hotline*, the headline for his column reads, "Attack on global ecological crisis must be focused." In his autobiography and biography he clearly states his motivations, beliefs, and criticism. In his current role as columnist and television show host he uses his background, education, and current awareness of crucial environmental situations to inform and heighten the consciousness of the public.

Suzuki is eager to involve teenagers in his environmental effort, as well. In a recent program of "The Nature of Things," an "Environmental Quiz" about acid rain and garbage was presented to the audience in their homes. The teenage actors in the CBC program "DeGrassi High" appeared on this program, as well as a Canadian teenager from Toronto whose letter-writing campaign concerning the pollution of a local pond has accelerated its clean-up. His interest in the involvement of youth extends to the Vancouver-based organization Environmental Youth Alliance, which links high school environment clubs. His books and all of the audio-visual material reviewed in this issue

of *YA Hotline* are most appropriate for Young Adults of all ages.

ECOLOGY ACTION CENTRE

The Ecology Action Centre is Nova Scotia's largest environmental group. Their office and library are located on the top floor of Veith House, a community-oriented non-profit social agency in north-end Halifax, which provides services to the low-income community. The social consciousness of Veith House is reflected in the activities of the Ecology Action Centre (EAC), which is now in its twentieth year of existence. Community action and involvement are encouraged by its weekly radio program, "Earth Action"; sponsorship of workshops, lecture series, and conferences; and assistance to other groups or individuals in their attempts to work with government or industry officials on environmental matters.

Students are reached by members of the EAC who speak at schools or assist teachers in answering questions about the environment. The Resource Centre Library is an extensive collection of environmental materials, open to students, journalists, and the public. It also serves as a distribution center for materials from other organizations, such as the Environmental Youth Alliance and the Nova Scotia Environmental Alliance, a network organization for university students.

Between the Issues, the bi-monthly newsletter published by the EAC, reports on local, provincial, regional, national, and international issues. Emphasis is on recycling and other practical activities, as well as controversies such as Point Aconi and protection of wildlife in Africa. Information on local and national conferences and workshops is also provided.

Sustaining Earth: A Bibliography of the Holdings of the Ecology Action Resource Centre, Halifax, Canada is the extensive (302 p.) subject bibliography of the Centre, compiled in June 1988, by Catherine Pross and Mary Dwyer Rigby. Six broad subject headings encompass the collection: energy, resource industries, pollution, changes in the biosphere, institutional responses to environmental issues, and human habitat and society. The bibliography may be purchased from the Centre. It was published as #44 in the Occasional Papers Series of the School of Library and Information Studies, and may also be ordered from this address:

Director
School of Library and Information Studies
Dalhousie University
Halifax, Nova Scotia B3H 3J5

More information about the EAC may be obtained from:

Ecology Action Centre
3115 Veith House
Halifax, Nova Scotia B3K 3G9
(902) 454-7828

A RECENT TREND: ECOFICTION

The current interest in all things environmental has encouraged growth in the green book trade. For the most part, these titles fall into the non-fiction category, but recent flights of narrative fancy have resulted in a new genre—one we affectionately label Ecofiction. These novels exercise traditional literary schemes to lure the reader, but add a healthy dose of ecological awareness to the plot to advise the young reader and elevate their awareness of the natural world. Weaving environmental concerns with an agreeable storyline can result in substantial rewards for both the author and the reader. A few examples of this innovative breed are considered below.

Philips, Ann. *The Oak King and the Ash Queen*. London: Oxford University Press, 1985. 171 p. ISBN 0-19-271495-3.

This stunning ecological fantasy is reminiscent of the Narnia tales of C.S. Lewis. Daisy and Dan are twelve-year-old twins who encounter a mystical land near their home in a quaint English village and become embroiled in a struggle between the forces of summer and winter. Summer is personified, as it were, by the Oak King and Ash Queen, while winter is exemplified by the Holly and the Ivy. The winter people are plotting against the summer sovereigns in an attempt to command the forces of earth, air, fire, and water. The children are enlisted by the Oak King and Ash Queen to aid in the return to a balance of power in the forest and restoration of the natural state of affairs.

While the allegorical characterization in the novel is far from subtle, the message is valid. The children learn that a disturbance in the natural status quo can lead to disaster and realize that humans may intervene to precipitate positive results in an endangered environment. Appropriate for young adolescents.

Katz, Welwyn Wilton. *Whalesinger*. Toronto: Groundwood/Douglas & McIntyre, 1990. 212 p. ISBN 0-88899-113-4.

Major, Kevin. *Blood Red Ochre*. Toronto: Doubleday Canada, 1989. 147 p. ISBN 0-385-29794-7.

It seems appropriate to consider these two titles together as they are both the products of well-known Canadian writers and, while their themes are disparate, they share some rather striking similarities. Both center on issues which might serve to raise the environmental consciousness of youthful readers and each employs the literary device whereby alternate segments are written from the somewhat ethereal point of view of characters removed from the core of the action—a maternal grey whale on the one hand, and a long-dead, fifteen-year-old Beothuk Indian boy (Dauoodaset) on the other. However, both novels overcome the cumbersome restraints inherent in such a demanding literary plot and reward the reader with powerful and poignant narrative.

Dauoodaset provides an insightful alter ego for David, the fifteen-year-old protagonist of *Blood Red Ochre*. In their individual worlds, both boys attempt to deal with the stark reality of family responsibilities, albeit Dauoodaset's unfortunate plight (which mirrors the genocide of his once noble people) is considerably more crucial than David's coming to terms with his own alienation from family and friends. While investigating the history of the Beothuk Indians for a school project, David teams up with Nancy, a newcomer to the small Newfoundland community where he lives. Nancy is unlike most of her peers and David is attracted to her dark and enigmatic beauty. Research for their projects takes Nancy and David to a small coastal island where, according to David's grandfather, a Beothuk Indian was known to have perished. Through the narrative of Dauoodaset, we become increasingly aware that his and David's fates are somehow inextricably entwined, and that Nancy's eagerness to get to Red Ochre Island is a vital counterpoint to their inevitable encounter. Kevin Major has crafted a fine and original story that serves to inform young and old readers alike about the untimely demise of the Beothuk culture without appearing overly didactic.

As one of two central characters in *Whalesinger*, seventeen-year-old Nick has escaped from the stifling atmosphere of his Vancouver home in an attempt to deal with the accidental death of his older brother and mentor, Richard. Nick's computer expertise lands him a summer job as research assistant to Dr. Jonas Anderson who, along with a company of oceanographic scientists, is camped for the summer near the San Andreas Fault on the coast of California. Unfortunately, Nick discovers that the leader of the expedition is the renowned conservationist who Nick blames for Richard's death. Two of the other Vancouver researchers, a married couple, are accompanied by their young daughters and a fifteen-year-old babysitter, Marty Griffiths.

Like David in *Blood Red Ochre*, Nick is at once attracted to Marty's quiet beauty. Marty suffers from an unusual learning disability which causes her reticence and self-deprecating behaviour. Through some unexplained phenomenon however, she is able to communicate with a lone grey whale and her calf and comes to identify with their solitary condition.

Nick and Marty's discovery of the fraudulent past and clandestine purpose for launching the excursion bring them together in an attempt to save the whales and expose the connection to Richard's death. Climactic and human passions collide as Marty and Nick are drawn further into a web of environmental intrigue.

Whalesinger is a novel of lustrous and poetic beauty. Mary and Nick's sensual tensions are particularly evocative and meticulously handled in light of the pressures of contemporary sexual mores.

NONFICTION REVIEWS

The Recycler's Handbook. The Earth Works Group. Berkeley, CA: Earth Works Press, 1990. 132 p. ISBN 0-929634-08-X (pb).

This practical "how-to" book grew out of the success of a previous book by the same authors—*Fifty Simple Things You Can Do to Save the Earth*. The basic premise of the Earth Works Group is "to provide information that helps individuals understand how their actions can make a difference."

The agencies, associations, organizations, and publications identified here are all in the United States; however, this book strives to be general in approach. It often advises the reader to "Check with your local recycler," since recycling practices, rules, and opportunities are very regionalized at this stage. Potential recyclers are urged to demand required services from local governments where they see a need.

This book does not claim to be the definitive work on recycling, but it offers the essentials and a fair representation of recycling possibilities. It "practices what it preaches" by being printed on "80% 'post-consumer' recycled paper" and notes apologetically that "the cover isn't printed on recycled stock" because of unavailability.

Although there are few illustrations, the format of this paperback book should appeal to YAs—clearly organized pages with manageable statistics and practical suggestions. Access to the information is possible though the table of contents and an index to materials. After attempting to define "Recycling" and giving advice on "Getting Started," the reader is introduced to "The Material World" of "Metal," "Glass," "Paper," "Plastic," "Organics," and "Other Recyclables." The book ends with ways of "Getting More Involved" followed by lists of names and addresses of "Resources" and a useful "Materials Index." Also, each chapter ends with lists of names and addresses for ordering supplies and publications for more information.

The tone of the book is upbeat and positive, although the statistics of garbage and waste of resources are inherently depressing. The light-hearted approach can be seen on the Contents page: "The Trash Man Cometh," "Glassified Info," "Sacks Appeal," "Vinyl Exam," "What a Load of Scrap," and much more.

The section "Starting a School Recycling Program" is of particular importance for YAs: recycling is profitable (one school earned $2,000 collecting aluminum cans). Also of interest to YAs would be "Getting a Job in Recycling;" the recycling field is ideal for budding entrepreneurs.

The actual practice of recycling changes attitudes. It develops lifelong good ecological habits.

Durrell, Lee. *State of the Ark, An Atlas of Conservation in Action*. Doubleday, 1986. 224 p. ISBN 0-385-23668-9.

This large format book introduces the planet Earth as a self-sustaining biosphere—and Ark. It shows, through charts, maps, and diagrams, the impact of humans on life support systems of air, climate, soil, and water. It looks at various ecosystems and the threats and pressures to which each is exposed. It divides the earth into regions and traces the special problems in each of these areas. Finally it outlines the conservation movement, both regional and global. This is an elegant book filled with useful information on many environmental issues. It would be very useful as a reference in a high school library. It would have applications in environmental studies, geography, biology, zoology, and social sciences. Highly recommended as a reference tool for the environmentally conscious young adult.

Hawkes, Nigel. *Toxic Waste and Recycling*. Gloucester Press. 1988. 32 p. ISBN 0-531-17080-2.

This large format book introduces the 12–14 year old to several environmental issues. It discusses the topics of toxic industrial waste, nuclear waste, domestic waste, and sewage. Common methods of disposal of hazardous material, burning, and dumping are discussed along with the potential problems with these methods. Recycling is mentioned as a viable alternative. With many pictures and being only 32 pages long, this book can only mention these issues very briefly, although many facts and figures are presented in a visually appealing format. It may be included in a library collection for young adults, but it will not likely appeal to those older that 13–14 years, because of its format and appearance as a "child" book. This may present some difficulties because its reading level is 8.5 (Fry test).

Griss, Paul. *The Daily Planet: A Hands-On Guide to a Greener Environment*. Toronto: Key Porter, 1990. 232 p. ISBN 1-55013-216-4 (pb).

This guide to living better environmentally is packed with practical how-to's for all member of our society. Although young adults are not specifically the focus, many of the topics are relevant to them and would interest them: how to be an environmentally-conscious shopper, driver, hunter, and gardener; how to get involved with environmental groups; and how to form your own environmental action group.

In non-scholarly, but authoritative language, Griss explains such concepts as global warming, acid rain, waste treatment, organic farming, and ozone depletion. He also tackles issues like energy conservation, deforestation, mining, water pollution, ethical treatment of animals, the fur debate, household chemicals, waste disposal options, and sustainable development.

This is an excellent reference source for both public and school librarians; it is current and informative and has a comprehensive index which provides access to the text. A bibliography and lengthy lists of organizations and agencies in Canada provide directions for acquiring further information. The information regarding individual environmental groups and government agencies is of specific use to Canadians.

Griss is upbeat in his enthusiasm for positive ways to improve our treatment of the environment—he does not beat us with all the bad things we, as humans, are doing to Mother Earth.

Bullock, David K. *The Wasted Ocean*. New York: Lyons and Burford, 1989. 150 p. ISBN 1-55821-019-9.

This book, sponsored by the American Littoral Society, a non-profit organization dedicated to preserving and enriching our sea coast habitats, deals with pollution and the environmental threat to sea coasts and the oceans. Although the book contains a lot of very technical information, it is clearly presented and easy to read. This will encourage the young adult to examine the damage done to the largest and most complex of all ecosystems. *The Wasted Ocean* also discusses several ways to help reverse this process, and many organizations committed to this goal are listed. The book will be a very useful guide in any library environmental series for young adults, since it clearly explains the problem, as well as suggesting ways to solve it.

Burnett, J. A., C. T. Dauphine, Jr., S. H. McCrindle, and T. Mosquin. *On the Brink: Endangered Species in Canada*. Western Producer Prairie Book, 1989. 190 p. ISBN 0-88833-298-x.

This attractive, large format book is an overview of the endangered species in Canada. The book is divided into various sections to correspond to regions of the country, with the endangered species of each region identified. There is also a section about how the various species are being assisted and brought "back from the brink." Finally there is a list of many government agencies that are responsible for endangered species in Canada. This is a very useful book for young adults, particularly those involved in environmental studies. Its large format is that of a reference book or textbook, but for this topic this is a practical way of presenting this information.

GAIA: An Atlas of Planet Management. Ed. Norman Myers. New York: Doubleday, 1984. ISBN 0-385-19071-9, 0-385-19072-7 (pb).

This atlas presents a tremendous amount of ecological and environmental information about our planet and its natural resources. The dedication reads: "To the poor of the world, denied their share of the world's rich resources."

The emphasis of the atlas is on what we can do as residents of the earth to preserve and wisely utilize its attributes, and to share renewable resources with those in need. The seven chapters feature essays on the land, ocean, elements, evolution, humankind, civilization, and management. Authors of the introductions to these chapters include Alvin Toffler (on civilization), and the Rainbow Warrior crew of the Greenpeace vessel (on the ocean). Of particular interest are essays such as "Haves and Have-nots," concerning the technology gap, development, and poverty, in the chapter on civilization.

The focus on appreciation and management of the earth, the clear presentation of factual information in essay form, and the striking photographs and drawings contribute to the excellence of this source. Thoughtfully designed and beautifully illus-

trated, this atlas is appropriate for students in junior and senior high school, as well as teachers.

Suzuki, David, with Barbara Hehner. Looking at the Environment. Toronto: Stoddart, 1989. 92 p. ISBN 0-7737-5255-2.

This is an informative, enjoyable book about the environment. Featured are our natural surroundings and how to enjoy and use them with care.

"We're All in This Together" is the title of the introduction. It is followed by information and exercises or experiments dealing with the environment, our food, water, marine life, waste, solar energy, and other interesting scientific and ecological topics. The experiments, or projects, labeled "Things to Do" are clearly explained, and a special printed symbol is provided for those which require adult assistance. Some of the "Things to Do" are quite straightforward and take only a few steps ("Bottle Music," p. 66 and "Energy Savers," p. 81, which uses water temperature to explain the principles of insulation). Others are more complex and time-consuming, such as "New Paper from Newspaper" (p. 75), which actually results in the creation of "new paper." Supplies for these projects are easily obtainable. The text for each topic is informative and interesting. Young Adult readers, particularly those in junior high school, will enjoy the projects. Readers of all ages will learn much about the environment and how to use it carefully from this book.

CANADA'S GREEN CRUSADERS

Mowat, Farley. Rescue the Earth! Conversations with the Green Crusaders. Toronto: McClelland & Stewart, 1990. 282 p.

Internationally renowned writer and ebullient Canadian commodore, Farley Mowat, brings the fractured Canadian environmental movement to light in this engaging conversational portrait. Mowat's self-proclaimed purpose is to "provide an introduction to a section of people in the movement and let them tell you in their own words what they believe must be done to ensure the survival in good health of a living world." He disclaims any intention of tendering a guide to the Canadian environmental movement in its myriad manifestations, but rather, offers insightful glimpses into the minds of key figures in various facets of the ecological community.

Mowat has divided the volume into three broad categories: Flag Carriers, A New Morality, and Mavericks and Activists. Each chapter embodies a conversation between Mowat and such ecological luminaries as Paul Griss (Chief Executive Officer of the Canadian Nature Federation), Brian Davies (of the International Fund for Animal Welfare), Dr. David Suzuki (Canada's leading ecological spokesman), and Elizabeth May (lawyer and green crusader). The conversations reveal personal doctrines and serve to outline the activities of those who value action over empty rhetoric.

While not specifically intended for an adolescent audience, youthful readers might appreciate this compilation from a recognized author and enjoy the parceled format which may be read a section at a time. In addition, the experience of these dedicated few might serve to inspire and encourage novice green crusaders.

Steger, Will and Jon Bowermaster. *Saving the Earth: Citizen's Guide to Environmental Action.* **Random House of Canada, 1990. ISBN 0-679-73026-5.**

The strength of this work lies in its clear presentation of the causes, effects, and solutions of the major environmental problems that exist today.

The authors have made excellent use of photographs, drawings, charts, and graphs to accompany the text. The result is an excellent resource book for environmental research projects or for general learning. The topics covered include: the atmosphere; the land; water; and the people. Within each of these chapters the subject is further divided into specific issues; for example, in the atmosphere chapter, the issues of global warming, ozone depletion, smog, and acid rain are all addressed. At the end of each chapter there is a reading list for further study, a list of relevant U.S. organizations to contact, as well as sections on suggested individual action and desired government action. The writing style is clear and succinct and is appropriate for all school-aged teens. The diagrams showing cause and effect are especially well done. This is a highly recommended reference tool for school and public libraries.

Harris, Mark D. *Embracing the Earth: Choices for Environmentally Sound Living.* **The Noble Press, 1990. 163 p. ISBN 0-9622683-2-1.**

This is basically a how-to book for environmentally responsible living, providing hundreds of simple, and sometimes obvious tips on how to reduce our impact on our environment. The book is divided into four sections: getting started; getting more involved; going all the way; and the directories. The coverage ranges from the basics of the three R's, to recipes for safe cleaning products (reduce, reuse, recycle), to tips for effective lobbying and protesting. The fourth section, the directories, lists only U.S. environmental organizations. The rest of the book is much more universal in its content. This book is very easy to read, either in whole or in small tidbits, presenting clear instructions while avoiding being preachy. A good starting point for the new green teen.

Pollution Probe. *The Canadian Green Consumer Guide.* **Toronto: McClelland & Stewart, 1989. 164 p. ISBN 0-7710-7162-0.**

The Canadian Green Consumer Guide is based on *The Green Consumer Guide* by John Elkington and Julia Hailes, first published in the United Kingdom. This guide provides direction for Canadian consumers of all ages, who wish to be environmentally responsible in their purchases. Coverage ranges from the basics of buying food and clothing, to transportation, to planning vacations and leisure activities. Each chapter provides basic information and suggestions up to very specific directives, such as which photofinishers recycle their chemicals. Each chapter is easy to digest and the reader's interest is constantly being enticed by the many boxes of facts, hints, and statistics. This guide is an essential source for any public or school library, for both the main circulating collection and as a reference source, and will likely appeal to many readers, from teens to seniors.

Marean, John, Robert Ritter, and John George. *Issues for Today: Canadian Environmental Concerns.* **Agincourt, ONT: GLC Silver Burdett, 1985. 105 p. ISBN 0-88874-038-7.**

This book presents four science-related social issues—acid rain, genetic engineering, herbicides and pesticides, and the greenhouse effect—and shows how science, technology, and society interact. These issues are presented in an objective manner; the reader is invited to evaluate the information and form his or her own opinions. Because the opinions of the authors are not offered, the tone of the text is impersonal. However, the layout of each unit provides good basic information and related facts, and examines the resulting controversies.

Profusely illustrated with black and white photographs and clear diagrams, it would be a useful source of ideas for science fair projects. Although designed for use in the classroom with directions for that usage, this book would be a valuable library addition for in-depth study of any of the four issues upon which it focuses. The lack of an index lessens its value as a reference source. This book is recommended for young adults because it encourages them to decide their own responses to these environmental issues.

Endangered Spaces: The Future for Canada's Wilderness. **Ed. Monte Hummel. Henderson Book Series No. 11. Toronto: Key Porter Books, 1989. 288 p. ISBN 1-55013-101-X.**

Endangered Spaces raises a fundamental question for all Canadians—how important is wilderness to the future of Canada?

The co-authors and photographers who collaborated to produce this work state that its real purpose is to "kick off a ten-year campaign to complete a wilderness network in Canada." For participants in this effort this includes supporting the Canadian Wilderness Charter and joining local organizations which protect wilderness areas. *Endangered Spaces* is published by the Canadian Parks and Wilderness Society, as a part of the Henderson Book Series.

To gain perspective on the future of Canada's wilderness, past actions are taken into account in the opening Part One: Learning from the Past. "Wilderness and the Canadian Psyche" and "Canada in a Global Context" question Canadian attitudes in the past towards wilderness areas. The political aspect of these issues is explored in Part Two: Current Issues and Perspectives, which includes articles by Elizabeth May and George Erasmus.

Provincial and regional priorities are considered in Part Three: The State of Wilderness Across

Canada Today. Part Four: Strategies for the Future includes the discussion of plans for conservation of these areas.

The truly breathtaking photographs of Canada's wilderness areas are as important a component in *Endangered Spaces* as its eloquent and informative articles. All aspects of caring for the wilderness are well represented: articles by authors such as Erasmus, Monte Hummel (general editor, and president of World Wildlife Fund Canada), and Harold Eidsvik (senior policy advisor at the Canadian Parks Service) contribute to the effort of including well-informed Canadian viewpoints.

Endangered Spaces would be well-used in school libraries by high school students, either as a reference book or as a general introduction to wilderness areas in Canada. Teachers will find much valuable information about Canada in general, specifically its wilderness areas. The organization is clear, the purpose is strongly stated, and the stunning photographs are most effective. Highly recommended for students and educators interested in preserving Canada's wilderness.

Suzuki, David. *Inventing the Future: Reflections on Science, Technology, and Nature*. Toronto: Stoddart 1989. 247 p. ISBN 0-7737-2354-4.

David Suzuki is well known to the Canadian public for his clearly stated, well-informed, often controversial views on scientific and political global matters. This is a collection of newspaper columns that were written in the past few years for *The Toronto Star* and *The Globe and Mail*. The articles are arranged in subject-oriented sections such as "The Great Code: Genetics and Society" and "Technology: Double-Edged Sword." Although an ecological consciousness pervades the book, the articles in four of the sections pertain specifically to the environment: "Warring Siblings: Economics and Ecology," "The Environment: The Scope of the Problem," "Rx for a Sick Planet," and the concluding section, "The Aboriginal Worldview." Examples of columns which discuss Canadian and international environmental issues are "Trouble in the Forest" and "Ecologists and Economists Unite!" Articles of environmental interest are also interspersed in the other sections. The focus of this review is on the contents which relate specifically to the environment.

Suzuki's columns on the environment are forthright, informative, and personally expressive. Each one is focused on a specific issue, such as the rape of the Amazon, Australian ecology, disappearing wilderness areas, and aboriginal ways of life. Suzuki is extremely well-informed and widely-travelled, and he is able to condense and relay his information and ideas to readers in a concentrated, readable manner. We know before we read his columns that he is first and foremost profoundly concerned and disturbed about what is happening to the environment of the world. But more than that, he wants us, the readers, to help right this situation—by keeping informed (as he is keeping us informed), by being active and ecologically conscious in as many ways as we can, and by keeping aware of and responding to disasters as well as improvements.

An historical perspective is also taken in such articles as "Children of the Earth," which includes an environmental speech from the American Chief Seattle in 1854. Suzuki has great respect for native and aboriginal peoples and their efforts to maintain their way of life. In fact, this book is dedicated to them. A feminist perspective ("Where Are All the Women?") and a concern for ethics ("Genetics after Auschwitz") are also expressed in two of the articles.

This is an excellent source for teachers, librarians, environmentalists, and ecologists for all backgrounds and purposes. Young adult readers (age 14 and older) would certainly be able to access information from the individual articles as well as the general overview. One effective use of the book would be to choose specific articles which relate to subjects which are featured in the classroom. *Inventing the Future* is a timely and valuable contribution by Canada's highest-profile spokesperson for the world environment.

Scared Stiff

YA Hotline, Issue No. 53, 1995

CATHERINE HOYT, DOREEN LANDRY, AND SHARON MACKINNON

HORRORS, HORRORS . . .

If romance and adventure are the stuff that dreams are made of, then what we're looking at here is the stuff of nightmares. There are numerous very early examples of the horrific in literature. We can look as far back as Petronius' *Satyricon*, Apuleius' *The Golden Ass*, and of course *Odysseus in the Underworld*. The medieval period gave us Danses Macabre and Dante's *Inferno*. But horror as a genre only began to coalesce around the end of the eighteenth century, primarily as a variation on the Gothic form of that time, which was a mixture of romance and the supernatural.

The horror genre in North America is normally traced back to Edgar Allan Poe, a master whose spine-tingling suspense and clever evocations of dread and impending doom continue to draw many readers. H.P. Lovecraft has become a more modern reference point for the genre. This consummate horror craftsman died in 1937, since which time his Victorian-style horror has sold prodigiously. In his book *Supernatural Horror in Literature*, Lovecraft says:

> The one test of the truly weird is simply this— whether or nor there be excited in the reader a profound sense of dread, and of contact with unknown spheres and powers; a subtle attitude of odd listening, as if for the beating of black wings or the scratching of outside shapes and entities in the known universe's utmost rim. (36)

For publishers, the adult horror novel has been a strong performer for decades. However, the 1980s saw a ten-fold increase in the publishing of horror books. Much of this product stepped well beyond the sinister and macabre into the grisly and gory. Many of the mostly paperback covers reflected this tendency with a typical red-and-black look of bloody knives, demonic and maniacal faces, or expressions of sheer unadulterated terror. Many Young Adults were buying, borrowing, and reading across the spectrum of adult horror. A 1988 Gallup poll indicated that the two dominant segments in the horror audiences at that time were (1) the young and male and (2) the adult, educated and at least half female. (Killheffer, 43)

A horror slump began in 1989, although certain authors who had emerged as masters of the genre—most notably Stephen King, Dean Koontz, Peter Straub, and V.C. Andrews—continued to ride high on the bestseller lists.

1991 has been identified as the beginning of the most recent mini-era in horror fiction. Dell launched its Abyss line dedicated to a more sophisticated, quality psychological suffering; madness and adult relationships pervade. Tanith Lee's *Heartbeat* and Dennis Etchison's *Shadowman* are Abyss novels. Carroll & Graf's new horror line tends to be more literary in nature. Thomas Ligotti's *Songs of a Dead Dreamer* and Brian Stableford's *Angel of Pain,* both Carroll & Graf publications, are more likely to be compared to Poe or Lovecraft. Berkley produces a quieter horror, often featuring, for example, a group of people up against an evil force. Phil Rickman's *Curfew* is a good example of this. Then, of course, there is Tor, whose products continue to give us the creeps.

The packaging of this 1990s horror product is more varied and subtle, without that lurid aspect of the 1980s. It is geared to more sophisticated target audiences and is a strong trend of the '90s in fact, luring readers who have not previously been horror fans. There is an obvious attempt at cross-marketing. Horrific novels dressed in tasteful, sometimes elegant jackets are being sold to a sizable segment of the reading public. However, sales of adult horror novels are still not what they were in the '80s.

Work Cited: Killheffer, Robert K.J. "Rising from the Grave." *Publishers Weekly,* 240, n38: 43–47.

THE NATURE OF THE BEAST: THE DEFINITION OF HORROR

Horror stories and the evil creatures, mental and psychological disorders that wreak havoc within them, have a hold on the North American imagination. North Americans are spending millions for the privilege of having themselves scared to death. Many of us can trace this fascination back to ghost stories around the campfire and the sleepover after dark.

The parameters of the horror genre are neither clear-cut nor constant. Horror fiction has long been included with science fiction and fantasy in magazines, anthologies, and guides. Science fiction and horror are often effectively combined, and many sci-fi authors also write horror. On the other hand, mystery / suspense novels often contain elements of horror and many works of horror depend upon a mystery plot. The distinction between psychological suspense and horror is fuzzy, and psychological suspense is often labeled horror whether or not there is an element of the supernatural or occult.

Whereas in pre-modern times, horror depended on beings with supernatural powers, against whom mere mortals had little recourse, more recently the genre embraces strange states of mentality. Megalomaniacs and psychopaths wreak havoc within the home or the broader community. The element of the occult has gained momentum in modern horror as well, much to the consternation of a large segment of our society.

The Magic Brew

The horror genre, then, embraces many themes and devices. Among them are:

* ghosts, ghouls and apparitions. These are especially popular in the short story medium.
* demonic possession and exorcism.
* satanism, demonology and black magic.
* witches and warlocks.
* reincarnation and possession (the principal area of crossover between horror and psychological suspense).
* vampires (came on strong with Bram Stoker's *Dracula* in 1897).
* werewolves.
* monsters (Mary Shelley's *Frankenstein* was written in 1818, *Dr. Jekyll and Mr. Hyde* in 1886).
* voodoo and witchdoctors.
* nightmares and hallucinations.
* paranormal powers.
* the supernatural and occult.
* transformation of people into other species, most frequently bats, cats and 'manimals.'
* souls sold to or somehow confiscated by the devil.

SHORT 'N' SWEET?!! THE SHORT STORY IN HORROR FICTION

The short story has retained its status as a favoured vehicle for the horror genre. Anthologies continue to be popular, some of which keep readers in touch with the old masters. *The Mists from Beyond* serves up Dickens, Stoker, Poe, Peter Straub, and others. David Hatwell's anthologies *The Dark Descent* and *Foundations of Fear* survey the history of horror. The Complete Masters of Darkness is a three-volume set edited by Dennis Etchison, and the list goes on. Some collections are composed of stories on a particular theme. *Deathport,* edited by Ramsay Campbell, focuses on a haunted airport. And for those who want the latest horrific offerings, there are the annual year's best: *The Year's Best Fantasy and Horror* (St. Martin's), *The Year's Best Horror Stories* (DAW), and *Best New Horror* (Carroll & Graf).

TO GRAB AND TO HOLD: THE IMPORTANCE OF COVER ART

Common to any category of fiction, but particularly to the horror genre, is the importance of cover art. It is especially vital before the author has become well known. The cover must grab and the content must hold. Much of 1980s adult horror featured lurid packaging characterized by black and red tones, bloody knives, dripping fingernails, demonic or maniacal faces, and expressions of sheer unadulterated terror. However, many imaginative techniques were being developed, including holographic art, die-cuts, and embossing, often combined with frightening or bizarre images. In more recent years, much of the packaging is more subtle and tasteful. All in all, the horror genre boasts some very innovative design. So much so that some of the cover art has become valued for its own sake.

WHITHER YAS?

Not least among fans of Stephen King, Dean Koontz, and V.C. Andrews have been Young Adults, whose reading tastes have encouraged the most notable development in 1990s horror fiction. In the late 1980s, as adult horror was going into decline YA horror novels were picking up steam, particularly in the realm of the series. The two best known and still the most popular YA series authors are Christopher Pike and R.L. Stine, whose *Fear Street* series took the YA market by storm. The popularity of Pike and Stine soon began to generate imitators, such as Daniel Ransom and Diane Hoh. In the '90s other YA horror series have been spawned, including *Terror Academy, Horror High, Nightmare Club*, and *Nightmare Hall*. The Point Series from Scholastic includes offerings from such increasingly popular YA horror authors as D.E. Atkins, A. Bates, Caroline B. Cooney, Richard Tankersley Cusick, Carol Ellis, Diane Hoh, and R.L. Stine. (Pike does not write for the Point series.) Stine and Pike are by far the biggest sellers, accounting for 60 to 70 percent of YA horror sales. Lists of Top Ten YA titles of 1993 and 1994 illustrate the extent of their popularity. American Top Ten YA lists sometimes include little other than Stine and Pike works, although Canadian teens appear to have somewhat more varied tastes.

It is interesting to note the poor representation of YA romance titles in the Top Ten lists. In fact, the romance series such as Sweet Valley High and Sweet Dreams, although still doing well, are not quite the performers they once were, and it would seem that the horror series have been putting the squeeze on them. One of the interesting things about the YA horror novel is its roughly equal appeal for both girls and boys.

A few series are intended for girls. *Vampire Diaries, Secret Friends,* and *Dark Moon* fall into this category, and tend to be romantic suspense with supernatural overtones.

Some series are actually characterized by publishers as thrillers. A case in point is Scholastic's Point Series, which has a red splotch under its name to designate the 'truly horrific' titles. The Point series is not the only one with a number of authors. Nightmare Club's author lineup includes adult authors writing under pseudonyms. Another series whose authors frequently use pseudonyms is Z-Fav/Zebra. This line has established a fan club whose members receive, among other things, author photos signed with pseudonyms and biographical information that does not indicate who these people really are.

Characteristics in Character

Most adult horror novels tend to be too long for YAs with less developed reading skills. So YA Horror, in keeping with YA novels in general, are short. Typically, they are fast-moving, with brief characterizations and good-looking protagonists. Most of them feature teenage WASPs in challenging and peculiar predicaments. Many of the protagonists are teenage girls who are smart, brave, and resourceful, rather than the hapless victims or helpless bystanders routinely constructed in years past. Inspiration for much of the cover art seems to have come from adult horror of the 1980s, although the pages within normally offer little in the way of gore. Love interests tend to be portrayed in romantic terms rather than sexual ones, although it is not difficult to find exceptions to this. Tongue-in-cheek humour is not uncommon, and supernatural and occult details may be used, sometimes with little regard for accuracy.

Recent decades have seen a shift away from reliance upon some supernatural forces of evil in the horror genre. True to this trend, YA horror is peopled with psychopaths, megalomaniacs, seemingly normal individuals with evil alter egos inhabiting their minds. Escapees from sanitoriums are a popular device, as is the possessed or obsessed teen who seeks revenge for some real or imagined rejection or other indignity. The revenge theme often infuses the story with strong mystery/detective or suspense characteristics. After reading a few of these novels, the astute reader detects an element of predictability, which may be one factor that encourages more mature teens with advanced reading skills to make the leap into adult horror.

At the lower end of the reading level spectrum are the young teens and preteens for whom R.L. Stine's Goosebumps has become a runaway favourite. In a February 1995 Coles Books list of the top 100 books of every type *other than* adult fiction, more than half of the top 25 titles were from the Goosebumps series, and 28 to 30 *Goosebumps* titles were among the top 100.

THE HORROR REFERENCE SHELF

Bleiler, Everett F. *The Guide to Supernatural Fiction.* Kent, OH: Kent State University Press [1983].

Burgess, Michael. *Reference Guide to Science Fiction, Fantasy, and Horror.* Englewood, CO: Libraries Unlimited, 1992.

Cox, Greg. *The Transylvanian Library: A Consumer's Guide to Vampire Fiction.* San Bernadino: Borgo Press, 1993.

Horror: 100 Best Books. Ed. Stephen Jones and Kim Newman. New York: Carroll & Graf, 1988.

Horror Literature: A Reader's Guide. Ed. Marshall B. Tymn. New York: Garland, 1990.

Justice, Keith L. *Science Fiction, Fantasy and Horror Reference: An Annotated Bibliography of Works about Literature and Film.* Jefferson, NC: McFarland, 1989.

Kies, Cosette. *Presenting Young Adult Horror Fiction.* New York: Macmillan, 1992.

Kies, Cosette. *Supernatural Fiction for Teens: More Than 1300 Good Paperbacks to Read for Wonderment, Fear, and Fun.* 2nd· Ed. Englewood, CO: Libraries Unlimited, 1992.

The Penguin Encyclopedia of Horror and the Supernatural. Ed. Jack Sullivan. New York: Viking [1986].

Reginald, Robert. *Science Fiction and Fantasy Literature 1975–1991: A Bibliography of Science Fiction, Fantasy and Horror Fiction Books and Nonfiction Monographs.* Detroit: Gale, 1992.

Reginald's Science Fiction and Fantasy Awards: A Comprehensive Guide to the Awards and Their Winners. 2nd· Ed. By Daryl F. Mallett and Robert Reginald. San Bernadino, CA: Borgo, 1991.

Science Fiction, Fantasy and Horror: 1984 [–1991]: A Comprehensive Bibliography of Books and *Short Fiction Published in the English Language.* Oakland, CA: Locus, 1986–1992. (8 vols.)

Supernatural Fiction Writers: Fantasy and Horror. New York: Charles Scribner's Sons [1985].

Selected Anthologies

Best New Horror. Ed. Stephen Jones. New York: Carroll & Graf. Annual.

The Complete Master of Darkness. 3 vols. Ed. Dennis Etchison. Penn Valley, CA: Underwood-Miller, 1991.

The Dark Descent. Ed. David Hatwell. New York: Tor Books, 1987.

The Horror Hall of Fame. Eds. Robert Silverberg and Martin H. Greenberg. New York: Carroll & Graf, 1992.

MacDonald, Caroline. *Hostilities: Nine Bizarre Stories.* New York: Scholastic, 1994.

The Mammoth Book of Terror. Ed. Stephen Jones. New York: Carroll & Graf, 1991.

The Mammoth Book of Vampires. Ed. Stephen Jones. New York: Carroll & Graf, 1992.

The Penguin Book of Horror. Ed. J.A. Cuddon. New York: Viking Penguin, 1985.

Year's Best Fantasy and Horror. New York: St. Martin. Annual.

The Year's Best Horror Stories. New York: DAW. Annual. (Their 20th Anniversary Edition was 1992.)

THE ATTRACTION OF HORROR

It isn't so hard to understand the attraction young adults have to horror. Their reasons are much the same as those of adults who enjoy reading from that genre. For many it is sort of an escapism, the thrill of being scared almost to death, without any real danger. When someone asked Stephen King why he made up such horrible things when there is so much real horror in the world, he said, "The answer seems to be that we make up horror to help us cope with the real ones." In today's world with so much crime, violence and uncertainty, readers can take a safe break from reality with a horror book that thrills and terrifies them at the same time. It is apparent that the attraction to horror movies is also a strong one. Horror movies draw an enormous crowd. Would we as librarians prefer that teens spend their time transfixed in front of the TV or in theatres watching horror movies, instead of honing their reading skills by enjoying a horror book? Reading has become an enjoyable activity for many teens, instead of a chore which has be forced upon them. Do we really want to squash this enthusiasm for reading?

HORRIFICALLY POPULAR YA AUTHORS

Though many teens read horror books intended for adults, the sheer length of these books precludes their being read by a lot of younger, less developed readers. Until recently when some new authors came on to the field, there was very little in the horror line to read for those readers who were past Lois Duncan but not yet ready to read King and Koontz.

Several authors have begun to write original horror paperbacks intended strictly for the YA audience, and their books have proven to be extremely popular with young adults. The two most successful of these authors are, of course, R.L. Stine and Christopher Pike. These authors are performing an important service by providing a sort of literary training for young YA readers who like horror fiction but can't quite cope with King and his buddies.

Though I can remember having children as young as 10 or 11 asking for a Stephen King book, that was largely before the whole Goosebumps and YA horror craze. Now it seems many of the youngest readers are content reading at their own level. Those who aren't good readers can also get in on the horror trend because now there are books available that they are able to read.

Even though the big names in YA horror (Pike and Stine), are extremely popular, that hasn't stopped many other YA authors from trying their hand at horror writing. There are numerous other writers who do have a following. Many of these popular authors, such as Caroline B. Cooney and Joan Lowery Nixon, did not start out writing horror. Caroline B. Cooney is chiefly recognized for her fiction (which appeals largely to a female audience) such as *Face on a Milk Carton,* a personal favourite of mine, along with numerous romance type novels. More recently she has tried her hand at horror with a trilogy: *The Fog, The Snow,* and *The Fire,* as well as other horror titles.

Nixon was first a mystery writer but now has also tried to move into the horror genre, with titles like *Whispers from the Dead, The Seance;* and *The Deadly Game of Magic.* Another popular author of gore and fear is Richard Tankersley Cusick, author of such favourites as *Teacher's Pet, Fatal Secrets,* and *Silent Stalker.*

Even the romance series Sweet Valley High is trying to cash in on horror's popularity. A red dot on the spine indicates *terror* making the book part of a special *terror* series, which is trying to appeal to young girls who like a little horror with their romance.

YA authors are also capitalizing on the increasing interest in vampires. Since the big movie hit *Interview with A Vampire,* YA authors have been trying to cash in on Ann Rice's fame. Dozens of vampire titles have popped up targeted for young adults. There are numerous novels simply entitled *Vampire* written by several different authors. Richard Tankersley Cusick has written *Vampire* and *Buffy, the Vampire Slayer.* But, perhaps most popular are the series such as Vampire Diaries by L.J. Smith, and Vampire Twins and Vampires by Caroline B. Cooney, which are extremely popular with teenage girls.

So, as you can see, there are lots of horror offerings aimed at or being read by young adults. Therefore they are an important part of any YA collection.

Yike! Pike!!

Though many adults and even some teens seem to lump Stine and Pike together, there are some differences between them.

In my opinion Pike writes at a more mature reading level. His books are longer, a little more horrific; and do have more violence and references to sex. Pike has a series called "Final Fiends" but most of his books are individual titles. Each Pike book features a cover showing a teenager or teenagers in distress and both the author's name and the title are printed in day glow colour.

It seems young adults know the difference between the two as well. Some read both; but very often we find a real R.L. Stine fan who does not like Pike; even more common is the Pike fan who does not read R.L. Stine. I once suggested a Stine book to a girl who was looking for one of the Pike titles (all out, of course) and she commented that she did not read Stine books. I asked her what the difference was and she said they just weren't as scary as Pike's. Well, thousands of readers do not agree, and R.L. Stine has become the 1990s craze.

R.L. Stine: The Craze of the 1990s

The famed Goosebumps Series by R.L. Stine are horror books for the younger reader, grade 4 or 5. They do not use sex or even much gore, but of course, there are scary things going on in order to scare the reader. That is the point isn't it?

However, R.L. Stine is best known by teens for his Fear Street series, though he also has numerous other series and individual titles. I have read at least a dozen R.L. Stine books and I really do not see anything wrong with them. I did not find any extreme or graphic violence, real sex, or even any swearing to speak of.

Actually, there are a number of Fear Street Series:

* Fear Street
* Fear Street Super Chiller
* The Fear Street Saga
* Fear Street Cheerleaders
* 99 Fear Street: The House of Evil

All of these books are read by thousands of teens across the continent.

Librarians everywhere voice the fact that they cannot keep them on the shelves. Young adults are lining up to buy and borrow these best-selling novels. What are we telling teens by trying to curb the one reading craze that has occurred among an age group which previously had a significant portion of which were a hard sell to the joys of reading? Many of these who are now reading YA horror might not be reading at all in the absence of that genre. What right do we have as educators and librarians to tell teens that their tastes and interests are not valid ones? Surely this is a drastic error on the part of professionals who should be striving to encourage reading interests in the youth of today's society.

TEN TREMENDOUS TERRIFIERS TO BOOK TALK: HORROR FOR YOUNG ADULTS

Athkins, D.E. *Mirror, Mirror*. Scholastic, 1992. ISBN 0590452460

Everyone wants to be beautiful, but is it worth dying for? Luci seems to have all the answers. Luci's mirror shows Dore's true beauty, doesn't it?

Bates, A. *Final Exam*. Scholastic, 1990. ISBN 0590432915

Kelly Frances doesn't know if she'll make it through finals. The pressure to do well and graduate is intense. But will Kelly pass the final exam? Her life depends on it! The pressure of finals is deadly for some people!

Cooney, Caroline B. *The Fog*. Scholastic, 1990. ISBN 0590416391

Part of a trilogy, Christina encounters evil when she leaves her home on Burning Fog Isle. She has to go to junior high school on the mainland. Boarding at the Shevvingtons' is proving to be a dangerous experience. Could something be going on at the principal's home; could it prove to be deadly?

Duncan, Lois. *I Know What You Did Last Summer*. Little Brown, 1973. ISBN 0316195464

That's what the note said. But how could any one know? There were only the four of them in the car that night, they were the only ones who knew, weren't they?

Duncan, Lois. *Killing Mr. Griffin*. Little Brown, 1978. ISBN 0316195499

The plan was to scare their teacher, NOT to kill him. But, now that Mr. Griffin is dead, the pact of silence is even more important. Susan should never have gotten involved. Now it's too late to back out of the group. She promised, and you should never break a promise; it can be deadly.

Duncan, Lois. *Stranger With My Face*. Dell, 1981. ISBN 0440983568

Laurie's perfect summer ends on a sour note when strange things start happening. Her boyfriend breaks up with her, swearing he saw her with another guy. Friends see her places, when she knows she wasn't there. Who's pretending to be her, who could look enough like her to fool her friends, even her family? Is it a ghost or someone even more scary? Will Laurie find out before it's too late?

Hall, John. *The Cheerleaders.* Harper, 1994.

Over the summer an old grade-school friend dies in a car accident. Holly's pretty, popular, and dying to become a cheerleader. How can she be getting phone calls and letters from the grave? The squad is getting smaller and smaller; will Holly survive the final cut?

Kuraoka, Hannah. *The Last Victim.* Avon Flare, 1994.

When Kelly moves into the house her parents are restoring, she's intrigued by the gold chain and piece of newspaper she finds under the loose floor board in her attic bedroom. They lead her to a string of murders. Has the real killer been caught? Or is the real killer someone she knows, watching her, loving her from afar, or is he nearer?

Nixon, Joan Lowery. *The Stalker.* Dell, 1985. ISBN 0440977533

Jennifer's determined to clear her best friend's name for a murder she's sure Bobbie didn't commit. But she'd better be careful; the murderer is still out there, and has been stalking her all along. Will the stalker be unveiled before it's too late?

Nixon, Joan Lowery. *Whisper from The Dead.* Delacorte, 1989. ISBN 0385298099

Since her near-death experience Sarah has had a special gift. When she moves into a new house where a murder recently took place, only Sarah senses the horror. Will she solve the mystery before it's too late?

GETTING THE GOOSEBUMPS: THE GROWING CONCERN ABOUT YOUNG ADULT HORROR FICTION

It seems that young adult horror fiction is scaring some adults more than it is scaring its teen readership.

Censorship challenges to titles by authors like Christopher Pike and R.L. Stine are increasing along with a general distrust of the genre and the effects it is having on those teens who read it.

Parents' groups, individuals, school board members, and others are voicing strong opposition to a series of books that children are devouring at a breakneck pace. Why are these people upset? What is it, exactly, that perturbs them about young adult novels that serve up suspenseful tales of the weird and sometimes unexplainable? A look at some recent challenges might reveal some of the answers to these types of questions.

In Halifax, in February and March of 1995, a group of parents were so concerned about the appearance of Pike, Stine, and L.J. Smith books in school libraries that they brought their concerns to the Halifax County District School Board. In a letter to that body, the parents (there were 3 of them) stated that they believed that by encouraging students to read books by these authors, the school system ran the risk of creating in its students unhealthy and harmful thoughts and behaviors. This same group also stated that the Goosebumps series (authored by R.L. Stine and intended for the preteen readership) possessed an ". . . underlying current of evil." In their letter they also cited a passage from a book entitled *Be Careful What You Wish For* that they deemed violent and inappropriate for a young audience. In it is described a strangling scene (prompted by one girl spilling pudding on another) in which the strangler's desire to harm is represented from the first person point of view. The same group of parents was interviewed on CBC's *Prime Time* news in a report filed by reporter Leslie MacKinnon. Interestingly, one of the parents objected to the books because they did not promote self-esteem.

The board, however, voted 6–3 against taking the books out of circulation immediately. The matter was referred for more consideration to an "education committee" whose job it will be to examine the issue more closely. That committee, at press time, was in the process of arranging its meetings and had not yet rendered its decision.

The concern about young adult horror fiction, however, is not isolated in Halifax. In fact, the concern about literature describing the inexplicable and the unknown can be seen in other parts of Canada. A survey conducted by Dave Jenkinson of censorship challenges in Manitoba public school libraries from September 1, 1991 to June 30, 1993, revealed some growing concern about materials containing supernatural elements. Having conducted a similar survey from 1982 to 1984, Jenkinson was able to gauge the change in fears from the time of the '80s survey to the '90s survey.

In the 1982–1984 survey, for example, the top reasons for challenges in the schools were based on the fact that the material was thought to be too mature for the readers or contained profanity. In the 1991–1993 survey, however, the two most dominant reasons for challenges were based on the fear that the titles in question contained elements of "Witchcraft and/or the Supernatural" or were "Violent." As Jenkinson himself states, "The 1982–84 concerns about materials containing 'Profanity' and 'Explicit Sex' have seemingly been replaced by the '90s fears that materials will contain elements of 'Witchcraft and/or the Supernatural,' or will contain 'Violence.'" The following chart provides a useful guide to the differences between the two periods.

TOP 10 REASONS FOR CHALLENGES IN SCHOOL LIBRARIES, 1982–84 AND 1991–93

1982–84	1991–93
1. Immaturity of Readers	1. Witchcraft/Supernatural
2. Profanity	2. Violence
3. Explicit Sex	3. Immaturity of Readers
4. Morality	4. Explicit Sex
5. Obscenity	5. Morality
6. Witchcraft/Supernatural	6. Nudity
7. Human Reproduction	7. Obscenity
8. Nudity	8. Profanity
9. Violence	9. Sexism/Role Stereotypes
10. Racism	10. Religion (Excluding evolutions)

The growing concern over materials containing elements of the supernatural also shows up in the authors and titles that were most frequently challenged in the 1991–93 investigation. Take the top two "Most Frequently Challenged Titles" from this survey as an illustration of this. In the 1991–93 survey, first and second place in this category went to Roald Dahl for *The Witches* and *Revolting Rhymes* respectively.

The question remains, however, as to *why* there is an increased opposition to titles of the type mentioned above? As Jenkinson points out in the Manitoba situation, the reason may have something to do with the removal of prayer from public schools. He feels that some of those interested in the removal of items containing supernatural elements might feel that if Christianity is not given a place in the public schools, then all other religions should be excluded as well.

Others might also try to explain the fear of the horror genre as a manifestation of the rising fear of crime. With its protagonists fighting forces of darkness and evil, horror literature contains elements of suffering and sometimes grievous physical harm. In the Halifax case, for example, the challenges came almost immediately on the heels of an incident at a local high school in which a male teen, armed with a shotgun, entered a school and, although unwillingly disarmed by a teacher, was apparently seeking out someone whom he wished to shoot and kill.

Admittedly, it is impossible to precisely discern the reasons for the fears that lead to censorship challenges. The only thing certain is that they will continue, be it horror fiction or not, and as educators, we had better be prepared for them.

Works Cited

Gee, Skana. "Thrillers Irk Board." *The Daily News*, Halifax, NS, March 1995.

Jenkinson, Dave. "The Changing Face of Censorship in Manitoba's Public School Libraries." *Emergency Librarian*. 22.2 (1994): 15–21.

SCARING AWAY THE CENSORS: SOME SUGGESTIONS FOR TEACHERS OF HORROR READERS

The whole language approach to English language arts has spawned a curriculum that allows students to read novels and short stories of their own choosing. The independent novel study, personal reader response journals, and uninterrupted sustained silent reading (acronymed as USSR) are elements of an educational format that makes room for the interests of the student. Thus, horror fiction is available in the libraries of our schools. Kids are reading them during USSR and responding to them for academic credit. As educators (and I firmly believe that librarians are included in this category), then we are faced with the question of their appropriateness. Do they promote the language and writing skills that our students need? Do they scare them and give them nightmares? Do they model violence? These are just a few of the questions which deserve answers in our attempt to better understand the relationship between horror fiction and the education system.

As indicated in the article in this issue entitled "Getting the Goosebumps: The Growing Concern about Young Adult Horror Fiction," the issue of challenges to public school's tolerance of young adult horror fiction is gaining increased attention. Scenarios like those in Halifax present complex problems to the teacher who wishes to make language arts relevant to her/his students' lives and interests while still managing to transmit to students the skills and concepts that they need. The purpose here, then, is to explore the options that are available to such educators. Should they throw out the books because they upset parents and, in so doing, risk losing the interest of the students? Is there any way that both groups can be appeased while still managing to teach something? Believe it or not, there are many ways in which horror fiction can be made relevant to the study of language arts.

As educators, then, what do we do? Undoubtedly, authors like Pike and Stine are not literary giants, yet there is little evidence that they do psychological harm to their readers. In Pike's *Remember Me*, there are plot inconsistencies, sentence fragments, and some poor grammar. As well, the plots are formulaic, the character development superficial, and the violence glaringly present. But do we ban them? Here in Nova Scotia, where the budget for school library acquisitions is zero (or near zero) across all of the province's school boards, do we begin to throw away the books that the students like and read the most?

What may shock some is the fact that these books do possess some measure of educational merit. The first of these is simply that the children actually read them. One Sackville area resource teacher reports that the students call Pike and Stine's works "page-turners" and seldom can put them down until they are entirely finished. Another junior high English teacher claims that reading the young adult horror authors actually improves her pupils' writing. They seem to have a much deeper appreciation of the concept of foreshadowing and pay more attention to narrative pacing instead of simply adapting the "reporter" style they tend to do naturally.

Indeed, plot lines and character sketches are still possible. For older, more mature readers, the genre provides an excellent departure point for the study of the classical concepts of catharsis: the Aristotelian theory that literature and art are activities engaged in because they provide the audience with an opportunity to experience tragedy at a comfortable remove from their real lives. In fact, the genre's standard portrayal of the protagonist as monied and "popular" might also provide an entry point into the study of the conventions of tragedy. Students might be asked if their favorite horror books would be as likable if the heroine/hero had been poor or "down and out" on his/her luck. The point, obviously, is to use literature that is interesting to students to turn them on to "literary" ideas.

In the same vein, as students' interests mature, they might become open to exploring related genres. To explore the connection between literature and psychology, students can be steered toward the "weird tale." Authors like Algernon Blackwood and H.P. Lovecraft created tales with more creatively developed plots and characters than one could find in any book written by Pike or Stine. Furthermore, reaching back to explore similar types of stories written and set in a different time also lends itself to cultural studies. Students might be asked to explore the social restraints and norms that are present in these works and compare them with those found in the horror literature of today. Some of the questions that could be asked are: How do the values of the respective protagonists differ? How are the settings different? Are the problems faced by the heroes and heroines in any way similar? In fact, in an effort to intellectualize the reading of these types of books, students might be presented with a literary critic's definition of art and asked to discuss their favorite horror book's qualification under the stated terms. The options are limitless and the horror genre, at the very least, *can* be intelligently examined and critiqued.

Admittedly, the gratuitous violence of some of these books should not receive sanction from the education system. But what message do we send teens when we limit their right to read instead of discussing the disturbing issues with them openly and honestly? Is it that we distrust their ability to judge and believe them incompetent of distinguishing fact from fantasy? What is surprising in this regard is just how sophisticated a readership we are dealing with: like the deconstructionists, a lot of students (at a young age) realize that, as readers, they are as responsible for the construction of meaning in a text as the author. Take the response of a grade seven student to the survey question "What do you think is scarier, seeing a horror movie or reading a horror book?":

> My opinion is reading the book is much more intense, you read descriptive words, and can picture everything in your mind, the pace goes as fast as you want to read it at. With a book, you read small details you probably would have skipped if you watched a movie. Reading exercises your brain more, and rays don't come off a book like they do a television. . . . You can take your book along with you almost anywhere. (quoted in Hansen, 124)

This is obviously a student who seems to control her text instead of letting it control her.

Making room for the interests of the students is a goal that all educators should embrace. And it is not an entirely new idea; there are documented examples of cases in which pleasurable reading for academic credit has been encouraged by the school. In one school, a program called the "Whole School Supplemental Reading Program" was implemented. Described in the 1993 *Journal of Reading*, this project involved the creation of a list of books which different teachers sponsored for credit in their course. Interestingly, on this particular school's list Stephen King's *The Eyes of the Dragon* appeared and was sponsored by the teacher of the school's Western Civilization course.

There are also ways for librarians to guide the horror reader while developing important communication and critical thinking skills. What about planning a library "celebrity monster dinner party"? Students can contribute a place setting that their character would enjoy and other culinary accoutrements befitting their anticipated guest (extrapolation, analysis, synthesis are the higher order thinking skills that are used here). Dramatic readings from good scary poetry or short stories can demonstrate that literature isn't boring; it affects you! A realization, we hope, that they will come to (and begin to look for) in other texts. Another activity, described in the September 1991 issue of *Bookmark*, is a "whodunit?" short story contest. In this activity, students were given a list of clues they had to use in their stories. The students' work was later judged by the English teacher and then by a selection committee.

Admittedly, students read about haunted houses and evil neighbors because they enjoy it. But the effort here is not to deaden that pleasure with an overly academic dissection of their reading interest. Rather, it is to demonstrate that the first response to literature is always affective and how the book made them feel is an important step in building meaningful interpretations of literature. For the teacher, then, who is interested in respecting her/his students' interests, these are just a few of the approaches that can be taken. Those who threaten to ban books often have little knowledge of the true aim of literature and are ignorant of the ideals of intellectual freedom. As Lou Willett Stanek believes, what students learn about society if their books are taken from them might be scarier than any of the young adult horror tales they will ever read:

> What students learn about the world when teachers are not daring is probably much more important than what we tell them or what they read. If English teachers are not willing to lead the fight for the student's right to think and judge for himself, censorship based on ignorance of the purpose of literature and the author's purpose will be perpetuated, and the English teacher himself/herself will become the censor. (143)

Resources

Gauthier, Michael and Elizabeth S. Smith. "Whole School Supplemental Reading Program." *Journal of Reading* 75 (1993): 55–56, 58–68.

Hansen, Eileen. "Censorship in Schools: Studies and Surveys." *School Library Journal* 34 (1987): 123–125.

Hopkins, Dianne McAfee. "Challenges to Materials in Secondary School Library Media Centres: A National Survey." *Journal of Youth Services in Libraries* 4 (1994): 131–140.

Jenkinson, Dave. "The Changing Faces of Censorship in Manitoba's Public School Libraries." *Emergency Librarian* 22.2 (1994): 15–21.

Jenkinson, Dave. "Results of a Survey of Challenges in Public and School Libraries." *Canadian Library Journal* (1986): 7–21.

McAloon, Noreen. "Selecting Books (From the Teacher's Desk)." *Journal of Reading* 37 (1993): 146–147.

McCarthy, Martha M. "Challenges to Public School Curriculum: New Targets and Strategies." *Phi Delta Kappan* 75.1 (1993): 55–56, 58–60.

Sacco, Margo. "Defending Books: A Title Index to Three Collections of Rationales." *ALAN Review* 20 (1993): 39–41.

Schrader, Alvin M. and Keith Walker. "Results of an Alberta Public Library Survey." *Canadian Library Journal* April (1986): 91–95.

Stanek, Lou Willett. *A Teacher's Guide to Censorship*. New York: Dell Publishers, 1979.

Webb, Anne C. and Carole Williams. "Developing Insurance Against the Censor." *ALAN Review* 20.2 (1993): 20–21.

Featuring Comics and Graphic Novels

YA Hotline, Issue No. 55, 1996

ILANA FERRIS, JACKIE JAMES, WAYNE PAQUET, AND KAREN PARUSEL

AMERICAN COMICS: A CHRONOLOGICAL HISTORY

The Early Years

19th Century—Comics began to appear in Sunday papers—Richard Outcault's *The Yellow Kid* involved in a bidding war as Joseph Pulitzer's *New York World* and William Randolph Hearst's *New York Journal* competed for the right to print

Dec. 12, 1897—Katzenjammer Kids created by Rudolph Dirks and appears in *New York Journal*—later becomes longest running cartoon

Nov. 15, 1907—Mutt and Jeff becomes first successful daily comic

1910–1931—Many cartoon books published with such characters as Little Orphan Annie, Dick Tracy, Popeye, Little Nemo, Krazy Kat, Tarzan, Mickey Mouse

January 1929—George Delacorte published *The Funnies No. 1*, the first four-color comic with a cover price of 10 cents

1933—Birth of the Modern Comic Format—Harry Wildenberg and Max Gaines of Eastern Color Printing saw plates of a comic and realized these could fit on a "tabloid page" to produce a 7½ inch by 10 inch book when folded. Published reprints of Mutt and Jeff and Joe Palooka in this format. Gaines and Wildenberg considered the "Pioneers of Modern Comics"

1934—Eastern Color hired Delacorte to market this new idea. He reissued his famous *Funnies No. 1* which became a hit in its new format and started to make a substantial profit by fourth issue

The Golden Era

June 1938—Superman debuts in Action Comics #1 published by DC Comics—became most famous comic of all—creators Jerry Siegel and Joe Shuster originally tried to sell it to United Features but they responded that it was "too immature"

May 1939—A new company called Detective Comics was formed and launched a new comic which soon included the character Batman, created by Bob Kane—due to Batman's popularity Batman #1 appears in 1940

1939—Timely Comics started and later became Marvel—The Human Torch and the Submariner created by Bill Everett and Carl Burgos

1939–40—By this time there were 60 different comic books and by the end of 1941 the number rose to 168 including: Flash, Green Lantern, Atom, The Hawkman, Green Hornet, The Lone Ranger, Captain Marvel, Wonder Woman

1943—25 million comics being sold a month and an industry worth 30 million dollars a year

1945–50—Shift to horror, western, crime, and romance comics—Hopalong Cassidy selling eight million copies

The Comics Code

1954—Dr. Fredric Wertham writes *The Seduction of the Innocent* in which he describes the damaging effects of comics on children—claimed comics encouraged unusual sexual acts, delinquent behavior, and learning disorders:

Robin is a handsome ephetic boy, usually showing his uniform with bare legs. He is buoyant with energy and devoted to nothing on earth or interplanetary space as much as to Bruce Wayne. He often stands with legs spread, the genital region discreetly evident.

April 1954—The U.S. Senate Subcommittee to Investigate juvenile delinquency set up and Wertham testifies—the result was the Comics Code, which was a response by the Comic Magazine Association of America Inc., which decided to self-regulate—massive restrictions were placed on comics—horror comics nearly disappeared, westerns had fewer gunfights—many publishers went out of business

1954–1969—18,125 comics published under the supervision of the Code—many publishers turned back to superhero stories which were easier to get published

1961—The "Marvel Age" of comics begins—Marvel dominates the next ten years with such titles as The Fantastic Four, The Hulk, Spiderman, Ironman, and The X-Men

1970s—The Comic Code began to be less rigorously applied partially due to successes such as an anti-drug Spiderman comic

1977—*Cerebus* published independently by Dave Sim and continues to this day—was grandfather of independent comic industry which currently published hundreds of titles

1980s—Very few large publishers outside of Marvel and DC remained—modern era begins

The '80s was the anything goes decade. Anything with ten adjectives in it was big. There was a big black and white boom. People began to accept that it didn't have to be Marvel and it didn't have to be in colour to be good.

—*Calum Johnston,*
Strange Adventures Comic Book Shop, Halifax

Bibliography

Fuchs, Wolfgang. *Comics: Anatomy of a Mass Medium*. London: Studio Vista, 1970.

Lee, Stan. *Origins of Marvel Comics*. New York: Simon & Schuster, 1974.

Santos, D. The Comic Page. http://www.loa.com//dsantos/pregold.html

GRAPHIC NOVELS: AN INTRODUCTION

Background

"There are *no* good comics," snapped an angry librarian in a professional journal in 1949. "Examine any one of them and you will find the subject-matter sensational, the language distorted, and the art worse than mediocre, to say nothing of the poor paper, the gaudy coloring, and the bad print" (Hunter, 455). How times have changed.

In the 1960s, sophisticated comic books, often elegantly printed and bound in hard covers, became fashionable in Europe and Japan. These, in turn, influenced American mass-market comic-book publishers and the two best known, Marvel and DC, started expanding into "graphic novels" in the 1980s. Competing with them were the independent publishers, who started producing graphic novels for a growing audience of mature readers (Johnson, 19–20).

Today's graphic novels, which are usually printed on high-quality glossy paper for crisper artwork, often go beyond the superhero/villain themes of mainstream comics. Science fiction, westerns, horror, mystery, and nonfiction are all well served by this format. The illustrations, sometimes awe-inspiring, range from black-and-white to full-color (Sherman and Ammon, 34).

The term graphic novels, however, is a misnomer that sometimes causes confusion and misconceptions (Sherman and Ammon, 34). To some, "graphic" implies explicit (as in sex and violence), and the books are not always novels. They are more often short stories, novellas, adaptations of longer works, or compilations of comic book serials. For this reason, the more accurate terms "trade comics" and "trade paperbacks" are frequently used.

Audience

Whatever you choose to call them, these books are truly unique in the way they marry words with illustrations (Weiner, 26). This special combination appeals to a varied teenage readership: disinterested and reluctant readers as well as accomplished ones. As Stephen Weiner noted, "Any librarian, upon visiting a comic book specialty shop, is immediately aware that the clientele consists primarily of teenagers, and that the activities the teenagers are engaged in are reading and discussing a literature they feel pertains to them."

Selecting Graphic Novels

One of the difficulties that librarians and teachers face when considering the purchase of graphic novels is the lack of reviewing sources. Although traditional sources such as *School Library Journal*, *VOYA*, *Library Journal*, and *Booklist* review graphic novels, they don't do so frequently. *Publishers Weekly* usually notes the publication of graphic novels and provides annotations.

The best way to keep up with the field, however, is through journals published by the comics industry. According to Weiner, *Previews* is the *Publishers Weekly* of the comics industry. In it are found listings and annotations for almost every comic book and graphic novel being released in approximately two months time. *The Comics Journal*, akin to *Library*

Journal, includes reviews, articles, and interviews with people instrumental in the industry. It also shows a definite bias against the mainstream (Marvel, DC, and Image). *Wizard* and *Overstreet's Fan*, glossy magazine/price guides, feature new releases and interviews with writers and artists, among other features. These publications are all issued monthly. Finally, *Indy*, issued six times per year, provides in-depth coverage of independent comics.

Whether or not they wish to become specialists in graphic novels, librarians should form a liaison with a comic book specialty shop. In good stores, managers and their staff, who are already comics experts, will not only know what is available and how to purchases it, they will guide librarians toward the "must buy" titles, identify "sleepers," and advise on which novels are attractive to which audiences, and why (Weiner, 270). Furthermore, the industry periodicals discussed above will usually be available through a comic specialty shop.

In selecting graphic novels, librarians should also ask young adults, perhaps those in their libraries or in local comic shops, what their preferences are. In most cases, they'll like the idea of adults asking them for advice. Askers might also be pleasantly surprised at how knowledgeable some of them are about the subject.

What to Acquire

Any librarians or teachers contemplating starting a graphic novel collection for young adults might want to consider beginning with the following four excellent books:

Maus: A Survivor's Tale. Art Spiegelman. Pantheon, 1986.

Maus II: And Here My Troubles Began. Art Spiegelman. Pantheon, 1991.

This Pulitzer Prize winning story is a narrative of Spiegelman's father's experiences as a Polish Jew during the Holocaust, and the son's attempts to reconcile himself with his father's past and present behavior. This two-volume set is one of the masterpieces of contemporary comic-book literature.

ElfQuest (Book 1). Wendy Pini. The Donning Company, 1981.

A well-realized fantasy about the Wolfriders, a band of elves in search of a new home in a savage Earth-like world. An excellent example of how graphic novels can do justice to fantasy themes.

Understanding Comics: The Invisible Art. Scott McCloud. HarperCollins, 1994.

The best examination to date of the historical development and perceptual traits of the comic book medium, presented in graphic novel format. Everyone who reads this fun book will learn a great deal about "sequential art."

COMICS IN THE CLASSROOM AND LIBRARY?

Why should any teacher or librarian consider the use of comics in their classroom or library? Here are just a few key reasons:

Comics in the Classroom

Popularity—Many YAs enjoy comics. They are entertaining. Using comics in your class is guaranteed to generate interest and excitement.

Connection—We often hear that school does not reflect the students' real life. Using comics is one way to make the connection between students' real lives and what occurs in the classroom.

Reading Interest and Levels—It is often a struggle to get many of our students to read. Whether trying to reach non-readers or readers with learning disabilities, comics can be a compromise that may get students reading. The graphic format and short length are not too daunting.

Unit Enrichment—Teachers are constantly looking for tools to enrich their units. Comics can be a unique tool to use in your class and have been written about virtually every topic. If studying the Holocaust in history you could use *Maus* to make the emotional connection and spark student interest. And if studying Japan in economics you could use *A Cartoon Introduction to the Japanese Economy*.

Gifted Material—If you have read a few comics, you know that some of the storylines are extremely sophisticated. For students needing extra challenge, the teacher could design a variety of independent studies focusing on comics and graphic novels.

Classroom Management—The most frustrating and time-consuming aspect of teaching is classroom management. No two students ever seem to finish assignments at the same time. Comics could be an effective classroom management tool. Most students enjoy them and would relish the chance to read a comic while waiting for the next activity or assignment. Comics could also be used as a reward for good behavior.

Language Arts—Teachers have been using music lyrics for decades as an addition to their language arts program. Students enjoy listening to the lyrics and begin to take notice of the poetic language being used. Many comics also use succinct, poetic language that could be analyzed in English class. Getting students to write and illustrate short comic book is another means of reaching reluctant writers.

Graphic Appeal—In virtually any analysis of artistic style comic books could be used as an example—whether analyzing Renaissance style in History or the influence of modern art on modern literature in English. All of these styles can be seen in modern comic books.

Tough Issues—Many comic books have been produced which deal with such sensitive issues as drug addiction and child abuse. These can be utilized to generate interest in these issues and to provide the necessary information YAs need to deal with these problems.

Comics in the Library

Door Crasher Special—comics are simply an easy way to attract young adults to your library.

The Mandate—Most librarians believe in providing what their clients want. The size of the comics industry clearly illustrates that they want comics.

Easy to Collect—For years librarians have been complaining that collecting comics was impractical due to their size and fragility. Now with the advent of graphic novels and trade paperback collections of comics they are easy to collect and handle.

A Stepping Stone—Some librarians consider comics and serial novels as fluff. However, they can be seen as a stepping stone to more sophisticated material. If young people are coming to the library to borrow comics they may eventually begin to borrow other materials.

Valuable Materials—It is also important to note that many comics and graphic novels deal with complex themes in a mature manner. We have already talked about such graphic novels as *Maus* and *The Watchmen*. But even many of the mainstream comics have their main characters deal with everyday problems and issues. It is time for librarians to take a second look at this popular and growing medium.

Alternative Materials for Non- or New Readers—Once again the small amount of text and visual details result in a pleasant read for non- or new readers. These materials could help supplement your literacy collection.

COMICS, CENSORSHIP, AND OTHER C-WORDS

The year is 1954. William Gaines has taken over his father's E.C. Comics and business is booming. All over the country the kids are eating up his titles. *The Vault of Horror. Tales from the Crypt. Weird Science. The Haunt of Fear.* All these are becoming standard teenage literary fare.

Gruesome titles, gory stories, detailed artwork to make even the least imaginative kid quake. Great Stuff. Or at least that's what readers and editors at E.C. Comics thought.

But not Dr. Fredric Wertham. In his book, *Seduction of the Innocent*, he exposed comic books as questionable and harmful. He claimed that comic books contributed to juvenile delinquency, violent crime, social unhappiness, and deviant sexual behavior.

The E.C. Comics were prime targets, of course, but not the only ones. Even the superheroes were not safe from his scathing criticism. Wonder Woman promoted lesbianism and Batman and Robin's bachelor status reeked of homosexuality.

What followed was a wave of controversy that swept the United States like a tidal wave. Everything from community bonfires to Senate Judiciary Committee hearings.

E.C. Comics owner, William Gaines, and editor, Harvey Kurtzman, tried to defend themselves but they were drowned out in the wave of anti-comics censorship.

The end result was the creation of the Comics Code and the Comics Code Authority. It proudly defended itself as "the most stringent code in existence for any communications media" (Witek, 48).

The Comics Code was a form of self-censorship. It established a code which dictated the content and look of comic books: "Guidelines of the authority prohibit displays of corrupt authority, successful crimes, happy criminals, the triumph of evil over good, violence, concealed weapons, the death of a policeman, sensual females, divorce, illicit sexual relations, narcotic or drug addiction, physical afflictions, poor grammar and the use of the words 'crime,' 'horror,' and 'terror' in the title of a magazine or story" (Witek, 48).

This pretty well finished off the entire E.C. Comics repertoire. The code was a perfect form of economic warfare. Most magazine distributors, fearful of parental protests, refused to sell non-Code-approved comic books. This once vibrant and sophisticated medium was instantly reduced to the "ill-crafted pap toward which most American comics tended anyway" (Siano, 43).

Only one of the E.C. comics survived the blast—*Mad* magazine. Only its larger, black-and-white format protected it from the censor's blade. Its social satire of American culture was a forerunner of the popular underground comics of the 1960s. Today, 40 years later, it still remains a cutting revelation of teenage rebellion. "It was the first to tell us that the toys we were being sold were garbage, our teachers were phonies, our leaders were fools, our religious counselors were hypocrites and even our parents were lying to us about nearly everything" (Siano, 43).

The renaissance of the comics in the 1960s as underground comics signaled the artists' creative control over their work, as well as economic control. Small independent publishers sprang up and took care of their own distribution, throwing off the constraints placed on them by the code. Novels such as *The Watchmen*, by Alan Moore and Dave Gibbons, *Sin City* by Frank Miller, *Love and Rockets* by the Hernandez brothers are just a few of the comic jewels produced.

These independent comics still managed to survive despite the power of the Comics Code Authority, but this does not mean that censorship is dead. Parents till complain about "adults only" and non-code-approved comics and graphic novels. In the United States comic book stores are being raided and literature confiscated daily (Siano, 43).

Here in Nova Scotia it is handled by an individual honour system. There are some comics that state on the cover that they are meant for mature audiences only. Most comic book store-owners simply use their own personal judgment to decide what they will sell to whom.

Some comic books contain pornographic or racist content. These materials are usually kept on a special shelf behind the counter.

Now there is a movement afoot to rate comic books, much as is done with movies. One store-owner here in Halifax says that he is very much against "rating" comic books. He says that if you go into a regular bookstore, "regular" literature isn't rated, so why should we rate comic books and graphic novels?

Another interesting battle is brewing in California over comic books. It involves how comic books are classified for tax purposes. The Board of Equalization in the state of California has ruled that comic book art does not qualify as an "original manuscript" (Siano, 43).

Art Spiegelman, who won a Pulitzer Prize for *Maus*, a two-volume graphic novel about the Holocaust, says that the implication here is that "comics are not literature, but simply a commodity" (Siano, 43).

Poems, music, even comic book scripts are not subject to sales tax, but comic book art is considered to be a commercial art and therefore is taxable. This is a blow to an art that already has so many handicaps.

One comic book writer has put the fight against this tax very clearly. Matt Groening says, "Comics are free speech, and you don't put a tax on free speech" (Siano).

The comic book and graphic novel have managed to survive a rocky childhood, filled with censorship from society and from within its own community. Despite the rigid format placed on it by the Comics Code, comics have managed to thrive as both an art form and an industry.

Today, inspired by the creative independence of the 1960s underground comics, you can find comic books stores filled with hundreds of great reads.

Excerpts from the Comics Code

"Scenes of excessive violence shall be prohibited. Scenes of brutal torture, excessive and unnecessary knife and gun play, physical agony, gory and gruesome crime shall be eliminated."

"The letters of the word 'crime' on a comics magazine cover shall never be appreciably greater in dimension than the other words contained in the title. The word 'crime' shall never appear alone on the cover."

"No magazine shall use the word 'horror' or 'terror' in its title."

"Scenes dealing with, or instruments associated with walking dead, torture, vampires and vampirism, ghouls, cannibalism, and werewolfism are prohibited."

"Profanity, obscenity, smut, vulgarity, or words or symbols which have acquired undesirable meanings are prohibited."

"Females shall be drawn without exaggeration of physical qualities."

"Passion or Romantic interest shall never be treated in such a way as to stimulate the lower and baser emotions."

The Wonderful World of Alternative Comics

What do you think of first when you hear the term comic book? Did you answer superheroes, Spiderman, Batman, Wonder Woman? That's what I thought until I went to my local comic book store and discovered another world—alternative comics. Alternative to what was my first question. The term refers to any comic book or graphic novel that is NOT a mainstream comic produced by one of the big publishers (Marvel, DC, Image) and is not in the superhero genre.

It was 10 to 20 years ago when characters were everything in comic books. It didn't matter who the artist was, in fact credit was never given. Walt Disney signed everything even though it was his artists that did the work. Now, much like in the film industry where audiences go to see their favorite

director, people are beginning to recognize individual artists and will seek out those comic books according to the artist's name, rather than the title. It is the creators not the characters (Batman, Spiderman) that are sought after. This marks a new trend in the comic book industry: the big companies are seeing the market for quality artwork. DC's subsidiaries, Vertigo and Paradox, publish comic books for their story and/or their art, not their superhero characters.

There are an enormous number and variety of comics and graphic novels that are produced by independent companies or artists. Some of these are breakaway companies from the big conglomerates, i.e., their creators used to work for the big guys but have now formed their own companies. Charles Vess used to draw fantasy comics for DC and Marvel. He now produces his own, the most well known of which is *The Book of Ballads*. David Lapham, former artist for superhero comics *Harbinger* and *Warriors of Plasm* now produces his own comic, *Stray Bullets*.

Another avenue of alternative comics is individual artists who have never worked for another comic book company going into business for themselves, such as Dave Sim who produces *Cerebus, The Aardvark*. Sim opened his own company, Aardvark Vanaheim, in 1977 and is the president. Over 200 issues later *Cerebus* is still a well-known and popular comic book.

Yet a third alternative route is the artist who creates her/his own comic, but rather than go to the trouble of self-publishing gives that part of the business over to another company. Drawn and Quarterly out of Quebec is such a company, much like a cooperative, and Mary Fleener is one of its artists.

Mary Fleener, a Seattle artist, has a comic book called *Slutburger*. Now don't go jumping to conclusions. The issue I read was grungy, but take into account the subject matter. This comic book is about the grunge band music scene in Seattle and she writes about incidents that have happened to herself and her friends. She is writing autobiographically. (The protagonist is a woman named Mary.)

Fleener's art is stunning, black and white, bold, brash, Picassoesque. I am told there is a man in Seattle who is so enamored with her art he had it tattooed all over his body. Whatever, as the teens say. This comic, along with Joe Matt's *Peep Show*, P. Bagge's *Hate*, and quite a few others, is characterized "for mature readers" as the titles well indicate. Indeed, these are for the older end teen range as well as for adults. However, the 16-year-old comics aficionados I talked to like them for the art. There are some excellent artists out there producing comic book art and they should be acknowledged. An important trend to note in the alternative comics field is that many of them are going to black and white. Often, as in Mary Fleener's case, the black and white is the most suitable for the art—it is stark and crisp. Most often, however, it is an economic impetus. Black and white is cheaper.

Graphic novels are another form of alternative comic book. Will Eisner's *A Contract with God* was first published in 1979 and is arguably the first graphic novel. Since then there are such works as Stan Sakai's *Usagi Yojimbo* (Rabbit Bodyguard), a story about a masterless rabbit samurai, Miyamoto Usagi, and his adventure in 17th-century Japan. A new graphic novel is *The Tale of One Bad Rat*, by Bryan Talbot, a well-known British writer of under-

ground comics. This is a brilliant story about a young girl named Helen who runs away from home because she has been sexually abused by her father and never wanted by her mother. It tells of her struggle and success in confronting her parents and finally dispelling the demons of her past. This is a victorious story, beautifully illustrated and a must for any school or public library. Talbot deals with the sexual abuse issue in a tactful, delicate, yet very realistic manner and will be read by young people. It is published by Dark Horse Books out of Milwaukie, Oregon, ISBN 1-56971-077-5.

In conclusion, you just can't take anything for granted in the world of comic books. What you *thought* it was is not what it actually *is*. Librarians and teachers need to be aware of this cornucopia of new works of art for their own sake, and even more importantly because lots of young people are reading them. And that is reason enough.

Bibliography

Hunter, Elizabeth K. "Comic Books." *Illinois Librarian* 31 (1949): 445

Johnson, Robin. "Comic Book Fan Magazines: Watching Pop Turn into Art." *Serials Review* 12 (1986): 19–20.

Sherman, Gale W. and Bette D. Ammon. "Beyond Superman: The Boom in Trade Comics." *School Library Journal* 39 (May 1993): 34

Siano, Brian. "Tales from the Crypt." *The Humanist* 54 (March-April 1994): 40–43.

Weiner, Stephen. "Creating a Graphic Novel Collection for the Public Library." *VOYA* 15 (December 1992): 26.

Witek, Joseph. *Comic Books as History*. University Press of Mississippi, 1989.

THE NEW NORTH AMERICAN COMICS CRAZE—MANGA!

"Picture yourself boarding a crowded bus or train in the United States and finding that almost everyone—from sweet old ladies to super-bad rappers to pin-striped young executives—is reading comic books. In Japan you'd be more surprised not to see this scene given the enormous variety and popularity of comics." (Magnier)

The Manga Industry

There is a new craze in the American comics industry—*"manga,"* which are Japanese comics. Surely this must be yet another example of those crafty and enterprising Japanese taking American technology, adapting it, and then selling it back to them in the form of a better product. After all, the comic book is an American icon. Superman and Spiderman are the stuff that legends are made of and have been around forever. Of course, "forever" in American terms is measured in decades while in Japan it is measured in centuries. In fact, the Japanese comics industry has a lofty and long tradition dating back over a thousand years.

Comics are currently more pervasive in Japanese society than they are in America. "In 1984 alone, 1.38 billion copies of Japanese comic books and magazines were sold nationally for 340 billion yen while in the United States approximately 39 million copies of American comics were sold" (Ito, 81). This trend has continued over the past ten years. "By 1994, annual sales of *manga* books and magazines had grown to 2.27 billion from 1 billion in 1980. There are now 500 new comic books published a month, compared to 80 a decade ago."

Some of this *manga* has made its way to North America and is growing in popularity. Marvel Comics began to translate the Akira series of comics in 1987 and have sold over two million copies in the United States (Comics Explosion, 40). They are bold, brash, more than a little off-beat, and have caught the attention of a whole generation of American comic readers. Let's take a closer look at its history and some modern themes.

Manga History

Emaki Mono. 9th-century Japan. The Heian Period. Buddhism and the Kana Syllabaries. Emperors and warrior Samurai battling for loyalty and territory. An artist decided to mix traditional artwork with the telling of history and stories. Emaki mono is born. "These scrolls (emaki mono) depicted epics, novels, folk tales and religious themes, employing techniques ranging from line composition to colorful scenes inlaid with gold" (Dyroff and Silbermann, 162). This emaki mono had many qualities of modern comics and became quite popular like their counterparts. The only things restricting their popularity were printing methods.

Kusazoshi. After many centuries the Japanese perfected block printing in the Edo period around the 17th and 18th centuries. A new pictorial literature was soon developed called Kusazoshi. It was originally developed for children of the lower classes, many of whom were illiterate and who had no taste for classical Japanese culture. However, it grew in popularity among all age groups and soon dealt with sophisticated themes. Kusazoshi was renowned for depicting explicitly violent scenes which stemmed out of the Japanese warrior tradition. Many of the techniques of the Kusazoshi are still evident in modern comics. It is from this period that the Japanese word for comic comes—"manga."

Kamishibai. One other fascinating artistic tradition that influenced the comics industry was Kamishibai (paper theatre), which existed for several centuries until about 1950. This art form required artists to draw their stories in a series of pictures without any dialogue. They would then travel the countryside and give performances with the pictures. Part of the performance included the artist hiding behind the pictures and speaking the parts of the characters in several voices. This art form has obvious parallels to comics. But its influence was even greater because "Many of the paper theatre artists later entered the field of mass comic production when they could no longer enter their profession" (Dyroff and Silbermann, 163).

After centuries of seclusion, the Japanese quickly became aware of the rest of the world with the arrival of Admiral Perry in 1853. In 1861 they began to publish *Japan Punch* for the English-speaking foreigners. Newspapers and magazines became interested in comics and began to publish installments of pictorial novels in the early 1900s. It wasn't until 1930 that the commercial production of comics in Japan got started. Even the government was supportive of this new industry since many of the comics possessed "an increasingly fascist tone until the end of World War II" (Dyroff and Silbermann, 163). After WWII comics became increasingly sophisticated and publishers started to target a variety of market segments in Japan, not just the shonen (young boys).

Gegika. There was a dramatic upsurge in comic interest in the 1960s with the development of a new type of comic called gegika (dramatic pictures). It was a new genre "with an intense, often sordid realism frequently focusing on lust and violence" (Dyroff and Silbermann, 163). This started as an underground type of comic attributed to an old paper theatre artist. It grew into the most dominant form of Japanese comic.

Modern Comics and Modern Themes

For many years the Japanese comics industry never encountered government interference or a comics code. "Actually, no official form of censorship exists in Japan. Editors execute this function as part of their job with a keen sensitivity for what the limits are, although it would seem to be the case that they are continually pushing these further" (Dyroff and Silbermann, 166). With the development of *gegika* and the long-standing tradition of explicitly violent cartoons and artwork, some modern comics have taken these themes to extremes. "Bordering on obscenity and revulsion, adult comics offer a strong mix of horror, crime, and pornography in which women are portrayed as sex objects for subjugation, or contrastingly, as monsters who subjugate men" (Dyroff and Silbermann, 166).

The end result was that the Japanese government stepped in and began to censor the Japanese comics industry. Their main concern was that children were reading the explicitly graphic and sexual comics. "In 1991, *Shuppan Rinri Kyogikai*, or Council of Ethics on Publication, decided that publishers should mark these adult comic magazines with a small round sticker with *seinen komikku* (adult comic) designation that it is adult material . . . . Between January and June 1991, there were a total of 2460 publications that were designated as harmful material" (Ito, 92).

It is interesting to note that while these comics certainly exist and are popular there are other Japanese comics that "stress the value of comradeship, collective loyalty, personal strength and are essentially moral with good invariably triumphing over evil" (Dyroff and Silbermann, 166).

Bibliography

"The Comics Explosion." *Publishers Weekly*. 239 n46 (October 19, 1992): 40.

Dyroff, H.D. and Herausgegeben von Alphons Silbermann, eds. *Comics and Visual Culture: Research Studies from Ten Countries*. New York: Saur, 1986.

Kinko Ito. Images of Women in Weekly Male Comic Magazines in Japan." *Journal of Popular Culture* 27 (Spring 1994): 81.

Magnier, Mark. "Comic Relief at the Newstand." *The Journal of Commerce*. Asia View column. July 19, 1995.

COMICS WITH GIRL APPEAL

The comic book, a medium that had its "Golden Age" over three decades ago, is making a comeback. Recent studies indicate that the percentage of adolescents reading comic books is substantial: for boys, the range is from 50 to 75 percent; for girls, 50 to 60 percent (McKenna, et al., 3319–324). This is less than during the Golden Age, but it is still a lot. So why does the popular belief that girls don't read comics persist?

Calum Johnston, owner of "Strange Adventures," a comic book shop in Halifax, confirms that girls *are* reading comics. "Any comic that has strong female characters has a female readership," he reports. "There are also some comics aimed directly at female readers."

Titles like *Archie*, *Bone*, *ElfQuest*, *X-Files*, and *Wonder Woman* appeal to girls of all ages. Mature readers are attracted to mainstream titles such as *X-Men*, *The Sandman*, and *Death*, as well as independents such as *Action Girl*, *Naughty Bits*, and *Love and Rockets*. Japanese *manga,* discussed elsewhere in this issue, also have a large female readership.

Action Girl (Slave Labor Graphics): This is an anthology showcasing female cartoonists. The comic is girl-positive and female-friendly, but never anti-boy. [Black and white]

Archie (Archie Comics): With family-oriented stories and perpetually teenage characters, this comic has had wide appeal for over 40 years.

Bone (Image): This charming character-driven fantasy presents the adventures of Fone Bone, his cousins, and their human companions, Torn and Gran'ma Ben. Originally an independent, *Bone* joined Image with Issue 21. [Black and white]

Death (DC Vertigo): This is a spin-off of *The Sandman*, described below. Despite her name and function, the character Death is a sympathetic and interesting figure. Recommended for mature readers.

ElfQuest (Warp Graphics): The Wolfriders are a band of elves living on an Earth-like planet in this well-realized fantasy adventure. Superior story telling and engaging characters highlight the series. [Black and white]

Love and Rockets (Fantagraphics): The Hernandez brothers produce a beautifully literate and artistic comic. Story lines vary, but feature young adult characters. Recommended for mature readers. [Black and white]

Naughty Bits (Fantagraphics): No topic is too controversial for artist/writer Roberta Gregory and her character Midge, aptly nicknamed "Bitchy Bitch." Recommended for mature readers. [Black and white]

The Sandman (DC Vertigo): This comic details the exploits of beings known as the Endless: Dream (also known as Morpheus), Destiny, Death, Destruction, Desire, Despair, and Delirium. Not gods, yet more than immortals, the Endless are responsible for the forces that govern our lives. Recommended for mature readers.

Wonder Woman (DC): The most famous Amazon in America is still fighting the forces of evil. See her story elsewhere in this issue.

X-Files (Topps): A recent entry into the market, this is a spin-off of the hit television series of the same name.

X-Men (Marvel): A band of mutant superheroes, both male and female, use their powers to help humanity while most normal humans hate them in return. This is the best-selling comic in North America.

Note: Several of the comic books and graphic novels we have referred to in this issue, including DC Comics' *Sandman* series, but not including First Comics' *Classics Illustrated* series, are "suggested for mature readers." This means the books do not carry the Comics Code seal of approval, and may contain subjects and depictions too intense for some young readers. While we recommend these books for students' personal reading, you may want to look into them yourself before deciding to use them in the classroom.

Work Cited

McKenna, M., D. Kear, and R. Ellsworth, "Developmental Trends in Children's Use of Print Media: A National Study," in J. Zutell and S. McCormick (eds.), *Learner Factors/Teacher Factors: Issues in Literacy Research and Instruction* (Chicago: National Reading Conference, 1991), 319–324, as cited in Stephen Krashen, *The Power of Reading: Insights from the Research*, Englewood, CO: Libraries Unlimited, 1993, 50.

VIRTUAL COMICS ON THE WEB

Online Comics

A whole new comics industry has exploded with the technological refinements of the Internet and the development of the World Wide Web. Artists from around the world now have instant access to their own publishing companies—WWW homepages. In a matter of minutes an artist can scan their comic and mount it on a server making it accessible to millions of web users. No more picky editors or aggressive competition. They draw, they edit themselves, and then they publish. This has resulted in a plethora of online cartoons being created. They range from single frame cartoons to lengthier comics. The topic matter is literally infinite. There are many online comics that young adults will find interesting and I will review two of the more appropriate sites later.

Probably the best way to find these comics is to begin with a comics hotlist. This is a list that simply describes various comics and where to find them. It is like an online bibliography. Several are in our list of comic-related web sites. They will link you to hundreds of various online comics, each of which will link you to other comics.

Like most other Internet sites these hotlists are plagued with incorrect or changing addresses so you need to be patient. If you find a comic that you like make a bookmark for that address so that you don't have to search for it every time. Also remember that graphics take a long time to load off of the web so choose your sites carefully. They usually tell you how large the file is next to the link.

Where to Go on the Web

The Big Problem with Marshall—by Pat Giles and Amy Spinthourakis

This is another excellent online comic with a neurotic main character named Marshall that YAs would certainly relate to. This page has yet to contain an archive but the cartoon is well worth examining. (http://www.panix.com/spydoor/Marshall/Marsh cov.html)

Comic Books Central

http://www.comicbookscentral

Claims to be best comic resource on the web. Lists new comics, e-zines, and has a handy reference desk with some info and history about comics.

The Comic Book and Comic Strip Page

http://dragon.acadiau.ca/~860099w/comics/comics. html

Claims to be the nexus of comics on the web. A hotlist of various other sites, online comics, the Comics Code, etc.

The Comic Page

http://www.dereksantos.com/comicpage/index.html

A catalogue of comics and an extensive history of comic book industry.

The Comic Strip (United Media)

http://www.unitedmedia.com/comics/

A promotional homepage for United Media cartoons. Useful information such as artist biographies.

Batman Homepage

http://batmanforever.com/welcome.welcome.html

Promotional site for the movie *Batman Forever*.

Sandman Homepage

http://www.holycow.com/dreaming/

Excellent graphics and biographical info on the writer Neil Gaiman.

Peanuts Homepage

http://www.unitedmedia.com/comics/peanuts

Just another promotional site but it does contain bio info for Charles Schultz.

In Search of Science Fiction

YA Hotline, Issue No. 56, 1997

LARA MCALLISTER, CARRIE-ANN SMITH, AND SUE WATSON

SCIENCE FICTION: WORLDS APART?

Science fiction and fantasy are the two branches that form alternate universe fiction. Both are considered to be literature of change.

Although the line between the two often grows fuzzy, there is one fundamental difference that sets them apart: the treatment of the laws of the universe. In fantasy, the story often takes place in a universe where some basic scientific law or laws are different than those of our universe. Science fiction on the other hand, takes place in our universe with all of its laws of science intact. Ursula Le Guin compared the two saying:

> The basic concept of fantasy, of course, is this, you get to make up rules, but then you've got to follow them. Science fiction refines the canon:

you get to make up the rules but within limits. A science fiction story must not flout the science, must not . . . deny what is to be known. (Gunn, 129)

Arthur C. Clarke also compared them saying: "Fantasy deals with things that can't happen, and we wish they would; science fiction deals with things that could happen and we hope they don't" (Gunn, 129).

Bibliography

Freer, Arlie. "Science Fiction for Children and Youth of the '80s: Trying the Future on for Size." *School Libraries in Canada* (Summer, 1984): 27.

Gunn, James and Milton T. Wolf. "Science Fiction: Disturber of the Literary Peace." *Library Journal* (Feb. 15, 1988): 128–131.

Nilsen, Alleen Pace and Kenneth L. Donelson. *Literature for Today's Young Adults.* 4th ed. New York: HarperCollins, 1993.

SCIENCE FICTION DEFINED

There are many definitions of science fiction written by various authors of the genre attempting to define their art. So perhaps the best way to be introduced to the idea of what science fiction is, is to hear from some of these authors.

"Science fiction is a literary response to scientific change, and that response can run the entire gamut of human experience."—*Isaac Asimov*

" . . . the history of concepts, not machinery"—*Ray Bradbury*

"What if?"—*Harlan Ellison*

"Science fiction, no matter how fantastic its content may seem, always accepts all of the real world and the entire body of human knowledge about the real world as the framework for the fictional speculation . . . the author's purpose is not to escape from reality but to explore seriously the complex and amazing manifold of possibilities which lie revealed in the future of our race—to explore them in the light of what we do now."—*Robert A. Heinlein*

"Science fiction . . . extrapolates the consequences of real or imagined discoveries in the sciences (physical, biological, and social) and embedded in it is a respect for fact."—*Mark R. Hillegas*

"It (science fiction) is an infinitely expandable metaphor exactly suited to our expanding universe."—*Ursula Le Guin*

To sum up, science fiction is a literature of change, of discontinuity. It is about concepts and questions such as "What if?" The genre is all encompassing and is open to the imagination.

Despite all the efforts to define science fiction, perhaps authors James Gunn and Milton T. Wolf have it right when they say, "We will not try further to define SF. Definitions restrict and the beauty of science fiction is that it liberates."

All quotations taken from Gunn, James and Milton T. Wolf. "Science Fiction: Disturber of the Literary Peace." *Library Journal* (Feb. 15, 1988): 128–131.

SCIENCE FICTION THEN AND NOW

It is not possible to pinpoint exactly when the first science fiction story appeared. There is controversy among critics as to who should receive the credit for writing the first science fiction book. Some critics claim that the genre began with the appearance of *Frankenstein* in 1818, calling Mary Shelley the "mother of science fiction." Others say that the genre started much earlier with the appearance of Lucian of Samosata's *The True History* in the 2nd century A.D. Other authors who have been credited with this achievement are: Swift, Aesop, Virgil, Homer, Heliodoras, Plato, and Cyrano de Bergerac. Despite the controversy, Jules Verne is generally considered the first major and widely read author of the genre.

The year 1929 is when modern science fiction was first developed. This achievement has largely been credited to Hugo Gernsback, creator of the first magazine devoted to science fiction, *Amazing Stories*. Gernsback deliberately avoided using pulp format and instead modeled his magazine on the science-hobby magazines from which it evolved. John W. Campbell was also influential in the development of modern science fiction. As the editor of the magazine, *Astounding Science Fiction,* now titled *Analog,* he established standards of literary excellence as well as scientific accuracy.

After World War II, science fiction began to appear once more in books. During this time, the paperback industry began to flourish, making science fiction more readily available to its readers. Due to the bombing of Hiroshima, which caused writers to realize the atomic age, and the prediction of the computer revolution to come, the gap between science fiction and reality began to close. Writers started to move away from scientific gadgetry and the far-away worlds seen often in the earlier works of science fiction, and began to focus on human reaction to scientific change.

Today more than 1500 science fiction and fantasy books are published every year. About half of these are new titles. Science fiction today also has the honour of being the most popular form of fiction on the market.

Young Adult Science Fiction

The history of science fiction for young adults dates back to the time of Jules Verne. Between 1863 and 1892, Verne published over sixty novels which, although they captured the adult audience, were largely aimed towards young adults. In the United States, science fiction was being published in dime novels familiar to that era. One of the most important science fiction series to appear during the nineteenth century was the Frank Reade stories. The series featured a boy responsible for the creation of many fantastic inventions.

In the early 1900s, many science fiction series aimed towards young adults were created. In 1906, Great Marvel Series published *Through the Air to the North Pole* by Roy Rockwood, probably a pen name for Howard Garis. This was the first of a nine-volume series. A year later, the Tom Swift series written by Victor Appleton, again a pen name for Garis, appeared. Published by Stratemeyer Syndicate, it was to become one of the most popular series of the twentieth century. Other science fiction series published during this time include *The Quest of the United States* (Hancock), *The Boy Inventors* (Bonner), two series called *Radio Boys* (one by Breckenridge and the other by Chapman), *Rocket Riders* (Garis), and *Radiophone Boys* (Snell). As one can probably tell from the titles of many of the stories, the science fiction novels written during the time were largely aimed towards the male audience. Females were considered to be both unsuited and disinterested in science and strenuous adventure.

It was in the 1950s that science fiction for young adults really began to have its success. This success has been attributed to several causes: "The pioneering work of Heinlein, who went on writing other good juveniles (his novel *Rocket Ship Galileo,* published in 1947, is considered the first American novel for teenagers to be worthy enough to merit serious attention); the emergence of a handful of genuinely talented writers, such as Andre Norton and Alan Nourse, who wanted to write for young audiences; the continuing development of preteens and teenagers as separate groups requiring their own reading material (most of the new titles were addressed to these groups); the growing popularity of science fiction, not only in novels and short stories but in the two media that drew teenagers as avid fans, film and comics . . . and the Sputnik phenomenon and resulting interest in space and its exploration, which rendered less suspect and flamboyant the speculation of science fiction" (Barron, 27). Since science fiction had become so popular much of the genre published during this period was not always of great quality. Publishers seeing the popularity as a way to make a profit were willing to publish just about anything as long as it featured young protagonists (or animals), that there was no mention of sex, and the story held some value, either educational or moral.

Since the 1950s science fiction for young adults has come of age. More themes are being explored and the sexism seen in the earlier works has become less prevalent. More women are contributing to the genre and more female protagonists are being introduced in the stories.

Bibliography

Barron, Neil, ed. *The Anatomy of Wonder: A Critical Guide to Science Fiction*. 3rd ed. New York: Bowker, 1987.

Clute, John and Peter Nicholls, eds. *The Science Fiction Encyclopedia*. London: St. Martin's Press, 1993.

Gunn, James and Milton T. Wolf. "Science Fiction: Disturber of the Library Peace" *Library Journal* Feb. 15, 1988.

Nilsen, Alleen Pace and Kenneth L. Donelson. *Literature for Today's Young Adults*. 4th ed. New York: HarperCollins, 1993.

SOME SELECTION GUIDES

One of the many challenges librarians have to face is deciding what materials to select for the library. With as many as 1500 science fiction and fantasy books coming out each year and the various types of multi-media available on the market today, the job of keeping up with this genre and trying to decide what to purchase is not easy. Perhaps it is the young adult librarian that has the toughest job when it comes to selection. The children's librarian can, for the most part, ignore adult and young adult materials, and the adult librarian can ignore most children's and young adult fiction (of course, there are going to be exceptions). The young adult librarian however, has to be aware of the young adult material in existence as well as the adult material available, as there tends to be a large crossover as to what young adults will read, especially it seems in the genre of science fiction and fantasy.

So what is available to help librarians decide on what to purchase for their collection? I have included some of the sources I have come across in my research that may be of help.

General Journals and Periodicals

Many of the general book reviewing journals will have some science fiction reviews; however, there is one in particular which I would like to draw your attention to: *Voice of Youth Advocate (VOYA)*, available from Scarecrow Press in Lanham, MD.

In addition to reviewing science fiction on an ongoing basis, *VOYA* includes a section devoted to the best science fiction of the year in each April edition.

Specialty Journals and Periodicals

Locus: The Newspaper of the Science Fiction Field. **PO Box 13305, Oakland, CA 94661 (monthly)**

Created in 1968, *Locus* is a monthly magazine devoted to science fiction materials. Its coverage includes: reviews of science fiction and fantasy materials, bestsellers lists, forthcoming books, multi-media, and interviews. It also keeps you informed of nominees and winners of science fiction awards, and has its readers evaluate science fiction books through an annual poll. This magazine would probably be the most useful of the three specialty magazines in selecting science fiction in either a school or public library.

Foundation: The Review of Science Fiction. **North East London Polytechnic, Longbridge Rd., Dagenham, England RM8 (3/year)**

Extrapolation. **Kent State University Press, Journals Dept., Kent (4/year)**

These two journals are more scholarly than *Locus*. They mostly contain essays about science fiction, however, some reviews are located at the end of the journals. The reviews are more detailed and scholarly than those of *Locus*.

General Sources

Some general materials that would make a nice addition to any science fiction collection include the following titles:

Aldiss, Brian W. *Trillion Year Spree: The History of Science Fiction.* **London: Victor Gollancz, 1986.**

Designed to serve in schools including science fiction in the curriculum, *Trillion Year Spree* provides a critical and historical account of the history of science fiction. It is considered to be one of the best general documentations of general science fiction in existence.

Barron, Neil, ed. *Anatomy of Wonder: A Critical Guide to Science Fiction.* **3rd ed. New York: Bowker, 1987.**

The *Anatomy of Wonder* provides the history of science fiction. It is divided into three sections: English Language Science Fiction, Foreign Language Science Fiction, and Research Aids. The first section includes a chapter devoted to children's and young adult science fiction. An annotated list of science fiction books and the age level the books are appropriate for is included at the end of this chapter. The final chapter provides a core collection checklist, a valuable resource for assessing or starting a science fiction section within a library.

Bleiler, E.F., ed. *Science Fiction Writers: Critical Studies of the Major Authors from the Early Nineteenth Century to the Present Day.* **New York: Scribner's, 1982.**

This book contains basic biographical information about authors contributing to the science fiction genre. It is divided into seven periods: Early Science Fiction; Primitive Science Fiction, the American Dime Novel and Pulp Magazines; Mainstream Georgian Authors; American Science Fiction—the Formative Period; the Circumbellum Period; the Moderns; and Continental Science Fiction. Included in the entries is a list of the authors' works and bibliographies to supplement the essays.

Clute, John and Peter Nicholls, ed. *The Science Fiction Encyclopedia.* **New York: St. Martin's Press, 1993.**

The Science Fiction Encyclopedia provides information on all aspects of science fiction. Its contents include articles on major writers, thematic articles which include identifying stories using the theme (this might be of particular use to teachers using science fiction in the classroom). Unfortunately the illustrations seen throughout its previous edition have been omitted in this edition.

Bibliographies

Bibliographies specific to the genre are available and can be found both in journals as a separate compilation and some general sources such as the *Anatomy of Wonder*. One that I found that seemed particularly useful is:

Justice, Keith L., compiler. *Science Fiction, Fantasy and Horror Reference: An Annotated Bibliography of Works about Literature and Film*. Jefferson: McFarland and Company, Inc., 1989.

This bibliographical compilation provides critical evaluations of secondary materials in the genres of science fiction, fantasy, and horror. It is divided into sections: General Histories and Criticism; Author Studies; General Bibliographies; Biographies, Autobiographies, and Interviews; Encyclopedias, Dictionaries, Indexes, and Checklists; Television, Film, and Radio; Comics, Art, and Illustrations; and Anthologies, Collections, and Annotated Editions. There are two appendices; the first is an evaluation of critical and bibliographical book series and the other is a suggested core collection checklist.

There are many other things the librarian should be aware of in the selection of science fiction materials. There are several awards that are given out in the field of science fiction and librarians should know the award winners. Science fiction collectors should not limit themselves to print sources.

Philip K. Dick Award—awarded to the best paperback original.
Nebula Award—for best novel, novella, novelette, and short story. It also has an award for grand master.
John W. Campbell Award—for the best science fiction novel of the year.
Theodore Sturgeon Memorial Award—awarded for the best science fiction short story.
Science Fiction Achievement Awards (Hugo)—awards the best novel, novella, novelette, short stories and non-fiction.

Librarians must be aware of science fiction epics being shown on the television as well as in the movie theaters, as often there will be requests for books about the movies.

The Internet also is a good resource to learn more about what is available and what people are reading. Why not hook into some news groups to see what people are talking about and make a habit of reading some of the science fiction reviews that are available on-line.

CAN YOU USE SCIENCE FICTION IN TEACHING WHILE AVOIDING "INTERGALACTIC SUBURBIA"?

We owe a lot to Mary Wollstonecraft Shelley. As the often credited first author of a science fiction (SF) novel, Shelley not only invented the (then unnamed) genre, but she used her book *Frankenstein* as a means to bring to the reading public ethical questions about creating life with science and technology. Since then, SF has taken us through a journey into outer worlds and back into our inner minds, as the space opera of the 1920s and '30s transformed into the new and very vivid cyberpunk writings. But, as many of us profess, SF is not our genre of preference and an understanding of the genre may largely escape us. Coupled with the proliferation of writings in SF, it becomes difficult to choose novels with which we can stack our shelves or use in our classrooms. So we may shy away from SF, convinced that it offers us only images of robots in altered worlds, androids in hyperspace, and mutants on post-apocalyptic Earth.

Being an educator, I had a special interest in diving into the SF literature to find out how I could use SF in the science classroom. Also, I have a particular interest in encouraging more young women into science, and was acutely aware of the "technology glorifying" image of SF, as a reluctant science fiction reader myself. So I embarked on a mission to investigate whether I could select novels that could be positive to both females and males, and which could be used in the science classroom. The following, borrowing on research from the Girls Into Science and Technology (GIST) project, is what I base my selections upon.

Science fiction, as science, has a number of strikes against it on the gender side of literary critique. It is a genre that has traditionally been produced by males, with males as the main characters, "masculine" concerns as central to the writings, a poor stereotype of the typical reader, and—during the "space opera" era—stuck in the glorification of technology and machinery, entirely disconnected with the ethics of science. The comparison of science and science fiction below provides a quick overview of the possible reasons that SF has failed to attract a larger female readership.

The first three points in this comparison have been to varying degrees challenged with the increase in the 1960s of women authors and with the changing image of women as protagonists. Pre-1960s SF novels presented what Joanna Russ called "intergalactic suburbia," remarking on the phenomenal lack of imagination in the genre regarding relationships (Lefanu, 112). Women were mostly absent or, if present, were largely secondary characters whose meaning was evident only in a relation to men.

The influx of women writers in the field and the changing nature of the protagonists have made it easy for a librarian or teacher to address these issues. Selecting more novels by women and/or with female protagonists can provide a different image of science fiction and science to a female reader. As Jane Donawerth notes, "Teaching science fiction by women offers a counterbalance to [the] causes of girls' lack of interest in science: worlds in which men and women participate equally in scientific discovery; role models in the portrayals of women scientists; and a mode of arousing interest in science, through literature, that is traditionally more congenial to female students" (42).

The latter point is important to consider when selecting novels thematically. Research by the Girls Into Science and Technology projects shows that females, when asked what scientific topics they would like to study, prefer those with some social implication, most often choosing the environment, the human body/health, or other topics with a practical application. Choosing science fiction by female authors or with a strong female protagonist, along with a theme that is of interest to young women, will be a start in attracting more females into both science and science fiction.

I was amazed to find how voraciously I read about a dozen SF novels within a couple of months when I started to look into the possibility of using SF to teach science. I selected novels or short stories in an attempt to redress the unequal participation in both. By far the most unanimously recommended by feminist critics and readers of science fiction are the novels of Ursula K. LeGuin, many of which raise questions about gender roles. I chose from a wide range of books including either female authors (both YA and adult authors: YAs read adult SF novels, too) or stories with strong female protagonists; those with a good dose of science content; those which contained science in a social context; and those centered on environmental issues.

Why Haven't Females Read Science Fiction as Much as Males? (A Comparison of Science with Science Fiction)

1. Image of Science Fiction as "Masculine"
   Science: historically associated with areas of knowledge accessible to men only: physics, math, astronomy, logic.
   Science Fiction: traditionally concerned with space exploration, machines, technology, robotics: areas not historically accessible to women.

2. Knowledge Producers
   Science: historically produced by male scientists.
   Science Fiction: written largely by male authors; protagonists are male.

3. Associated Gender Identity Incompatible with Societal Expectations
   Science: stereotypical elderly, greying, balding male scientist image or spinster female.
   Science Fiction: stereotypical young nerdy, computer-obsessed male reader.

4. Knowledge Unconnected with Social Reality (Important to Females)
   Science: impersonal, objective, knowledge where personal experience is not valid; research often not concerned with implications for society.
   Science Fiction: technology and science historically glorified, relationships sparse or absent.

Works Cited

Donawerth, Jane. "Teaching Science Fiction by Women." *English Journal* (March 1990): 39–46.

Lefanu, Sarah. *In the Chinks of the World Machine: Feminism and Science Fiction.* London: The Women's Press, 1988.

Whyte, K. *Girls into Science and Technology: The Story of a Project.* Boston: Routledge and Kegan Paul, 1986.

Resources for Teaching Science Fiction by Women

Yntema, Sharon K. *More than 100: Women Science Fiction Writers.* Freedom, CA: Crossing, 1988.
   Includes a list of writers of YA novels.

Sargent, Pamela, ed. *Women of Wonder.* New York: Random, 1974.
   Includes a history of women writers.

Kessler, Carol Farley, ed. *Daring to Dream: Utopian Stories by United States Women 1836–1919*. Boston: Pandora, 1984.

Anthology of short stories.

Harding, Jan. "The Making of a Scientist?" *Perspectives on Gender and Sciences*. London: Falmer, 1986: 169–67.

Examines barriers to female achievement in science.

RECOMMENDED SCIENCE FICTION

The following is a "starter" list of female positive books recommended for use in high school classes.

Eva by Peter Dickinson (Delacorte, 1988. ISBN 0385297025) is the often hated, often loved novel of a teenaged Eva who wakes up in the hospital after a terrible car accident to find that her mind has been transferred into another body—that of a chimpanzee. The novel provides a great opportunity for discussion and research-based activities around genetic engineering, animal rights, ecology, and the value of human life over other animals. The book's devotion to the primatologist Jane Goodall, and the interesting descriptions of chimpanzee behaviour provide a basis for researching primate behaviour. Written for an older YA audience, its strong, young female protagonist, the large number of female scientists, and the presentation of science in a context adds to the possibility that it will entice young women into SF reading and scientific exploration.

The Keeper of the Isis Light (Atheneum, 1980. ISBN 0689308477) by Canadian author Monica Hughes centers on 16-year-old Olwen, raised by her guardian robot, who must welcome settlers to her planet. The novel raises important ethical questions about genetic alteration of humans, prejudices because of physical difference, and colonization. Descriptions of the planet's atmosphere and geography could be used as jumping off points for students to create their own planet and environment in a creative writing exercise. With both a female protagonist and author, the novel can serve as a model for females to be active participants in both the understanding and the production of scientific knowledge.

Crisis on Conshelf Ten by Monica Hughes (Copp Clark, 1975. ISBN 0773010424) is an excellent book for bringing the connection between science, resource use, and politics into the classroom. The story takes place in 2005, when the earth has colonized the moon and the ocean for resources. Written for a younger YA audience, the novel has good cross-curricular possibilities for maritime studies units, as it is full of marine biology, conservation, and environmental issues, including a small dose of eco-terrorist activity for discussion.

The Word for World Is Forest by Ursula K. Le Guin (Berkley Publishers, 1972. ISBN 0399117164) presents an opportunity to discuss the harsh realities of human (read male, in Le Guin's portrayal) morality with respect to environmental degradation, racism, and war. Humans, who colonize a forested planet inhabited by peace-loving people, force the inhabitants into slavery and wreak havoc with the forest. Le Guin's admission that she was very angry when she wrote this book during the Vietnam War gives an indication of the ethical possibilities for classroom discussion the book provides.

Dinosaur Planet (Ballantine, 1978. ISBN 03453319958) is a novel of planetary exploration written by Anne McCaffrey. Varian, the young scientist of the future, co-leader with Kai of the expedition sent to explore the planet Ireta, discovers more than just dinosaurs on the planet. The Heavyworlders, half of the group's personnel, have reverted to their primitive carnivorous selves, and are threatening the lives of all. The book relies on the sciences of geology, paleontology, and geography to describe the planet, and biology to make vivid the descriptions of the dinosaurs. The capable females in the story rely on their scientific knowledge to survive the mutiny which results.

SCIENCE FICTION AND TEACHING: LESSON IDEAS FOR PETER DICKINSON'S EVA

Activity #1: Class Discussion on Environmental Ethics

In the modern world, we justify the use of animals for experimentation, the cultivation of animals for consumption, the sacrifice of animals for organ donation, the destruction of habitat, and extinction of species for economic ends. The following classroom discussion activity, centering on the question "Why do we value *human* life above all other?" could be used to introduce environmental ethics with the novel *Eva*.

1. Before reading *Eva*, explore your personal feeling about the value of other species. Write in your journal about your attitudes/experiences/knowledge about non-human species. Do you go fishing? Hunt? Eat meat? Cut down trees? Kill mosquitoes? Feel free to write about any aspect of your beliefs, but be sure to examine the origin of your beliefs, i.e., why do you feel and behave the way you do.

2. After reading *Eva*, and with reference to page 80 (where Eva challenges her father's beliefs about chimps), break into groups of four and discuss the following: Should we value human life above other species? If so, why? If not, are we justified in sacrificing some life to ensure the survival of our own? Where do we draw a line of "justification"? Report your group's discussion to the class.

Activity #2: Human Ecology

As a follow up to the first question, and with page 115 as a reference (where the effects of overpopulation are described), organize a debate on the following: humans have developed artificial means to ensure the survival of their population, causing the extinction of many other species in so doing.

Pro: humans, as the "most intelligent" animals on Earth, have a right to control and alter their environment to ensure the survival of the species.

Con: humans are animals like any other and as such, must not alter their environment because it upsets the ecological balance of the Earth and causes the extinction of other species.

Activity #3: Genetics Speculation

Before arriving at page 82, where the answer to the following question is revealed, ask the students to speculate, using their knowledge of heredity and genetics, whether chimps born of Eva would have human characteristics. Would a chimp born of Eva have human behaviour?

Activity #4: Animal Behaviour

Read about Jane Goodall's research on primate behaviour. Is the animal behaviour described in *Eva* consistent with real chimpanzee behaviour? Study the behaviour of one primate of your choice (e.g., baboons, gibbons, gorillas) and write a story, article for the *National Geographic*, manual for a zookeeper, etc., which is based in factual information.

Teens on the Infobahn

YA Hotline, Issue No. 57, 1997

ANNETTE ANTHONY, CAROLYN CARPAN, ALISON CREECH, RHONDA O'NEILL, MICHELLE PAON, AND MARY V. THORNTON

EDITORIAL

Just as Elvis and the Beatles launched the cultural revolution of the fifties and sixties, the Internet has transformed the lives of today's YAs. Parents and those who work with teens have seen the world go from hi-fi to sci-fi in two generations. The old Smith-Coronas and television antennas have been replaced by state-of-the-art keyboards, monitors, and modems. Today's teens perceive the Internet the way their parents did the television—as a source of amusement, entertainment, and a way to connect with the world.

This issue of *YA Hotline* looks at the Internet and how it influences the lives of today's teens. Despite the opportunities afforded by the Net, the negative aspects of this medium dominate the news. We have tried to look at both the benefits and the drawbacks of cyberspace as it continues to influence the lives of young adults.

This project started off with a brainstorming session in which our team created a very long wish-list of topics for articles. Some of the themes fell by the wayside or unraveled as our research or happenstance lead us down more interesting paths. Numerous individuals provided us with professional insight, interviews, and information. We would especially like to thank the following:

Our Professor, Vivian Howard, Dalhousie University
Janice Fiander, Halifax Regional Library
Betsy McDonald, Central Branch—North York Public Library
Subscribers to the PUBYAC listserv

IF YOU BUILD IT, TEENS WILL COME: CONSTRUCTING A LIBRARY WEB PAGE FOR YAS

So you want to build a YA Web page? If you are looking for an HTML primer read no further, this article is not for you. If you are thinking about building a web page or have been asked to build a web page read on.

The World Wide Web has been with us for several years now. It is a seemingly chaotic place filled with both promise and danger. Teens are out there right now browsing through text and graphics, chatting on chat lines, gaming, setting up their own web pages and doing whatever else they find interesting. A web page is one way to introduce teens to the best sites out there and by doing so, leading them away from less desirable sites.

Before implementing a web page it is important to spend time thinking over your reasons for wanting a web page. Do you want to post information about your library and your services to YAs? Do you want to include book lists and program information? Do you want to create a directory of useful sites so that YAs are able to locate useful information easily? Are you trying to create a fun spot on the web that teens can call their own? What about web zines and chat lines, do you want to create local ones or link to established sites?

Hardware and a Space to Call One's Own

On a more practical note, physical requirements include having the necessary equipment and a space

on a server to mount your web page. As far as the necessary equipment is concerned you will need a computer with Internet access—the more the merrier. Ideally the computer(s) will be located in the YA section of the public library or in an easily accessed spot in the school library. Good systems are becoming more reasonable in price. High-end monitors, a fast internal clock, RAM, video cards, sound cards, and other peripherals add to the web experience. When making a decision to purchase, get the best system you can afford and make sure that it is upgradeable.

Finding a server on which to mount your web page is something else you may need to consider. If you are part of an environment with its own server, this is not such a big consideration. If you do not have a server of your own, it will be necessary to create an alliance with another organization (one that has a web server). Freenets, educational organizations, other libraries, community groups, or an Internet service provider (ISP) are options which may or may not be open to you. Take a good look at local web pages to see where they are mounted. The authors of these pages may be able to point you in the right direction.

Web Pages

LION—Librarians Information Online Network

Network: an information resource for K–12 school librarians.

http://www.libertynet.org/~lion/lion.html

This site contains information of interest to school librarians. The Internet Forum provides useful information and tips for creating web pages.

Young Adult Librarian's Help/Homepage

http://yahelp.suffolk.lib.ny.us

The young adult librarian's help/homepage is a micro index to the vast amount of resources available on the World Wide Web. It is not a review, recommendation, or endorsement of these links/pages, but only a find tool to be used by librarians for professional development and/or used by those putting together pages for young adults in their libraries.

Virtual YA: Public Libraries with YA Webpages

http://www.suffolk.lib.ny.us/youth/virtual.html

A lengthy directory (created by Patrick Jones) of YA web pages.

Calgary Public Library—N.F.A., a page strictly NOT FOR ADULTS

http://calgarypubliclibrary.com

Bright and humorous, this page combines library information, local information, and links to other sites. A good sample site.

Toronto Public Library . . . teen zone . . .

http://www.tpl.toronto.on.ca/teen/teen.htm

This web page is more subdued than the Calgary web page, but well laid out. The standard topics are covered: books and authors, homework help, arts and entertainment, career information. Teen zone central links to both fun and serious sites for teens.

The Internet Public Library—Teen Division

http://www.ipl.org/teen/

Links to many sites covering arts and entertainment, books and writing, career and college, clubs and organizations. Computers and Internet, dating issues and conflicts, general homework help, health, math and science, politics and history, sports, and style.

Planning

As in planning any other service or program, a needs assessment should be undertaken. What are teens looking at when they come to the library to surf the web? The quickest way to find out is to ask them. Survey students at the local schools, in the library, or wherever you find them (chat lines even). At the same time, spend time following the highlighted links on the web to see what was of interest to teens (provided they have not been cleared). This might not be effective if Internet access is on a terminal shared by other patrons of the library. If you have a Young Adult Advisory Committee, have them suggest sites and ask other teens for interesting site suggestions. After your web page is implemented, you may place a recommendation form on the page to solicit ideas from young adults.

Who Will Create the Web Page?

After planning the web page (or while planning the web page) you will need to decide who is going to implement it. Will it be the YA librarian or other public services staff? Is there a technophile in the library? Will someone outside the library do it? Are there any cyber teens in the neighborhood?

When it comes to computers, "Young Adults" are often miles ahead of the "Adults." I remember logging into a bulletin board a few years back and talking to the sysop (system operator). I found out that he was 14 years old! At the time I thought this was amazing. Since then I have heard similar stories from other people who have encountered even younger sysops. It is the same with the WWW—many teens are setting up their own pages. If you find that you have local talent, use it! You might even consider bringing web authoring to your library as a program first. Afterward, have the participants try their hand at creating the web page. You could make it into a contest or strike up a YA web page committee. Try to get YAs involved as soon and as much as possible. In a recent article, Patrick Jones tells us that of the libraries he surveyed "every library that involved young people in page creation documented positive results."

Spinning Your Web

The bulk of web pages today are created using HTML. Java and CGI increase the functionality of many web pages and should be taken into consideration depending on what you wish your web page to do. The following definitions were taken from the Free online dictionary of computers, (http://wombat.doc.ic.ac.uk/foldoc/index.html). More detailed information about each is available in both print and web sources.

HTML (Hypertext Markup Language): A Hypertext document format used on the World Wide Web. Built on top of SGML, "tags" are embedded in the text. A tag consists of a <, a "directive" (case insensitive), zero or more parameters, and a ">." Matched pairs of directives, like "<TITLE>" and "<TITLE>" are used to delimit text which is to appear in a special place or style.

Java: A simple, object-oriented, distributed, interpreted, robust, secure, architecture-neutral, portable, multithreaded, dynamic, buzzword-complaint, general-purpose programming language developed by Sun Microsystems in 1993. Java supports programming for the Internet in the form of platform-independent java "applets."

CGI (Common Gateway Interface): A standard for running external programs from a World Wide Web HTTP server. CGI specifies how to pass arguments to the executing program as part of the HTTP request. It also defines a set of environment variables. Commonly, the program will generate some HTML, which will be passed back to the browser but it can also request URL redirection. The CGI program can, for example, access information in a database and format the results as HTML.

Finding Inspiration Online

One of the best ways of broadening your web authoring repertoire is to seek out examples from the web itself. These can range from existing YA pages to unrelated (but well-designed) sites. It will also be useful to look at examples of bad web pages so that you know what to avoid. Check out Vincent Flanders' Web Pages That Suck (http://www.webpagesthatsuck.com). He's on a mission to rid the web of bad design "one page at a time."

When a good page is found which serves as an example of a specific web authoring technique, view the underlying HTML coding to learn how it was done. In Netscape, choose View from the menu bar then choose "Page Source" to see HTML coding or choose "Page Info" to see how the page is layered. Netscape Communicator allows you to create or edit web pages while connected to the World Wide Web, offering drag and drop ease. For further information about this capability check "Help Contents" under Help on the Netscape menu bar. If you are using Microsoft Explorer (version 3.02), HTML coding may be displayed by selecting "Source" under "View" on the menu bar.

HTML Primers on the Net

Web authoring "primers" are also found on the WWW itself. In fact they will often be found on the Internet before they will be found in books. Pages containing web authoring information can be found by performing searches or by linking through other relevant pages. Suggested starting points include Yahoo, http://www.yahoo.com/Computers/Internet/World_Wide_Web/ and the Web Mastery site at the University of Illinois at Urbana-Champaign which is clearly laid out and useful.

This site also gives us a lengthy list of HTML editing tools and conversion programs: http://union.ncsa.uiuc.edu/HyperNews/get/www/html/guides.html.

Books

World Wide Web technologies continue to expand at a rapid rate. A trip to a local Chapters book store provided evidence in support of this statement. Specific titles will not be suggested due to the mercurial nature of publishing in this field. Newer titles (perhaps even newer authoring technologies) are likely to be available by the time this issue of the *YA Hotline* is distributed. It is better to go to a local bookstore (computer book store) and carefully browse the latest offerings before making a purchase.

Linking to Other Web Sites

When deciding which links to include on your web page it is important to keep in mind the purpose of your web page and its audience. Links may be found in a number of ways; it is important to check several to ensure broad coverage. Read the "Surf for" column in the *School Library Journal* and check the other professional literature for reviews of web sites. The Scout Report is an alert to new Net happenings. The web page is located at http://scout.cs.wisc.edu/scout/. Listservs may be useful in alerting you to new sites, so subscribe to the listservs which are relevant to your field. Scout Report has a listserv as well—subscription information is located at http://scout.cs.wisc.edu/scout/report/subscribe.html.

Have teens alert you to the sites they find which could be included on the web page. You could even have them fill out a suggestion form from the web page. If a topic or theme arises which deserves web pages which meet your criteria, update your site!

Maintaining Your Web Page

It is important not to forget about the web page after it has been set up. Links need to be checked frequently so that they are removed when they are no longer valid. What better reason to keep the number of links from your page at a manageable level. Link to the best and most current YA sites. Link to other directories of YA web sites, but be sure to provide a brief note outlining the nature of the directory at the linking site. Trends change, so be sure to update your web page periodically to reflect current YA interests and current technology.

Works Cited

Taken from the *Young Adult Librarian's Help/ Homepage* at (http://207.160.160.231/ya/whatitis.htm) 09/12/97.

Jones, Patrick. "A Cyber-room of Their Own." *School Library Journal* (November 1997): 34–37.

See Jackie L. Carrigan, "Evaluating Internet Resources" (Focus on Technology), *Youth Services in Libraries*, summer 1997 p. 423–425, for a succinct look at evaluation of web resources. This article discusses evaluation of the source of information, currency and bias, appearance and ease of use, and lists several Internet sites where you can find further discussion of evaluating web sites.

"YA HEAVEN": AN INTERVIEW WITH BETSY MCDONALD, NORTH YORK PUBLIC LIBRARY

Gateway is the orientation department for the library, and has fifteen Internet terminals. Right beside this part is the HUB—a marvelous area for teens, with four jukeboxes, three VCRs and all the other bells and whistles. (YA heaven!)"

—*E-mail communication from Betsy McDonald to Michelle Paon, November 8, 1997*

The introduction of the Internet into libraries has meant a whole new set of responsibilities and opportunities for the Young Adult Services Librarian. One such professional is Betsy McDonald, Senior Librarian—Youth Services, with the Central Branch of the North York Public Library in Ontario, Canada. A graduate of the University of Toronto, Betsy keeps in close contact with her YA public and provides guidance for the YA collections of North York Public Library.

Betsy and I met over the Internet, when she answered a request I had sent to PUBYAC, the listserv discussion forum for Children and Young Adult Services in Public Libraries. When she described how her branch used Internet terminals, as well as other electronic equipment in the YA area, I was eager to learn more. In keeping with the theme of this issue of *YA Hotline*, Betsy agreed to be interviewed via e-mail. With only a few minor technical hitches, the interview was successful carried out between November 25 and December 8, 1997.

Betsy, can you briefly describe your library?

The North York Central Library is a large 7 storey circulating branch, located directly at a subway station stop. Our clientele is drawn from the neighbourhood, but also from all over the Toronto Metro area.

Do you have a philosophy of service to YAs that you feel is particular to your library?

I don't know that our philosophy is unique, but we do want our YA collections to reflect our community in all its ethnic and lifestyle diversity, and encourage teens to use our resources. Our staff strives to be non-judgmental, knowledgeable and approachable.

Can you describe the Gateway and HUB areas?

The Gateway Services part of the department is designed for orientation to the library and much of the new technology, such as Internet and CD

ROMs. The HUB is the young adult area, with all manner of books, magazines, comics, CDs, videos (for borrowing and in-house use on our two VCRs), 4 jukeboxes, and board games.

What does the word HUB mean or stand for? Is it an acronym or just used to designate the central spot for YAs?

HUB—the name of the YA department—simply indicates the centre of the action, where all is happening for teens.

I take it the area which contains the Internet terminals is in Gateway (general) area. How do the YAs gain access to the Internet? Must they sign up for a time in order to use the machines?

Yes, the Internet terminals are in the Gateway end. We have fifteen terminals at this time. Ten of the terminals must be signed up for ahead of time, for one hour's search time per day. Five of the terminals are available on a first-come, first-served basis.

What sort of policy do you have in place in terms of YAs using the Net? (I'm thinking of parents who might object to a YAs choice of surf sites.)

The YAs are free to visit any site they choose. It is up to the parents to monitor where their son or daughter goes on the Net.

Do you use any form of filter to control Internet access? If so, what type?

No, we do not use any filters at NYPL.

What kind of privacy is afforded YAs while they use the Internet? Can others view the material they are accessing?

All the monitors are in full view of other users. A few terminals have "privacy screens" on them, which allow only the person sitting directly in front of the monitor to see what is on the screen.

Is there any restriction in terms of number of hours YAs can spend on the Internet as compared to other users?

Our rules are the same for all users. Mind you, there are always folk who manage to find ways around our rules . . . and with our staff changing frequently on the desk, we may not notice . . .

Do you have any idea of the kind of use YAs make of the Internet (e.g., recreation, reference, research material for school projects, summer job ideas, etc . . .)?

It seems as though there is a lot of use for recreation—following up on areas of personal interest such as sports, entertainment figures, e-mail, chatrooms, MUDs. There is some use for school projects as well. Sometimes teachers specify that the assignment must include an Internet segment (or not!).

Do YAs generally use the Internet alone, or in pairs or groups?

I find the YAs will often get deeply engrossed, on their own, in what they are looking at, such as a MUD. But mostly, the YAs are a very gregarious bunch and sit together in twos and threes or more, talking and kibbutzing. YAs who did not know each other before have become new friends.

What kind of interaction occurs between YAs and adult users? Any conflict over amount of time YAs use the terminals?

Occasionally adults will come to the desk complaining that they have "real research" to do, and those teenagers are just using the chatrooms, and can't we get them off . . . ? We have to explain that any user can utilize their hour any way they like—we are not judgmental, right?

Here in Halifax, users can go to the public library in order to access their accounts on the Chebucto FreeNet. Do you allow e-mail access/BBS use on the Internet terminals?

We have the Toronto Freenet on our terminals, but in all honesty, this is seldom used. All patrons prefer setting up their own e-mail accounts on such free web-based e-mail systems as Hotmail or Rocketmail. The Internet evolves to meet the needs of those who use it!

Can YAs listen to auditory material from the Internet terminals? (e.g., sound clips from rap bands)?

Yes, some of our terminals are equipped for sound.

Do you provide headphones to allow them to listen to sound clips on the Internet terminals?

Yes, headphones are available.

Are YAs taught how to use the Net or do they pick it up on their own?

Many YAs have somehow soaked up what they need to know to use the Internet. However, we do provide basic help from the desk, and we offer classes for the public in basic and advanced Internet searching (one-hour sessions). We also instruct many school classes, at the request of their teachers.

Do YAs have the opportunity to teach other YAs or adults how to use the Internet (on either a volunteer or a paid basis)?

YAs often teach other YAs and adults too, on an informal basis, as the need arises. We don't do this on a formal basis. We considered it at one time, but the YA who wanted to do it just didn't have the maturity to handle the teaching on his own. He tended to take over and do the searches for people instead of letting them do their own thing. I believe this idea could work though, given a mature and well-trained young adult.

Do you incorporate the Internet in separate YA programming apart from the individual use made of it (for instance—"How to Create Your Own Website" or YA career info. program)?

At this very moment, we have a "Design Your Own Web Page" program for YAs (two sessions) and adults (one session) running. Due to concerns over security, we are restricted to using the website "Angelfire" rather than getting into full HTML programming.

How do organized youth groups use the Internet in your library (e.g., Boy Scouts, Junior Achievers, Pathfinders, youth church groups, etc . . .)?

Organized youth groups have not requested to use our facilities, but this suggestion gives me food for thought.

How do YAs perceive the information they find on the Net? Do they accept it as true, or do they discriminate between what might be a reliable source and what might be a hoax/front/joke/unreliable?

When Internet users enter WWW searching via the NYPL homepage, they must read and accept the library's "Public Internet Access Policy" before they can proceed. This states that the library is not responsible for what a person might find on the Internet. However, people can bypass this by entering a URL in the "Open Location" box directly.

When we get the chance, as in a class visit, we clearly state that each individual must judge for him/herself what they find there, based on specific criteria.

How is Gateway separated from HUB area? How is HUB area subdivided or partitioned?

HUB is really only separated from Gateway by a movable partition of bookshelves. The HUB has function areas, with like media grouped together (e.g., books in one part, audiovisual in another). The seating bench for the jukeboxes forms another divider.

How did the HUB come to be developed or created?

The HUB was always conceived of as an integral part of the design of the library when it was opened ten years ago. The architects were Moriyama and Teshima. Raymond Moriyama also was responsible for the Metropolitan Toronto Reference Library and the Ontario Science Centre. The prominence given to the young adult area demonstrates the high level of commitment accorded this age group by the North York Public Library.

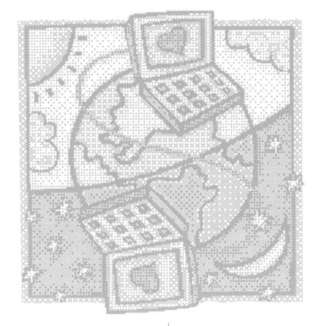

What's available on the jukeboxes? Can I take it that they're free of charge?

We have up-to-date hits and golden oldies on 45s in our four jukeboxes. We have to order them from a supplier in the U.S. Yes, you can take it that listening to the music is free of charge!

I take it they're equipped with headphones. Can more than one person listen to the same selection at one time?

There are four listening outlets for each jukebox, making sixteen in all, installed along a permanent wall which also forms the back to the sitting bench. This means that up to four people at a time can listen to the same juke. All jukes have different titles on them.

Is this the same arrangement for the VCRs—that is, more than one person can wear headphones and share the tape but other YAs in the area wouldn't overhear?

We started out with an arrangement with the VCRs where the YAs could watch/listen to the videos either with or without headphones. There were six listening outlets for each VCR. The difficulties would come when more than six kids wanted to watch at the same time, and believe me, that time came often. We finally gave up on the headsets. Now we just have to monitor the sound levels so they don't disturb each other too much. Dueling VCRs!

What kind of VCR tapes do you have available?

We have videotapes that YAs (and others of course) can borrow and take home to watch. They are mostly feature films, old classics, sports bloopers, and the like. We maintain a small collection of videos for the in-house machines. We obtain these from Criterion Pictures, on a lease basis, and so they can be very up-to-date. They all have Public Performance Rights and are suitable for all ages, since we often get small children accompanying their older sisters and brothers.

I understand you've hosted visits by librarians who would like to use your branch as a model for their own. Can you tell us about these visits?

We live in "YA Heaven" here, and we know it! Word gets around, and we often have inquiries by phone or letter about our resources and services. We are always happy to talk to anyone about the HUB. This past fall we had a visit by a YA/Children's co-ordinator from Brooklyn, New York. She and her architect flew up to examine our YA area, since she had heard via the grapevine what we had. She's in the position of renovating and wanted to get some ideas. Very flattering!

I'm going to play devil's advocate here and ask how all of these toys encourage YAs to read books—any stats on that?

OK, you devil's advocate you—all our "goodies" certainly encourage YAs to see this place as their own, and the Internet has brought in a whole new crowd. The flow of traffic is high.

In spite of all the peripheral collections and the technology, our book collections remain central and integral. Reader's Advisory and training for this is a priority. We believe in ever-changing and varied book displays. In everything we do, we try to tie books to whatever else is going on.

Since we have always had this mix of media and books it is hard to say if now having the Internet has caused circulation to rise. To add to the excitement, we now circulate CD-ROMs from our department, so the stats get blurred. It is our feeling that allying Gateway with the HUB has created a synergy that has energized both departments.

Editor's note: As of May 1999, the North York Public Library site merged with the Toronto Public Library site. See http://www.tpl.toronto.on.ca

FILTERING THE INTERNET

Do you know what your child is looking at when he or she is on the Web? Not all parents sit with their children while they are on the Web. The growth of sites that are believed to be dangerous to children has led to a new growth industry: blocking access to Internet sites. If you have questions about the term "filtering," ask yourself the following questions:

When you access the Internet, do you have access to any website you choose, or does the terminal have filtering software on it? Are you able to determine this without actually looking for an offensive site?

Filtering is the hot topic among educators, librarians, and administrators as each tries to decide how best to protect children and young adults from accessing inappropriate Internet sites.

Saying this, several other questions arise: Which sites are inappropriate? How does one define inappropriate? Do you realize that if you or your organization purchase filtering software for your computers, it is the manufacturer of the product who determines which sites are inappropriate?

Does a decision to put filters on the terminals mean you are being selective, or does it mean you are censoring the contents on this medium? This depends on your point of view. Most articles about filtering take a stand one way or the other (authors seem to see filtering as a black and white issue without any shades of gray).

This article hopes to provide the reader with some of information about filtering. Along with the resource guide also in this issue of the *YA Hotline*, we hope to give you enough information to let you make up your own mind about the issue.

Most of the discussion about filtering takes place on the Internet itself. For this reason, it is necessary for the reader to analyze sites at least as closely as the magazines or talk shows that discuss the issue. Be advised, however, that typing in only the key words "filtering and Internet" on some search engines might lead you to some of the pages you might want to avoid.

What Is Filtering?

When discussing the Internet, filtering pertains to the blocking of certain websites as dictated by software designed for that purpose. There are several commercial software packages on the market that promise to limit user access to inappropriate sites. "Inappropriate" is usually defined as websites that use pornography, especially that involving children, extreme violence, or advocate hate groups. If you look on the Web, or if you examine any one of the computing magazines on the market, you will be able to discover the names of these products and be able to read about them.

You should be aware, however, that not all filters are created equally. This, in fact, is one of the major concerns expressed about filters. Some are less effective than others in blocking unwanted sites. Opponents to filters claim that this could leave organizations open to lawsuits.

Filters work in several ways. Some block key words such as sex, breast, or homosexual. This type of filter is considered crude by industry standards and is also considered the least effective type of filter available. Other filters examine the descriptors that webmasters attach to their pages to advertise their contents. Without such descriptors, no one would be able to locate a website.

The third type of filter employs a stop list of URLs (Web addresses). A computer terminal with software cannot access sites flagged by the software. Conversely, this type of filter may also contain a list of sites that have been inspected and approved by the manufacturer of the software. Any sites not on the list cannot be accessed.

Whichever filtering technique the software utilizes, companies which design filters invest large amounts of money developing their products. In order to protect this investment, they often refuse to divulge information about which sites, stop words, or URLs are being blocked. For this reason, the user rarely knows exactly what is being blocked. Many opponents to filtering believe that websites with political beliefs different from those of the software manufacturer are also blocked. Some sites that are said to be blocked by some filtering packages are the homepages of NOW (National Organization of Women), as well as sites hosted by gay and lesbian groups.

In addition, some filtering software can be programmed to block sites based on age. A parent can program a terminal to limit a ten-year-old access to certain sites, while they can give their fifteen-year-old more leeway in viewing sites.

Filtering and Libraries

As a matter of principle, the American Library Association (ALA) opposes filters because they violate the First Amendment, but this does not mean that library boards and trustees refrain from putting filters on Internet terminals in both public and school libraries.

Some libraries refuse to put filters on their Internet terminals. They also refuse to restrict access to terminals to any group. Other libraries, however, place filters on the Internet and also require that parents accompany minors. Minimum age requirements for unaccompanied minors range from twelve to seventeen.

A third group has entered the filtering fray. The Platform for Internet Content Selection (PICS) is calling for voluntary rating of sites by their webmasters. PICS calls for webmasters to voluntarily employ labels that conform to certain conventions. This would, in effect, ask them to label their sites based on content. If publishers fail to comply with voluntary labeling, outside agencies can label the site. This format has proved so attractive that many of the major computer and software manufacturers have announced that they have products compatible with PICS (Resnick and Miller, p. 87). Using PICS means that sites can be blocked based on the material, the user, or even the time of day.

Selection can be made based on a sliding scale, claim Resnick and Miller. The parent (or employer) can set a scale based on violence, language, or sexual content. Developers claim that this format can be easily adapted for different languages.

Whether or not your organization decides to use filters, it is in everyone's best interest to understand this issue and to read the position papers of the various groups that are helping to formulate national policies for the Internet. Sooner or later this issue will come to the local library, business, or school.

Bibliography

ALA. Resolution on the Use of Filtering Software in Libraries. www.ala.org/alaorg/oif/filters.html. [Accessed November 11, 1997].

Resnick, Paul and James Miller. "PICS: Internet Access Controls Without Censorship." *Communications of the ACM.* Vol. 39, No. 10, 87–93.

Resnick, Paul. "Filtering Information on the Internet." *Scientific American.* www.sciam.com/0397issue/0397resnick.html. [Accessed November 11, 1997].

Schuyler, Michael. When Does Filtering Turn into Censorship? www.infotoday.com/cilmag/may/story2.htm. [Accessed November 21, 1997].

THE PROS AND CONS OF FILTERING

Filtering software is used on computer terminals to prevent users from accessing sites that are considered inappropriate. There is no question that parents have the right to use this software to police their personal computers. Putting this software on library computers, however, is very controversial. The official position of the ALA states, in part, that:

> The use of software filters which block Constitutionally protected speech in libraries is inconsistent with the United States Constitution and federal law and may lead to legal exposure for the library and its governing authorities. The American Library Association affirms that the use of filtering software by libraries to block access to constitutionally protected speech violates the Library Bill of Rights.
>
> —*Statement of Library Use of Filtering Software—American Library Association/ Intellectual Freedom Committee, July 1, 1997 (http://www.ala.org/akairg/oif/filt.stm.html)*

Along with its position statement, the ALA has issued guidelines that are designed to help both libraries and patrons understand some of the problems associated with the use of filters on the Internet. These guidelines include the following:

1. Most libraries are public institutions, this means that they are, in effect, government institutions. As such, the First Amendment (freedom of speech) forbids them to deny access to information based on a particular viewpoint or content.

2. Filters limit access to sites other than those that have been deemed illegal. They also block access to legal sites that are protected by the first amendment. Therefore, legal information is being denied to users along with the illegal.

3. Filters are designed by commercial manufacturers. By using these products, the views of the manufacturer are imposed on the entire community.

4. The criteria for blocking sites are vaguely defined and are applied subjectively.

5. Due to the methods employed to block access, sites are blocked accidentally along with those that are meant to be blocked.

6. Filtering products are not flexible enough to serve the needs of a community with diverse perspectives. They are often designed to be used in the home and respond to the needs of parents. Because filters require libraries to deny access to information, they run contrary to library mandates.

7. The role of librarians is to advise and help users select appropriate sites, but it is the role of parents to determine what information should be denied to their children. This should be limited to their own children. It is not the role of the library to act in loco parentis.

8. Using filtering software implies that all access to restricted information will be denied to users. In fact, this software is not sophisticated enough to accomplish this goal. This would leave the library potentially legally liable if users were able to access such sites due to the limitations of filtering technology.

9. Laws already exist that prohibit the use or dissemination of child pornography. These laws protect both libraries and their users.

Not all librarians or library boards agree with this position, however. A number of librarians are now using filtering software. One of the most vocal proponents of filtering within the library profession is David Burt, a librarian from Oregon. He has developed his own website called Filtering Facts that counters the claims of the ALA. This site includes several sections including Fighting Facts, Anti-Filter Sites, News Items, Friendly Sites, and What's New. One of the most interesting parts of this page is his section called Responses to Arguments Against Filtering (www.filteringfacts. org/resp.htm).

In this portion of the site Burt answers some of the arguments of the ALA. Some of his answers are paraphrased here:

Argument: Filters block all sites that contain certain key words.

Response: The filters can be turned off on some software packages. Instead site selected blocking is used to deny access.

Argument: Filters block sites about sex education, AIDS, and other controversial topics.

Response: Many filters use stop words to block sites. In addition, however, these programs also have broken the stop words down into subjects. These can then be deselected for access.

Argument: Filters rely on a list of banned sites that is denied to the public.

Response: These lists of sites are expensive for the manufacturers to develop. They are kept from the public to protect the product rather than to keep the contents secret. If the list were made public, the value of the program would be diminished.

Argument: Filters allow outsiders to decide what sites are selected for viewing.

Response: Many libraries have out sourced their selection process for years. Using filters is not any different than letting the vendor select books for the library.

Argument: The size of the Internet makes it impossible for filters to be entirely accurate.

Response: Filters are not 100 percent accurate, but they work very well on pornography. Libraries should warn parents that filters cannot guarantee that inappropriate sites will not be accessed.

Argument: It is not the librarian's job to decide what is appropriate. They should let the user decide what is appropriate.

Response: Librarians decide every day what patrons may or may not have access to every time they make a decision regarding library materials. Users are allowed to decide what materials are appropriate within an already pre-selected group of materials.

Argument: Librarians do not act in loco parentis.

Response: While librarians do not act in the place of a minor's parents, they do try to screen children from materials that are not appropriate for them. Communities assume that libraries have minimum standards that are designed to protect children. This means that pornographic materials will not be made available to minors.

There are additional arguments both for and against filtering, but the Filtering Facts homepage was paraphrased for this discussion because it was found to be representative of these opinions.

Many other sites on the Internet also discuss filtering. The web site for "From Now On," which describes itself as a "monthly electronic commentary on educational technology issues," provides a well-thought-out strategy for allowing students' access to the Internet (without using filters) while still respecting the values of each family.

This site stresses guidance as the appropriate tool to teach students how to use the Internet responsibly. These guidelines would provide students with pre-viewed sites to complete homework assignments. While completing such assignments, students would be expected to confine their searches to these sites. Providing students with previewed sites not only meets the requests of the most conservative of families, but it is also a good tool for maintaining order in the lab, instructing students in effective searching techniques, and for teaching them critical thinking skills as they evaluate sites.

Students would be required to have parental permission to conduct free searching. Only students with such permission would work together. They would also have access to the computers at times different from the students without such permission. Students found violating any of the lab rules, including accessing illegal or offensive sites, would risk losing privileges or face other punishments.

This article has outlined only a few web sites that discuss the pros and cons of filtering. One could spend a great deal of time researching filtering. Each article will be pro or con, and none will say that these are sometimes appropriate and sometimes not. It is up to administrators, teachers, and parents to do what they think best, but they should do their homework first. Do not depend on sites that use scare tactics regardless of the slick graphics.

Most of all, know your children, know what your library policies are, and find out how your schools use the Internet. The knowledge that you acquire about this issue is the best defense for your children, your library, and your school.

Bibliography

"ALA: Resolution on the Use of Filtering Software in Libraries." *ALA Homepage* www.ala.org/ alaorg.oif/filt res.html. Accessed November 11, 1997.

"Responses to Arguments Against Filtering." *Filtering Facts* www.filteringfacts.org/resp.htm. Accessed November 21, 1997.

From Now On. Vol. 4. No. 10 June 1995. www. fromnowon.org/frojune95.html.

12 Reason Why Schools Should Avoid Filtering

* Filters do not work very well.
* Filters may work too well.
* Filtering draws the attention of young adults to sexually explicit material.
* Funds used to buy and maintain filtering programs could be used to acquire software for students' course work.
* Filters may create false security.
* Filters may increase liability.
* Filters may violate family values.
* Filters may violate community values.
* Filters may violate civil liberties.
* Manufacturers of filtering software may define obscenity too narrowly.
* There are better ways to protect our children. Guidance, not censorship, could be provided.
* Young adults can learn to filter for themselves.

From: "A Dozen Reasons Why Schools Should Avoid Filtering," *From Now On: The Educational Technology Journal*, 5 (March–April 1996): 12–14.

PARENTAL EMPOWERMENT AND THE INTERNET

Many libraries state in their Internet access policies that they are not responsible for what users may access on the Internet. The American Library Association (ALA) states that it is not the place of libraries to enforce parental restriction or to block access for any group of users to electronic information. Yet the Internet contains a lot of controversial, pornographic, inaccurate, or offensive material— material that may be considered inappropriate, not just for young adults, but for many other people. Libraries believe the responsibility lies with parents, and only parents, to monitor and restrict a child or young adult's access to the Internet.

The World Wide Web is a very recent phenomenon. Even four or five years ago, there existed chat rooms and gophers, while the World Wide Web only became a household term in the early 1990s. Only recently has the Internet become an everyday thing, to be found in schools, homes, and libraries across North America. With technology this new, many young adults are much more at home than their parents with the Web. According to the ALA, "Libraries may need to help parents understand their options during the evolving information revolution." If parents are supposed to be responsible for determining what they wish their children to access electronically, they need to know what can be accessed electronically.

Many librarians feel that libraries need to play a role in this process of parental empowerment. Parents need to be familiar with the Internet, with what it can be used for, with its strengths and weaknesses. For parents who wish to become informed, the library is a possible resource. The Internet itself contains many sources that advocate parental empowerment and suggest ways for parents to understand their child's Internet usage.

One of the most important things is to sit down with your child or young adult and get them to show you the Web. Spend time with them while they are online. Chances are the average 15- or 16-year-old in North America has been exposed to computers and the Internet at school. This may not be true of parents. The Internet may or may not be present in the workplace. It may or may not be something that the parent has to deal with.

There are also web sites (which your teenager may show you how to access!) written specifically for parents. The New York Public Library has a site at http://www.nypl.org/branch/safety.html that offers the following advice:

1. Have your child show you how to access the Internet
2. Spend time with them when they are online
3. Explore the wide range of information that is available and discuss with them which topics you consider off-limits
4. Keep the lines of communication open so that you can talk to your children, and they will recognize your interest in what they are doing as genuine
5. Monitor the amount of time your child spends with the computer. Excessive use of online services, especially late at night, may signal a potential problem. The same parenting skills that apply to the "real world" also apply while online
6. Set your rules for the use of the Internet

As with any information on the Web, it is important not to accept any of these sites at face value, but to read carefully and to be aware of who is sponsoring the site. Sites may be sponsored by non-profit organizations, by businesses, by libraries, and by individuals, to name a few, and this may influence the information that you find there.

Here are just a few of the available Internet sites for parents:

A Parent's Guide to Supervising a Child's Online and Internet Experience

http://www.cais.net/cannon/memos/parents.htm

This is version 1.1, last updated: March 4, 1997, by Robert Cannon, Esq. Bear in mind that CAIS is an Internet service provider. This article starts with some definitions of common Internet terms. Again, the author explains some of the risks with Internet use. He suggests filtering software, but also points out that such software may filter out material which you find desirable.

Child Safety on the Information Highway
http://www.safekids.com/child safety.htm

This site contains the full text of a brochure called *Child Safety on the Information Highway* written by Lawrence J. Magid and published by the National Centre for Missing and Exploited Children in the United States. In his introduction he says:

"Whatever it's called, millions of people are now connecting their personal computers to telephone lines so that they can 'go online.' Traditionally, online services have been oriented towards adults, but that's changing. An increasing number of schools are going online and, in many homes, children are logging on to commercial services, private bulletin boards, and the Internet. As a parent you need to understand the nature of these systems."

Lawrence J. Magid is a syndicated columnist for the *Los Angeles Times*. The brochure covers the risks involved in Internet access and suggests to parents basic rules they should insist on.

Netparents.org: Resources for Internet Parents
http://www.netparents.org

This is a site that describes the various electronic ways in which parents can limit or monitor their child's access to the Internet. Netparents.org covers things such as:

Stand Alone Blocking Software Resources
    provided by online service providers
    and ISPs
Internet Content Rating Systems
Starting Points for Kid-Friendly Net Access

The site also provides links to a number of other sites that might be of interest. Again, sites need to be evaluated carefully. Netparents.org provides links to the various filtering software. However, they paint a rather positive picture of filtering software and do not bring up many of the negative issues that have been raised elsewhere concerning this issue.

Children Online: The ABCs for Parents
http://www.childrenspartnership.org/

This site is good for parents who are just beginning to use the Internet. It gives information on exactly what the Internet is and explains how it works. It also provides age-appropriate-guidelines for children using the Internet and includes the following categories:

What Is the Information Superhighway?
What's At Stake—Why Computers
    Matter to Your Child
What Does Using Computers Actually
    Do for Your Child?
When Is Your Child Ready?

A Parent's Guide to the Internet and How to Protect Your Children in Cyberspace
http://www.familyguidebook.com/book/contents. html

This contains the entire text, online, of Perry Aftab's book *A Parent's Guide to the Internet and How to Protect Your Children in Cyberspace*. The book includes:

Part I   Outfitting Yourself for Cyberspace
           (everything you need to know to get
           online)
Part II   The Dark Side . . . Keeping Things in
           Perspective

This book covers almost everything a parent would want to know, and it's right there online.

INTERNET ACCESS POLICIES

Internet access or Internet use policies are a very important issue in libraries today. Libraries without policies have been caught off guard when parents or other library patrons made complaints. What is an Internet access policy? What does it include?

An Internet access policy defines what a library considers as acceptable use of its Internet facilities. While the American Library Association (ALA) opposes any policies that restrict access to library materials or services, or that discriminate against any category of user, providing Internet access without some sort of policy has proven to be nearly impossible. The ALA believes that each library should formally adopt a policy that is developed from its mission and goals and that it should periodically re-examine that policy. The policy should allow for reasonable restrictions placed on the time, place, and manner of access. Acceptable use policies should ensure broad access, citing as few restrictions as possible. The ALA states that "Only parents and legal guardians have the right and responsibility to restrict their children's and only their own children's access to any electronic resource." The ALA believes that libraries, while they may need to help parents understand their options, should not be in the position of enforcing parental restrictions. The library does not act in loco parentis.

So what are libraries including in their Internet access policies? Policies vary from library to library. Many of these policies are available on the Internet and can be viewed as examples. Most policies lay out the administrative details, including things like length of time you may use the Internet terminals, whether or not you must sign up, and if there are any fees. Many policies will state that a minor needs parental permission, although this is contrary to the official beliefs of the ALA. Some policies state that children may only use the Internet when accompanied by their parents.

The majority of policies act as some sort of a disclaimer. Statements such as this one from the Ottawa Public Library's website are quite common:

> The Public Library has no control over these resources nor does the library have complete knowledge of what is on the Internet. Information on the Internet may be reliable and correct or it may be inaccurate, out-of-date or unavailable at times. The Internet may contain material that is inappropriate for viewing by children. Parents or guardians are expected to monitor and supervise their children's use of the Internet.

Other policies, such as this one from an American library, are much blunter about things:

> The library has no control of the Internet and its resources and assumes no responsibility for the quality, accuracy, or currency of any Internet resource. The Internet may contain material of a controversial nature. Individual Internet usage will not be monitored by Library staff. As with other Library materials, parents are responsible for their child's use of the Internet; any restriction of a child's access

to the Internet is the responsibility of the parent/guardian.

Libraries are also using their Internet policies in the same way as collection development policies to protect the library in the case of censorship challenges. A statement supporting the ALA Bill of Rights might be made. The New York Public Library provides links to ALA statements including the Library Bill of Rights, the Freedom to Read Statement, the Freedom to View Statement, and the Interpretation of the Library Bill of Rights: Free Access to Libraries for Minors and Access to Electronic Information Services and Resources. The policy states that these statements guide the library.

In an article in the November 1997 issue of *American Libraries* entitled "Internet Policies: Managing in the Real World," Karen Hyman provides some advice to libraries when trying to cope with Internet access. These include:

1. Pick a common-sense approach and give it a try.
2. Focus on customer service.
3. Keep your mind open.
4. Avoid accepting or repeating hearsay.
5. Find common ground—don't avoid or misrepresent facts just because they don't fit your own personal theories.

Works Cited

American Library Association. "Questions and Answers on Access to Electronic Information, Services and Networks" http://www.ala.org/alaorg/oif/ifqanda.html.

Hyman, Karen. "Internet Policies: Managing in the Real World." *American Libraries* (November 1997): 60–62

Tenopir, Carol. "Online Use Policies and Restrictions." *Library Journal* (July 1997): 33–34.

TO CENSOR OR NOT TO CENSOR?: A RESOURCE GUIDE FOR LIBRARIANS, PARENTS, AND TEACHERS

This resource guide offers a wide range of sources and views about censorship and the Internet. For your information, I have indicated if an organization or author is obviously pro-censorship or pro-intellectual freedom.

Web Sites

The Internet Advocate: A Web-based Resource Guide for Librarians and Educators Interested in Providing Youth Access to the Net

http://www.monroe.lib.in.us/~lchampel/netadv.html

This resource guide is maintained by Lisa Champelli, Children's Librarian, Monroe County Public Library, Bloomington, Indiana, USA. The author of this site is pro-intellectual freedom.

Provides information and links to sites about:

- how to respond to inaccurate perceptions of pornography on the Net
- how to promote positive examples of youth Internet use
- how to develop an "Acceptable Use Policy" and examples of AUPs from schools and libraries
- understanding filtering software and safety/censorship issues
- contacting organizations committed to electronic freedom of information
- how to become familiar with Internet resources for libraries

The Internet Filter Assessment Project (TIFAP)

http://www.bluehighways.com/tifap/

The purpose of The Internet Filter Assessment Project (TIFAP) was to study Internet content filters from the perspective of libraries. Participants in the project were both pro- and anti-filtering. All participants agree that filtering tools must be tested in order to determine their usefulness. TIFAP does not endorse or reject filtering.

Provides information about TIFAP including:

- the TIFAP summary report
- articles about TIFAP in the press
- information about filters that were tested by TIFAP

American Library Association Office for Intellectual Freedom

http://www.ala.org/oif.html

The American Library Association supports the rights of youth to gain access to information in any format, including information available on the Internet. The ALA promotes intellectual freedom.

The ALA Office for Intellectual Freedom offers information on censorship and Internet filtering software:

- ALA Library Bill of Rights
- ALA Intellectual Freedom Committee Statement on Library Use of Filtering Software
- ALA Council Resolution on the use of Filtering Software in Libraries
- access to electronic information, services and networks: an interpretation of the Library Bill of Rights (questions and answers)
- text of *Intellectual Freedom Action News*
- links to the Citizen Internet Empowerment Coalition web site that includes the text of the decision of the Supreme Court of the United States that overturned the Communications Decency Act on June 26, 1997, and reactions to this decision

Filtering Facts

http://www.filteringfacts.org/

Filtering Facts is a non-profit organization working "to protect children from the harmful effects of pornography by promoting the use of filtering software in libraries." The Filtering Facts web site is maintained by president and founder of Filtering Facts, librarian David Burt. Burt advocates censorship using filtering software.

The Filtering Facts web site includes information about:

- legal issues regarding filtering in libraries
- links to organizations supporting and opposing filtering the Internet
- recommended filtering products
- full text articles from the popular press and Filtering Facts about filtering
- how to respond to those who oppose filtering

Net Parents Organization: Resources for Internet Parents

http://www.netparents.org/

The Net Parents Organization web site is produced and maintained by the Center for Democracy and Technology and the Voters Telecommunications Watch. This organization promotes censorship via filtering. This web site provides information to parents about the Internet including:

* availability of filtering software
* Internet service providers
* Internet rating systems
* resources including book titles and links to web sites

Enough Is Enough

http://www.enough.org/

Enough Is Enough is a non-profit organization run by president and founder Dee Jepsen and executive vice president Mariam Bell. This organization is committed to protecting "children and families from the dangers of illegal pornography and on-line predators." This organization is pro-censorship and pro-filtering.

Provides information about:

* pornography on the Internet
* legislation and legal issues about pornography on the Internet
* family friendly resources on the Internet

Fear and Loathing in Cyberspace

http://www.ccn.cs.dal.ca/~aa331/fearloath.html

Fear and Loathing in Cyberspace was created by Erez Segal (Dalhousie MLIS). It is intended to provide access to allegedly controversial web sites including sites containing hate literature and pornography. This site could be useful for parents, teachers, and librarians who wish to become aware of hate literature and pornography available on the Internet.

This site provides:

* links to hate literature and pornography available on the Internet
* links to watchdog services, such as the Watchdog Online Sex Site Hotlist Service
* links to legislative documents and articles about censorship, with particular attention to censorship and electronic media

Peacefire: Youth Alliance Against Internet Censorship

http://peacefire.org/

Peacefire is an organization of youth against censorship of youth on the Internet. Concerns of Peacefire include self-rating Internet systems, legislation, and Internet filtering products. Peacefire is active in the fight for the rights of youth including free speech and the opportunity for youth to view material online without interference. This organization promotes intellectual freedom.

This site includes:

* reports on filtering software
* the Cyber Rights and Digital Liberties Encyclopedia (CRADLE)
* links to articles about libraries and Internet filtering in the popular press
* links to other organizations supporting intellectual freedom on the Internet

Platform for Internet Content (PICS)

http://www.w3.org/PICS/

The Platform for Internet Content (PICS) project is a voluntary Internet rating system. PICS is a platform on which other rating services and filtering software have been built.

This web site offers:

* introductory information about PICS
* information for web site authors, parents, schools, employers, the media, and PICS developers
* responses to frequently asked questions about PICS

Student Association for Freedom of Expression (SAFE) Home Page

http://www.mit.edu/activities/safe/

The MIT Student Association for Freedom of Expression (SAFE) supports intellectual freedom including freedom of speech and other forms of freedom of expression.

This site includes information about:

* labelling and rating systems on the Internet
* links to other organizations supporting intellectual freedom on the Internet

Blue Ribbon Campaign for Online Freedom of Speech, Press and Association

http://www.eff.org/blueribbon.html

The Blue Ribbon Campaign for Online Freedom of Speech, Press and Association promotes intellectual freedom on the Internet. This site provides information and links regarding:

* intellectual freedom and freedom of speech on the Internet
* Internet censorship legislation in the United States, Australia, Germany, Greece, and South Africa

* blue ribbon graphics to download and add to your web site

IF IT'S ON THE NET, THEN IT MUST BE TRUE!: EVALUATING WEB RESOURCES

Every day, young adults consult the Internet for information. Some may do so to research a school report or presentation on which they are working. Teachers report that increasingly more references in students' papers cite web pages as resources.

As well, youth are surfing the Net for information unrelated to school, such as how to find and use birth control, when will the Tragically Hip be touring in their province again, or what are the latest in fashion trends from Europe. Whatever the reason for consulting this medium, it is important that these youth are informed as to how to evaluate properly and judge what is "out there" on the Internet.

The question then arises—are young adults critically evaluating the information they find on the Internet? An extensive search on this topic, conducted on Dialog, the Internet, and postings to a young adult librarians' mailing list, produced very little. There were literally hundreds of sites and articles on web evaluation, but this search produced little on how *youth* evaluate such sites. It was then decided that in order to find out, it was best to go directly to the source itself—teens who use the Internet.

An informal survey was carried out at an urban high school (population approximately 800 students). Thirty surveys were completed; however, it should be noted that approximately fifty teens were approached to complete the survey. Out of the thirty respondents, twenty-eight had used the Internet.

Some of the survey's findings:

Age of respondents: 15–19 years; average age—
16.48 years old
Grades: 10–12

How often do you use the Internet?
One to three times per week: 13
Daily: 6
Did not quantify their answer: 9
("not often": 6, "a lot": 3)

Where do you use the Internet?
Home: 19
School: 19
Library: 8

What do you use the Internet for?
Homework: 23
Fun: 19
Chat lines: 8
Games: 6
Other: 7 (e-mail: 6, music: 1)

The remainder of the survey solicited the opinions of these youth on:

* how they judge what they find on the Web
* how reliable is the Internet as a source of information
* why they would choose to look up information on the Internet rather than use a book
* whether information on the Internet is more reliable than what is printed in books.

The responses were varied and information was gathered from both sides—those who were critical and those who were not.

When asked how they judged the information on the Internet, some of the common responses were: "by company or informer," and "it is generally useful, but you have to sift through so much useless junk before you can find what you are looking for." Others simply replied "interesting," "useful," or "informative," which did not provide a lot of answers. The most common complaints were the advertisements which were found, and problems using the search engines. One respondent stated that "I don't like it when they put advertisements about joining cults and stuff because it's not good."

Complaints about using search engines included finding "Error 404" messages and having to wait up to twenty minutes for a search result only to find out the results were not what they wanted.

The youth's views of the reliability of the information on the Internet was found to be directly linked to the other two questions: why would you use the Internet rather than books, and is the information in books? Eleven respondents judged the Internet to be more reliable than books, eight were very wary of the information found on the Net, and the remaining nine stated that their evaluation depended on factors such as who published the information and where it was found. For the pro-Internet side, the common theme for deeming the Internet as the more reliable source of information was that it was up-to-date, had information from around the world, and it had information that they could not find in books in their library. Those who were skeptical claimed that they "just don't trust them," "[the information] is fairly useless [because] anything with that word [search term] in it shows up but it is not necessarily on the subject," and "I can't just depend on the Internet . . . it's not that reliable."

Those who stated that their evaluation depended on the author, the information sought, and the location provided some very good reasons for questioning this medium. Some of the responses included, "Well, in books the publishers and authors have their names there, so it is more reliable, but . . . if you use Yahoo and come to a site, you should have no problem"; "Some information is more reliable but some things they write on the Internet are false facts, I find it very annoying"; and " I would usually use both sources to back each other up."

One respondent seemed to be quite critical of all resources stating, "The Internet is probably fairly reliable, but as with any form of media, you can't believe everything you read."

A mixed grouping of opinions and thoughts indeed!

There are valid sites out there on the Internet, just as there are those which are dubious. As well, the Internet can fill in certain gaps in library collections, especially on current statistics and information. The key is to help youth evaluate what they find on the Internet and teach them to think about their findings critically. How can we do this? As with our printed media, we can teach students and young adult library users to ask critical questions: who wrote the information, does the author state his or her credentials (including previous publications and position), where does the information originate (is it a personal web page or is it part of a university department or company's findings), and when was the information published?

Both teachers and librarians can assist young adults by showing them how to examine the information they find—both in print and on the Internet. Part of this evaluation can begin before the user ventures out onto the Net. Students and library users can be presented with criteria for evaluating online information and checklists for judging what they find. These youth must be instructed on how to use such guidelines and then be allowed to judge for themselves if the information they find is relevant. Such guidelines can be found online and a list of these is provided at the end of this article.

Unfortunately, the material found on the Internet does not find its way to editorial boards or review committees, although some journals are now publishing reviews of web sites, and libraries are providing users with lists of sites reviewed in-house. It is unlikely that the information found "out there" on the Net will ever be forced through editorial boards or committees, so in the meantime we must teach our youth the value of critically evaluating the information found.

WEB ZINES: WHERE TO LOOK FOR YA ZINES

Young adults like magazines because of the following characteristics:

- they are visual
- they appeal to short attention spans
- they speak to developing special interests
- they are viewed as socially acceptable reading material
- they give information on important stuff (sex, love, etc.)
- they cover fads/celebrities
- they are at an easy reading level
- teens don't have to read them at school (no pressure)
- they allow teens to dream/fantasize/set goals
- they make teens laugh, cry, emote, think, and relax

YA web zines have all this and more. In addition to matching the advantages given to magazines in general, web zines have their own distinct advantages. Benefits of web zines include such things as:

* low cost
* highly visual
* can include multimedia (sound, video, etc.)
* can link to other relevant sites
* teens can submit material (not limited to letters to the editor)
* teens can start new web zines
* may be accessed by a number of YAs (depending on equipment)
* high interest and fun
* may be interactive
* variety (many zines catering to different teen interests)

Though there are many advantages to web zines, there are several drawbacks as well:

* sites disappear
* sites may not be updated regularly (fluctuating publication schedule)
* quality of information found on web zines may be suspect

Finding Web Zines

When looking for web zines you need to be resourceful as there is no single source of information. The following locations contain links to a number of YA web zines:

The Young Adult Librarian's Help/Homepage contains a large selection of clickable links to various YA zines. This page is updated frequently. See http://yahelp. suffolk.lib.ny.us

On Yahoo, magazines are listed under the Society and Culture heading, e.g., http://www. yahoo.com/Society_and_Culture/Cultures_and_ Groups/Teenagers/Magazines/ or http://www. yahoo.com/text/Society_and_Culture/Magazines /Youth/ or http://www.yahoo.com/Society_and_ Culture/Age_Groups/Teenagers/Girls/Magazines/

Reviews of web zines may be found in the professional literature and on listservs. Surf other YA web pages for links to web zines, and check the counters on any zines you find to see how much traffic the site receives. Talk to teens as often as possible about the zines they like and whether they would be interested in starting a zine. For school librarians, publication of a web zine could become an ongoing project coordinated between the library and the English department.

Sites to See

The following web pages were functioning at the time of writing.

Blast
http://www.explode.com/
Published monthly. Contains featurettes and standard articles.

Circle J
http://www.cts.richmond.va.us/heaventek/ circlej.htm/
Christian e-zine containing poetry, stories and links. Back issues are archived

daisyface, the zine
http://www.geocities.com/Paris/4840/index.html/
Includes letter from the editor, poetry café, pen pal network, and more.

Spank!

http://www.spankmag.com/

Includes feature articles, columns, and regular articles. Appears to be updated monthly.

Write Teen

http://members.tripod.com/~JennaRose/writeteen-1.html/

This site gives a choice of viewing styles, choose from classical, wild, or picture free. Contains stories, advice, poetry, and articles.

NET-PLOTS: THE INTERNET AS AN ELEMENT IN YA NOVELS

With the development of the World Wide Web (WWW), use of the Internet has grown exponentially, and young adults have taken their place among those who have become its most avid users. For those YAs who have the advantage of being connected, the Internet can touch on many aspects of their lives. The Net can be harnessed to research homework assignments, download computer game software, hear a favorite band's latest release, or meet other teens through chatrooms. YAs have developed their own websites, set up school homepages, and published their own poetry and stories via electronic magazines.

Alert to new interests among westernized teens, YA fiction writers have kept pace with this cybersurfing trend by including the Internet in their novels and short stories. The story lines range from realistic fiction to sci-fi and from horror to romance, but now include characters who use chatrooms, browsers, e-zines, and webpages.

Over the past year, publishers have launched at least four YA series novels that include the Internet in the plot. In some of the titles (*cyber.kdz*), most of the book revolves around chat sessions (dialogue) between characters. In other selections (*danger.com*), the e-mail or chatroom messages are lightly interspersed throughout the text and traditional narrative is dominant. Some of the series books (*@café, cyber.kdz*) follow the lives of a particular set of characters, with each new edition in the series focusing on one of the teens and a new story line. In other series books (*danger.com*), each issue introduces a fresh set of characters and a new story.

Some books offer a light recreational read while others, such as *Bottom Drawer,* treat more weighty issues—in this case, suicide and gay/lesbian themes. Sometimes the Internet plays an important role in the plot (*Search for the Shadowman*), while at other times its presence is incidental.

The following list of Net Novels was compiled with help from *Global Books in Print, Voice of Youth Advocates (VOYA)* magazine, amazon.com, and barnesandnoble.com websites and through suggestions from subscribers to the PUBYAC listserv. The Net novels available to YAs range from those for a middle school readership to those in junior/senior high and beyond. Those which might suit older YA tastes include titles by Card, Greenberg, Lewitt, McCarthy and Watkins.

Net Novels

Balan, Bruce

Cyber.kdz :1—In Search of Scum, Avon Camelot, 1997. (0-380-78514-5)

Cyber.kdz :2—A Picture's Worth, Avon Camelot, 1997. (0-380-78515-3)

Cyber.kdz :3—The Great NASA Flu, Avon Camelot, 1997. (0-380-78516-1)

Cyber.kdz :4—Blackout in the Amazon, Avon Camelot, 1997. (0-380-78517-x)

Cyber.kdz :5—In Pursuit of Picasso, Avon Camelot, 1998. (0-380-79499-3)

Cyber.kdz :6—When the Chips Are Down, Avon Camelot, 1998. (0-380-79500-0)

Boyd, David

Bottom Drawer, Rubicon, 1996. (0-92115-658-8)

Card, Orson

Ender's Game (revised edition), Tor, 1994. (0-812-55070-6)

Ciencin, Scott

Faceless (Lurker Files #1), Random House, 1996. (0-679-88235-9)

Know Fear (Lurker Files #2), Random House, 1996. (0-679-88236-7)

Nemesis (Lurker Files #3), Random House, 1997. (0-679-88506-4)

Incarnate (Lurker Files #4), Random House, 1997. (0-679-88507-2)

Apparition (Lurker Files #5), Random House, 1997. (0-679-88634-6)

Triad (Lurker Files #6), Random House, 1997. (0-679-99635-4)

Clancy, Tom

NetForce (series of 18 proposed YA novels), Berkley, 1998.

Cooney, Caroline B.

Wanted! Scholastic, 1997. (0-590-98849-2)

Cooper, Susan

The Boggart, Aladdin, 1995. (0-689-80173-4)

Craft, Elizabeth

Love Bytes (@café #1), Archway, 1997. (0-671-00445-X)

I'll Have What He's Having (@café #2), Archway, 1997. (0-671-00446-8)

Make Mine to Go (@café #3), Archway, 1997. (0-671-00447-6)

Flavor of the Day (@café #4), Archway, February 1998. (0-671-00448-4)

Cray, Jordan

Gemini7 (danger.com #1), Aladdin, 1997. (0-689-81432-1)

Firestorm (danger.com #2), Aladdin, 1997. (0-689-81431-3)

Shadowman (danger.com #3), Aladdin, 1997. (0-689-81433-X)

Hot Pursuit (danger.com #4), Aladdin, 1997. (0-689-81434-8)

Stalker 5 (danger.com #5), Aladdin, 1998. (0-689-81476-3)

Doyon, Stephanie

It Had to Be You (Love Stories #10), Bantam, 1996. (0-553-56669-5)

Greenberg, Martin H. and Larry Segriff, ed.

Future Net [anthology], DAW, 1996. (0-886-77723-2)

Lewitt, Shariann

Interface Masque, Tor, 1997. (0-312-85627-X)

Mazer, Harry

City Light, Scholastic, 1988. (0-590-40511-X)

McCarthy, Wil

Murder in the Solid State, Tor, 1996. (0-312-85938-4)

Nixon, Joan Lowery

Search for the Shadowman, Delacorte, 1996. (0-385-32203-8)

Don't Scream, Delacorte, 1996. (0-385-32065-5)

Tolan, Stephanie S.

Welcome to the Ark, Morrow, 1996. (0-688-13724-5)

Watkins, Graham

Interception, Carroll & Graf, 1997. (0-786-70354-7)

BOOK REVIEWS

Balan, Bruce. *Cyber.kdz:1—In Search of Scum.* Avon Camelot, 1997. 163 p. 0-380-78514-5.

In *Cyber.kdz,* a new YA series by author Bruce Balan, seven teens from around the world have become friends through the Internet. Ranging in age from ten to sixteen, they share their computer savvy to solve mysteries and depend on each other for emotional support. In the first of the series, Balan interweaves two stories. Josh, the group's Seattle connection, runs away from home to try to deal with his parents' recent breakup. Meanwhile, against the wishes of the kids, Deeder (in Amsterdam) tries to trace a deadly virus-producing scum and put him out of business. When the scum discovers Deeder's presence in his system, the kids must work quickly to prevent disaster—and they must find Josh in order to crack the scum's security code.

Balan infuses this story with both suspense and humour. I found myself laughing out loud quite a few times—a good sign, I suspect. The kids are likeable, smart, and multidimensional, with occasional soulful insights—Josh explains his pent-up emotions as "kind of like if you got a real slow modem and the buffer gets full . . . next thing you know, your system crashes." The story reads quickly and is composed of both traditional narrative and cyber-chat between the kids, who log on from France, India, Rio, Amsterdam, and the USA.

Balan, who has a background in software design, writes with the easy familiarity of someone who knows the wire. He includes just enough jargon to highlight the technical smarts of these cyberteens. The book includes a glossary of computer slang and foreign words, as well as website addresses for both Balan and the Cyber-kdz. *Cyber.kdz* (six titles currently available) is a series that would appeal to young- to mid-YAs, whether or not they have yet taken a ride on the information highway.

[The websites themselves are well designed, entertaining, and extensive. They include excerpts from the *Cyber.kdz* books as well as information about Balan and his availability for school talks and other public appearances. Balan has given the site a very personal feel, with many comments and photos, including my favourite—a great shot of his cat Bacardi.]

Cyber.kdz site: http://cyber.kdz.com/
Bruce Balan website: http://cyber.kdz.com/balan/index.html

Boyd, David. *Bottom Drawer.* Rubicon, 1996. 122 p. 0-921-15658-8

Fifteen-year-old Mac Kuper is rescued from a Toronto Go-Train track minutes before the train roars past. Through a series of interview transcripts, online conversations, memos, and narrative, Boyd guides us through the incidents that have resulted in Mac coming to the decision to end his life. Mac's father actually committed suicide in the same way when Mac was only six years old. Mac then lived in a difficult relationship with his mother and stepfather. His private world revolved around his chatroom alias, "MacKid," his Internet friend, "2Cool," and the treasures hidden in his bedroom's "bottom drawer."

Boyd incorporates two powerful symbols in the book. One is the character of Holden Caulfield (from Salinger's *The Catcher in the Rye*), a protagonist with whom Mac is fascinated. The second image is one from an Alex Colville painting—a dark horse running towards the light of an oncoming train—". . . confused and desperate, powerful yet powerless, running to meet destiny head on." Mac holds firm to the belief that his father had bravely met the train in the same way. It is only when tragedy again touches Mac's life that he realizes that this running has actually meant running *away*.

It is unfortunate that the cover art does not reflect the theme and quality of the book. The photo of a boy seated at a computer, eyes intent on the screen, reminds me of a computer store ad. Although I can't speak for today's female YAs, as a woman I can't say that this cover would have called out to me, even though the story would be appreciated by teens of both genders. A cover reproduction of the Colville painting may not have been possible, but more appropriate artwork could have conveyed the sensitive issues, psychological elements, and train/horse imagery present in the story.

Cray, Jordan. *Gemini7 (danger.com #1)*. Aladdin, 1997. 196 p. 0-689-81432-1

"Surfing the Net can be hazardous to your health"—so warn the *danger.com* novels, each of which introduces a new set of characters. In *Gemini7*, the first of the series, Jonah has grown tired of being seen as a couple. His steady girlfriend, neighbour, and classmate Jen begins to pale when compared with some of the female chatroom friends he meets. When one of them, a dream-girl named Nicole, makes an appearance in Jonah's small town, strange things begin to happen to his family and friends. As the days of summer roll on, Jonah must choose between the unpretentious, pragmatic Jen and the beautiful, but manipulative Nicole.

Gemini7 is written primarily in first-person narrative with only a few instances of cyberchat occurring in the text. It has a mild psychological/suspense theme and was certainly able to give me a creepy sense of foreboding at certain points in the story. A quick read for any fan of YA mystery or suspense, the book includes a *danger.com* website address, as well as a teaser-style excerpt for the next issue (five titles currently available). The story also offers the added bonus of a male perspective on romance.

[Run by Simon and Schuster for its Aladdin Paperbacks line, the website includes excerpts from the books, a conversation with the author and depictions of the book covers. Although not as extensive as the Balan site described in this column, the page does allow visitors to link to other series titles by Simon and Schuster, including *Extreme Zone* and @café.]

Danger.com website: http://www.simonsays.com/kidzone/net-scene/ns_danger.html

Youth and Athletics

YA Hotline, Issue No. 58, 1997

GILLIAN ANDERSON, JACQUELINE GREENOUGH, AND CAMERON METCALF

HACKING AT NO PAIN TO GAIN

Initiation, violence in sports, over-competitive teens. We have ignored the touchy topics to conduct a moderately positive approach to adolescents and sport today: our interviews and reports speak for themselves, indicating where the real issues are.

It feels like I've just regained consciousness. I'm being suspended and jounced in mid-air. I can make out a banner at about eye level, close to my face, which I have subconsciously started trying to read: its lettering appears backwards so I'm having trouble understanding the blurry message written on this banner, waving like a ribbon at the end of a 100-meter dash. I concentrate, letter for letter, M, O, O, L, E, H, T . . . If I had a mirror to reflect the phrase, it would have to read—more concentration—"Fruit of the Loom."

Fruit of the Loom?

Suddenly things start to click, explaining that nonstop sensation of pain where the sun don't customarily shine, that momentary lapse of consciousness. I am awash with cramping discomfort and humiliation as I formulate a dawning realization: because that banner isn't a banner at all, it's actually the waistband of a pair of underwear—underwear that belongs to (and is currently being sported by) yours truly; because with my Asics Tigers sneakers dangling a foot above the ground, there's four guys trying to take off my underwear in a set of rudimentary jerks. Their unorthodox approach is illogical and has scrotum-stretching repercussions for me, the wearer.

This is my initiation to junior high school volleyball.

I don't feel any anger although I resent my mother for having decided I would enter grade nine with a new batch of underwear added to my wardrobe. This particular pair, brand-spanking-new, refuses to give up a stitch as it is tugged and grappled. This is problem-atic, because initiation protocol dictates that a rookie's underwear be ripped upwards until it is torn from his person.

I wish I'd kept an older, worn-out pair to wear today; some frayed and faded little number that could easily relinquish its weak elasticity and fabric so I could break free in relative comfort. I wish my guardian angel would stop laughing at my predicament and float down with some scissors to snip me from this uncertain doom.

Alas the wretched angel never comes to offer assis-tance and my teammates reluctantly give up. My new department store garments have outmatched their destructive energy.

Half laughing, half crying, I pull out the second pair of underwear I'd brought along to change into, just for the occasion when I knew they would end up getting me. There is a fresh wave of incredulous laugh-ter from the volleyball team, they can't believe I had the foresight to bring extra clothes.

The act itself is called ginching or giving someone a wedgie, a shnoogie. Every new member of the team was to be ginched, wedgied, or shnoogied, until his underwear (as I've said) was ripped right off him. I was the last on the team to be ginched. Sporadically, week after week, one or two guys would fall prey to get-ting initiated. A couple of rookies would get hit after practice, sometimes they'd get someone after we'd soundly walloped another school during one of our var-sity games. Even some of the smaller second-year play-ers were subject to repeated counts of the shnoogie—just for the fun of it. They finally got me at the concluding season tournament, a one-hour bus ride away from home.

Pick any school, any sport, you'll find this spe-cial treatment is more common than the instances of sweating palms at a school dance, but it stems from the same thing. The anxiety of boys strug-gling to fit in.

There are lots of issues that surround the nature of sports. It's no easy task to assemble a magazine that incorporates all the themes and concerns fac-ing young people who regularly compete. Such ele-ments vary from sport to sport, from level to level of competition. With the multitude of sports and degrees of athleticism, we have chosen to provide select perspectives of the face of athletics by address-ing coaching, the pressures of individual sport, the desire to acquire an ideal body image, and the out-look of athletes who are in the introductory stages of something that could become very competitive for them in the future.

Sports represent many stages and skills required to reach a further goal down the line. It might mean working on your basketball shot so you can someday make that unlikely three-pointer in the last desperate seconds of a game or perfect-ing a flip turn so you can shave a few eighths of a second off of your best swim time. Everyone plays sports for different reasons too: they represent recreational pastimes; a chance to blow off some steam; occasions to get together with friends.

Clearly, not everyone shares a common enthu-siasm for sporting life, but this magazine's content goes well beyond everyday jock talk to reach wide-spread appeal, whether you are directly involved in athletics, or not. For those readers who have tradi-tionally considered themselves "ungifted" in the area of athletic prowess, for those readers who can unthinkingly get on with their day without first diagnosing last night's hockey results, there is a lot to be enjoyably learned from the interviews, reports, book reviews, and short story that follow.

This introduction serves as your initiation to our publication. You've made it. You're qualified to go on. And we would like you to read further.

IN PURSUIT OF PERFECTION: YOUNG ADULTS, SELF-IMAGE, AND SPORTS PARTICIPATION

Females: Thin Is In

One need only turn on the television and watch the typical images of today's perfect movie stars, models, and athletes to realize the societal belief that "thin is in" for females, and "strong, muscular, and lean" are imperative characteristics for the ideal male. Today's youth are under tremendous pressure to meet these criteria in order to feel good about their physical self and to feel worthy of society's acceptance.

The pressure to be slender is especially overwhelming for teenage girls. For example, in a recent *Maclean's* article, five adolescent girls from Rosedale Heights Secondary School in Toronto comment on the pressure they feel to be thin. "Two of the girls say they used to starve themselves for three and four days at a time, enduring dizzy spells. 'People said it would shrink your stomach,' explains Tiffany Ruffolo, 16. She finally quit fasting after she fainted" (Nemeth, 44).

Indeed, many teenage girls, those involved and those not involved in sports, are in mental turmoil at this difficult age. Puberty is beginning, consequently changing their bodies from girls to women. Through this natural progression, body shape changes as body fat increases. "Hence, feelings of reaching menarche (puberty) and developing secondary sex characteristics . . . may be a warning sign as well as a risk factor for the development of eating disorders" (Sundgot-Borgen, 414). These painful feelings are summarized in the following excerpt written by Naomi Wolf, a popular feminist writer:

> It is dead easy to become an anorexic. When I was twelve I went to visit an older, voluptuous cousin. "I try," she said, to explain the deep breathing exercises she did before bedtime, "to visualize my belly as something I can love and accept and live with." Still compact in a one-piece kid's body, I was alarmed to think that womanhood involved breaking into pieces that floated around, since my cousin seemed to be trying to hold herself together by a feat of concentration. It was not a comforting thought. . . .
>
> My cousin looked me over. "Do you know how much you weigh?" No, I told her. "Why don't you hop on the scale?" I could feel how much my cousin wished to inhabit a simple, slight twelve-year old body. That could only mean, I thought, that when I was a woman, I would want to get out of my own body into some little kid's. (Wolfe, 12)

Concerns about image is something most young adolescent females share. However, for those who are involved in sports, particularly in the areas of gymnastics, figure skating, and swimming, a slim body type resembling that of a twelve year old is usually a prerequisite, and allows for continuance in the sport. For some, body image is not an issue as they were naturally blessed with a suitable body for their chosen area of sport. However, these cases are the exception rather than the rule as it is impossible for a young girl to predict what type of body she was destined to have before the onset of pubertal changes. Thus, for the great majority who wish for success at an elite level, when puberty begins, so do eating disorders. This finding was established in a recent study as was reported, "a significant number of eating disordered athletes felt they had reached menarche too early. . . . Even though the athletes had reached menarche at an expected time, they felt burdened because they competed in sports where late menarche is more common and extra weight is thought to impair performance and detract from appearance in the eyes of the judges (gymnastics, modern rhythmical gymnastics, figure skating, sports dance, diving, etc.) (Sundgot-Borgen, 415).

Through intense training and dieting the female athlete struggles to maintain a body type that is not her own. A startling statistic reports that 62 percent of female athletes involved in gymnastics at the elite level have eating disorders, compared to about 2 percent of the general population (Nemeth, 45). This statistic is distressing, and ultimately problematic for the aspiring female athlete who is intentionally altering her eating habits. She is making harmful choices at a time when appropriate nutritional habits are important to foster developmental health and sustain a level of energy and strength that will propel her into achieving success with minimal chance of injury. Yet with restrictions on her eating habits, and a regimented training program, she is apt to experience long and short term health problems. To explain, it was mentioned a late menarche was common with participation in certain sports, such as gymnastics. However, this does not happen out of simple coincidence as "intense training suppresses estrogen production delaying puberty and causing 18 and 19 year old athletes to resemble 12 year olds." Further,

lack of estrogen also decreases bone density, putting them at risk of fractures and osteoporosis (Gilbert, E4). Stunted growth is also an obvious possibility and reality for these athletes.

Childlike characteristics are prized in these sports. Young, impressionable athletes will strive for these qualities if it means achievement and acceptance, regardless of physical or mental consequences. Therefore, other "key players" must be targeted to help change this unreasonable, unhealthy outlook or approach. Parents and especially coaches are guilty of pushing these youngsters beyond their limits. Truly, "to perform for the coach, who is often a key figure in the athlete's life, young athletes may feel driven to lose as much weight as possible by whatever means possible, and may dread the alternative: remaining heavier than the 'ideal'" (Sundgot-Borgen, 415). Young athletes must be treated as human beings rather than machines. They do have feelings, they can get hurt, and there can be long term effects from maintaining inadequate diets. Accordingly, little girls should be allowed to develop as intended, and reap the benefits of success as their true selves, instead of feeling coercion to shape or mold themselves into an almost impossible ideal.

Males: Bigger Is Better

Young males feel similar social pressures to conform to societies ideal. One need only flip through the pages of *Sports Illustrated* to view the perfect masculine identity; a tall body frame, bulging biceps, a chiselled chest, and a washboard stomach. Teenagers see these images on a daily basis, "as portrayed in pop culture, the new man is Saturday night-primed, his hard body a turn-on to women and a threat to other men. And that is precisely what a lot of teenage boys want. But their bodies are still developing, so the only quick way to achieve that ideal look is by turning to anabolic steroids to get what nature did not supply" (Nemeth, 47).

"Anabolic steroid use among adolescents has become a major health issue for physicians, coaches, teachers, and others who deal with athletes" (Rickett, 724). This, as mentioned earlier, results from the host of *established side effects and adverse reactions* such as this list which was taken directly from Mishra's 1991 article. Other possible side effects include:

acne
abdominal pains
fetal damage
unexplained weight loss/gain
genital changes
hives
coronary artery disease
nausea and vomiting
water retention in tissue
chills/fever
sterility
vomiting blood
oily skin
euphoria/depression
liver tumours and disease
bone pain
stunted growth
diarrhea
death
impotence
breast development in men
muscle cramps
aggressive behaviour
headaches, fatigue

urination problems
gall stones
sexual problems
high blood pressure
kidney disease

Additionally, in women:
male-pattern baldness
hairiness
voice deepening
decreased breast size
increased body hair
menstrual irregularities

Recent statistics suggest that approximately 83,000 Canadians between the ages of 11 and 18 now use steroids to achieve "what nature did not supply." This is compared to 250,000 adolescents in the United States. Inevitably, this drug abuse is a serious problem, with serious side effects. Unfortunately, young users don't foresee any problems in the future, they only see the short term benefits. "Dr. Arthur Blouin, a psychologist at the Ottawa Civic Hospital who is studying the similarities between steroid abuse and eating disorders [believes] 'they are willing to risk the side-effects of steroids to avoid the negative perception that they are too small and weak'" (Nemeth, 48).

Small and weak, these characteristics or traits are frightening prospects for the average North American teenage male. These features can lead to failure in sports, failure with girls, and being deemed a failure in the eyes of society. Small and weak are attributes that scare many teenagers into using these dangerous substances.

So what are steroids and how do they affect the body? Anabolic steroids are the synthetic version of the human hormone known as testosterone.

Natural testosterone, found in varying levels in both males and females, stimulates and maintains the male sex organs. It also stimulates development and growth of bone and muscle, promotes skin and hair growth, and can influence emotions. "In males, testosterone is produced by the testes and adrenal gland. Women have only the amount of testosterone produced by the adrenal gland—much less than men have. This is why testosterone is often called a 'male' hormone" (Mishra, 26).

Steroids were first introduced by researchers during the 1930s as a measure to rebuild and protect the body from autoimmune diseases which attack body tissues. However, it wasn't until the Olympic Games during the 1950s that the athletic community discovered the drug had performance enhancing capabilities, and took it in large doses. Since this time we have learned of the serious side effects associated with steroid use, yet despite our knowledge of the drug and its adverse effects, the sale of steroids has ballooned into a hundred-million-dollar-a-year black market (Mishra, 27).

When ingesting or injecting anabolic steroids, the body is tricked into believing that testosterone is being produced, and this high level of synthetic testosterone gives the body a false boost. Thus, muscle mass and physical strength is increased at a fast pace, as is overall stamina, allowing the athlete to compete above and beyond the average physically fit male or female. This phenomenon will be maintained for as long as the user continues steroids.

With all of the well-established and well-publicized side effects, why do young adults decide to use steroids? There are several reasons or ideologies the experts believe are important factors that urge adolescents to use them. "One answer is social pressure. Many young men feel they need to look masculine, that is, strong and muscular. Bodybuilding stresses such exaggerated muscularity that some men and women are tempted to abuse anabolic steroids to increase muscle mass and definition. And then there's the 'winning isn't everything-it's the only thing' philosophy common in so many school athletic programs. Some student athletes feel so pressured to succeed in their respective sports that they resort to steroids for help. Another reason, say many experts, lies in the basic nature of young people not to concern themselves with long term effects. The desire to make the football team to impress peers is much more immediate than the future prospect of possible damage to the liver, heart, and other vital organs" (Mishra, 27).

The adolescent's tendency to believe he is immortal, or to feel "nothing bad will ever happen to me" also encourages young males with athletic ambition to give steroids a try. However, if they were to seriously look down the road to the future, perhaps they would realize a brief moment in the spotlight is not worth a lifetime of illness.

Works Cited

Gilbert, Susan. "The Smallest Olympians Pay the Biggest Price." *The New York Times,* 28 July 1996, E4.

Mishra, Raja. "Steroids and Sports Are a Losing Proposition." *FDA Consumer,* 25 (1991) 25–7.

Nemeth, Mary. "Body Obsession: In an Era of Waif-like Models and Beefy Heroes, a Vocal Anti-diet Movement Is Urging People To Set Realistic Goals." *Maclean's*, 2 May 1994, 44–52.

Rickett, Vaughn I. "Human Growth Hormone: A New Substance of Abuse among Adolescents?" *Clinical Pediatrics*, 31 (1992) 723–26.

Sundgot-Borgen, Jorunn. "Risk and Trigger Factors for the Development of Eating Disorders in Female Elite Athletes." *Medicine and Science in Sports and Exercise,* 26 (1994) 414–19.

Wolf, Naomi. *The Beauty Myth*. Toronto: Vintage Books, 1990.

GYMNASTICS: FRIEND OR FOE?

The artistic beauty, grace, and challenges of gymnastics are just a few of the reasons children and young adults become involved in this sport.

Gymnastics, according to four gymnasts from the Valley Flip Flop Gymnastics Club in Port Williams, Nova Scotia, is a great sport. "I love the challenge of learning new and more difficult moves," explains Julia, age 12. "Especially when you are the only one at school that can do multiple back flips, or when all your classmates keep asking you to do another back walkover. It's fun."

For, Amy, also 12, it is the thrill of competition that keeps her interested in gymnastics. "Gymnastics wouldn't be the same without competing," says Amy. "It would just be learning different moves. There would be no reason to put them together into a routine . . . boring!" Yet when asked about competition, all four girls admitted that competing is intimidating. As Elizabeth explains, "It is hard to do a routine in front of an audience, especially at the larger meets when there are 40 girls competing in one category." "There are all these people watch-ing you make a mistake," continues Leah. "Yet it is wonderful to do well, and even if I don't do well I know there will be another meet in the near future." Practicing 3 to 4 times a week is not easy for these girls but they all love it. "I would practice everyday if I could!" exclaims Leah, although interrupts Julia, "It is sometimes a drag practicing on Saturdays because you miss a lot of birthday parties, or if you are at a sleepover, you have to leave right after breakfast."

According to Jennifer Leung, the coach at Valley Flip Flop's, "Gymnastics is a visual sport that increases body awareness, flexibility, strength, agility. This helps develop poise and self confidence as the girls are more aware of how they present themselves. The benefits of gymnastics, especially the speed and power, are carried over into the other sports the girls play like soccer and figure skating."

"Competitive gymnastics is usually a short-lived interest for girls," Jennifer explains. When gymnasts reach 16 or so they develop other interests that take time away from gymnastics. High school offers a new assortment of team and individual sports a person can play. Also, at puberty girls' bodies change and grow heavier which makes competing in gymnastics harder. In gymnastics a girl's strength has to be more than her body weight. Extra weight changes the balance of the body and it takes more strength to get up in the air, more time to do the moves, and it is harder to land. When these factors are multiplied by gravity the chance of injury increases.

Although gymnastics tends to be dominated by younger females, competition is set up by age level or by skill level. So you could be very young and very good and thus compete by skill level, or older and compete by age level. This arrangement helps alleviate stress on the athletes who feel they have to reach a certain skill level by a certain age. To even consider training to become good enough for the Olympics, these 12 year olds at Valley Flip Flops would have to practice up to 6 times a week at a larger gym in Halifax and then would probably have to move onto an even larger gym in Toronto or Vancouver. An improbability for Julia, Elizabeth, Amy, or Leah, but they don't care. For now they are just enjoying participating in a sport in which they have made great friends and are having a great time.

If gymnastics is such a good sport, why has it received such negative attention in the past five years? One reason is the 1994 death of American gymnast Christy Henrich. Christy died from complications arising from anorexia nervosa. This event forced people to make the connection between eating disorders and sports such as gymnastics and figure skating. Another reason is the publication of *Little Girls in Pretty Boxes* by Joan Ryan, which describes gymnasts and figure skaters afflicted with eating disorders and injuries. In 1995 both Canada and the United States set up task forces to look into the serious problems that seemed to be plaguing female gymnastics. The American College of Sport Medicine identified the Female Athlete Triad, which is defined as "the inter-relatedness of disordered eating, amenorrhea, and osteoporosis, disorders that may lead to significant health problems." Five main factors appear to affect an athlete's tendency to develop disordered eating problems:

1. Most gymnasts are young females and studies have shown that self esteem in pre-adolescent and adolescent girls is dramatically less than the self esteem levels of elementary girls.
2. Elite gymnasts tend to have personality traits that include striving for perfection and obsessive behavior. These traits correlate with those found in girls who suffer from eating disorders.
3. Gymnastics is a subjectively judged sport and while there are no points that relate to body size, gymnasts feel they have a better chance of winning if they have a body type similar to previous champions. This is a problem especially in cases where it is simply not possible for the gymnast to have the body she perceives necessary in order to win.
4. There is a lack of knowledge about the Female Athlete Triad by parents; this combined with an over emphasis by parents on a child's performance, can contribute to the problem.
5. The elite athlete's environment is often one that is highly evaluative and one that is characterized by negative feedback. These two factors can put an athlete at risk.

To address these problems both countries now have sport psychologists on call, nutritionists, and a support network for an athlete to use as she needs. This has been done to help athletes learn to eat properly for their level of training and competition. But children don't usually prepare their own food, so it's been recognized that parents and coaches must take an active and very supportive role in the lives of elite gymnasts.

In Canada, by the time coaches are coaching at the elite level they have gone through three or four levels of certification. They have been exposed to advanced degrees of education, consisting of information on ethics, exercise physiology, nutrition, and the energy source needs of the athlete. So they are very aware of potential problems.

Canada, because of its small number of elite athletes, has a better chance of monitoring an athlete's well-being. Also in Canada most of the gymnastics clubs are non-profit organizations with a volunteer board of directors who hire a coach. This coach is an employee and while having high performance athletes may attract more people to the club it does not increase a coach's personal wealth. This contrasts with the United States in which most are coach-owned clubs. Thus the coach runs the club as a business and making money is the goal, not necessarily the well-being of the athletes.

In Canada the developmental system is based upon both skill level and age level. So a gymnast could compete in an age group or by skill level. This elevates some of the pressures to achieve a certain level at an early age. It gives gymnasts time to develop their skills.

To protect gymnasts, the *Federation internationale de gymnastique* is raising the minimum age that girls may go to world championships or the Olympics from 15 to 16. Coaches in the United States have developed methods of training older athletes that have resulted in improved performance and an increase in the length of competitive careers. These older gymnasts should provide a more mature image of a gymnast which will hopefully aid in ending the preoccupation younger athletes have with body image.

Despite the negative attention that gymnastics has received it is important to realize that for the majority of girls participating in gymnastics it is a healthy activity that offers them the opportunity to make new friends and to develop agility, flexibility, and body strength. Just ask Leah, Amy, Elizabeth, or Julia, and they'll tell you.

References

Chui, Grace. *Gymnastics, Figure Skating Address Serious Issues*. Action Bulletin. Autumn, 1995. Online. Internet. March 1997. Available at infoweb.magi. com/~wmnsport.

Supplementary Task Force. "Preliminary Report 1995, USA Gymnastic Response to the Female Athletic Triad." *Technique,* 15 (9) 16–22.

For more information about the sport of gymnastics look up the home page of Gymnastics Canada Gymnastique at www.gymcan.org or the home page of USA Gymnastica Online at www.USA-gymnastics.org.

SPORT NUTRITION FOR THE ADOLESCENT ATHLETE

Adolescent athletes are considered a unique group because of their special nutritional needs. All athletes are encouraged to follow the rules of healthy eating to help their performances, both in training and in competition. However, bad eating habits may occur during adolescence as increasing independence and peer pressure influences food selection. Sports related expectations combined with an obsessive focus on weight control may set the stage for eating disorders like anorexia nervosa or bulimia nervosa. The primary requirement for the athlete in training is to consume a well-balanced, nutritionally complete diet that will meet the additional nutrient demands imposed by a training load. Power and endurance athletes need a high carbohydrate diet that will enable intensive training to be sustained on a daily basis. The athlete who is training hard also has an increased demand for energy and protein. This requirement can be met by enjoying a variety of nutritious foods that will provide the body with all the protein, vitamins, and minerals that it needs. The athlete's diet should be low in fat and high in carbohydrates with an adequate amount of protein. The body's preferred source of energy comes from carbohydrates. Adolescents should be getting 50 to 55 percent of their total calories from eating carbohydrates, and most of these calories should come in the form of complex carbohydrates. A person's body breaks down carbohydrates and stores them in the liver and muscles as glycogen. During physical activity glycogen is the first item the body turns to for energy and because of this many athletes will load up on carbohydrates before a competition as a way of building up the glycogen stores in their body. To do this athletes train hard for the first six days before competition, and eat mostly fat and protein. Then for the last three or four days before the event, the athlete switches to eating mostly carbohydrates and trains very little. Carbohydrate loading is not a good idea for young athletes since their bodies have not finished growing and they need to maintain a balanced diet. Besides carbohydrates, adolescent athletes need protein that should come from low-fat animal sources like poultry and fish, low fat dairy products, and a variety of plant food. It is not necessary to increase the recommended amount of protein when in training. Extra protein does not make an athlete stronger or faster, in fact, extra protein is stored as fat and can actually hurt an athlete's performance.

According to the American Dietetic Association, iron and calcium levels need special attention especially for athletes competing in endurance sports where body fat content is maintained at low levels. Adolescents are at increased risk of iron deficiency because of their increased growth, lower energy intake, inadequate dietary iron intake, and exercise-related iron loss. Female athletes have an additional iron loss through menstruation. By intervening when iron levels are low, athletes can avoid iron deficiency anemia and the accompanying decline in their athletic performance.

Calcium levels on average are low for adolescents but adequate calcium is necessary for prevention of osteoporosis and bone fractures. Preventive dietary measures can be taken to reduce the risk of bone disorders by improving overall diet (especially calcium) at a time when bones should be forming at their maximum rate.

Water is also a very important aid to athletic performance; although water does not itself produce energy, it does prevent dehydration. Dehydration is one of the greatest threats to health especially when superimposed on performance demands. Drinking a glass of cold water (cold water is absorbed faster) before, during, and after a sporting event is the best advice for all athletes. It is good practice to drink 10–14 ounces of water 1 to 2 hours before an activity and then to drink another 10 ounces of water 10 to 15 minutes before the competition. For exercise that lasts longer than an hour and/or is performed in high temperatures and humidity, is it more effective to drink a sports drink or dilute fruit juice. Commercial sports drinks should taste good, contain 6 percent to 8 percent carbohydrates, and be rapidly absorbed into the body. Even low levels of dehydration will impair performance, especially in adolescent athletes who are sensitive to the effects of dehydration.

To help improve their competitive edge many teens may consume a variety of so-called sports enhancing substances. Amino acid and other protein supplements are not recommended for adolescent athletes. Most supplements have no more protein than a serving of meat or a glass of milk. They are an expensive way to give the body extra protein; protein that the body does not need if it is already receiving a balanced diet. For the athletes already meeting the nutritional needs of their body through a well-balanced diet, taking vitamin and mineral supplements will not enhance their performance and taking too much of certain vitamins and minerals can actually harm the body. Unsupervised use of vitamin, mineral, and other supplements raises safety concerns and cost issues. When these substances replace a good nutritional diet, health and performance could be jeopardized.

It is important that parents, coaches, and teachers take the time to encourage sound nutrition practices that promote optimal growth and development in adolescents.

Through nutrition education, coaches, parents, and athletes can be made aware of the consequences of extreme weight loss methods and learn to recognize eating disorders. Healthy alternatives for achieving a competitive weight should always be promoted.

Before a competition is it recommend to eat a "pre-event" meal to keep an athlete from becoming hungry when competing. This meal should be eaten not less than one hour before a competition or practice and could include the following:

* 1–2 hours before: fruit or vegetable juice, low fiber fresh fruits (peaches, plums, cherries).
* 2–3 hours before: fruit or vegetable juice, fresh fruit, breads, bagels, english muffins (don't use cream cheese on the bagel because high-fat foods take longer to digest and can cause nausea in some younger athletes).
* 3–4 hours before: fruit or vegetable juice, fresh fruit, low-fat yogurt, breads, bagels, english muffins, peanut butter, lean meats, baked potato, pasta, or cereal with low fat milk.

Athletes come in different sizes and shapes, and follow different types of training programs. While they may all follow these nutrition rules, their meals may look quite different. Athletes who train strenuously for many hours each day will need to eat large amounts of carbohydrates and kilojoules.

Big, tall athletes will need to eat more than petite athletes such as gymnasts. Many athletes need to organize their meals to fit around their training or competition schedules. A survey of the typical evening meals eaten by some different athletes are presented as examples:

Male Basketballer

The male basketballer is playing a game at 9:00 P.M. and therefore needs a pre-game meal and a post-game recovery meal. Being nearly 6 foot 10 inches tall and weighing nearly 100 kg, he needs to eat plenty of kilojoules to maintain his large size. The pre-event meal (5:30–6:00 P.M.) tops up carbohydrate stores and fluid levels. Is eaten about 3 hours pre-game so that he feels comfortable on court:

* 3–4 cups of noodles with tomato-based pasta sauce
* 2 slices of bread
* small bowl of fruit salad and a glass of fruit juice

The post-game meal (10:00 P.M.). Recovers fluid and carbohydrate levels that were depleted by the game. Is eaten as soon as possible after the game to help with rapid recovery and avoids overeating since this may cause discomfort while sleeping.

Sports drink immediately after the game. At home:

* 2 rounds of toasted ham and tomato whole-meal sandwiches (minimize the margarine)
* big banana smoothie 500–750 ml (made with skim milk, banana, skim milk powder, and 2 tablespoons of low fat ice-cream)

Female Gymnast

A female gymnast needs to eat small meals. She needs to keep her energy (kilojoule) intake low to maintain a trim shape and low body fat level. Her energy requirements are low because she is small and because her training program is low in intensity. Even though she trains for many hours each day, most of this work is based on skill strength and flexibility with only short bursts of high intensity work. She chooses her food carefully to achieve maximum nutrients for minimum kilojoules—particularly by eating nutritious foods that are low in fat.

* small serving of lean meat—grilled, all fat removed
* medium potato, boiled

* medium serving of three different vegetables (example, carrots, beans, broccoli)
* 200 g carton of low fat fruit yogurt

Male Marathon Runner

The male runner eats plenty of carbohydrate foods to support his daily training program, since carbohydrates provide the preferred fuel for his muscles. Although he is light and low in body fat (65 kg) his energy requirements are high because of his heavy energy expenditure in training and competition. He is careful to drink plenty of fluids in his training sessions—water and/or a sports drink—and to continue to rehydrate at his evening meal.

* medium serving of lean meat, grilled, fat removed
* 3 cups of noodles and 1 large potato—boiled
* 1 cup each of other vegetables (e.g., same vegetables as gymnast)
* 2 slices of wholemeal bread
* big bowl of fruit salad with 200 g carton of low fat yogurt
* 2 glasses fruit juice (plus plenty of water)

Male Rower

The male rower has a big frame (85 kg) and trains strenuously for 3–4 hours each day. Thus he has very high needs for energy and carbohydrate. To help increase his food intake without making him overeat and feel uncomfortable, he may need to eat two evening meals with a gap of a couple of hours in between. Like the basketballer he may also make himself action-packed fruit/milk smoothies. Drinks like these are full of nutritious kilojoules but are compact and low in bulk: nutrition THAT DOESN'T

HAVE TO BE CHEWED! He is also careful with his fluid intake, knowing that he sweats heavily while he trains.

Meal 1 (7:00 P.M.) Same as evening meal for marathon runner.

Meal 2 (9:30 P.M.) Big bowl of cereal with reduced fat milk and fruit banana smoothie same as for male basketballer.

Sample menus taken from *Nutrition for Athletes* by Dr. Louise Burke, Consultant Dietitian at the Australian Institute of Sport.

Bibliography

International Scientific Consensus Conference Monaco. 18/20 February 1995. "Nutrition in Athletics Consensus Statement. World Forum on Physical Activity and Sport." National Center for Health Fitness. 1995 [Online]. Available at www.healthy.american.edu/world-scitrack.html. (20 Mar. 1997)

Jennings, D.S., and S.N. Steen. *Play Hard Eat Right: A Parents' Guide to Sport Nutrition for Children.* Minnetonka, Minn.: American Dietetic Association and Chronimed Publishing, 1995.

Nemous Foundation. "Answers to Your Questions about Sport and Nutrition." Kids Health Organization. 1996 [Online]. Available at http://kidshealth.org/. (15 Mar. 1997).

GIRLS ARE PART OF THE TEAM NOW

According to the Women's Sport Foundation girls who participate in athletics are eighty percent less likely to get pregnant, 92 percent less likely to become involved with drugs, and three times as likely to graduate from a college or university. Sports are important! (McConnell, 15).

In addition to the above benefits playing sports is an empowering experience for young girls. Through it they learn to be leaders and team players.

During adolescence girls experience tremendous social pressure to conform, to "fit in." Through becoming involved in athletics adolescent girls learn how powerful their bodies can be. Sports can help a girl develop a positive self image based on what she is capable of and not what others think of her.

If this is the case, then why do 72 percent of girls drop out of athletic programs by the time they are 14, a rate six times that of boys? (McConnell, 15). A study done by the Canadian Association for Health, Physical Education, Recreation and Dance (CAHPED 1996) showed that in physical development, girls at puberty on average reach a plateau in their physical activity patterns which then start to decline. Once girls reach high school they become involved in other activities and interests that distract them from sports. Girls also cited lack of opportunities in athletics, lack of time, and a perceived lack of necessary skills as other reasons why they drop out of sports.

Girls need to be encouraged to continue in athletics during their adolescent years, and the '90s is the time to do this. No longer are girls confined to sports that rule out physical contact. No longer are they only participating in individual sports that emphasize beauty and poise. Girls are now on the soccer fields and basketball courts. Girls and women now have choices as broad as their interests.

Physical education programs in schools can provide an excellent opportunity to reach all young females. But to be effective these programs must ensure equality between the athletic opportunities for girls and boys. Physical education programs need to examine existing resources and curriculum. They need to analyze the attitudes of teachers and coaches. Parents, teachers, and coaches all have a role in promoting gender equality in sports (CAH-PED 1996).

Teachers can promote gender equality in sports by:

✳ including activities in courses that promote a wide variety of physical activity,

✳ using respectful non-sexist language,

✳ choosing females as group leaders,

✳ allowing girls to choose single sex groupings if desired.

Parents can help encourage their daughters to participate by:

✳ encouraging their children to be physically active,

✳ participating in activities with their children, volunteering to coach at the school or community,

✳ encouraging high school girls to choose optional physical education classes.

Coaches can:

✳ lobby schools to provide equal access to facilities, equipment, scheduling, and budget allotment for female and male teams,

✳ ensure that both boys and girls learn the basic skills to enable them to participate,

✳ use non-sexist language,

✳ encourage females to pursue careers in physical education and sport.

The benefits of sports for adolescents are too important for society to ignore. Exposure to team sports means girls learn how to bond with their teammates, practice networking skills, and receive the kind of training that brings success in organizations. "Girls are making the teams and team sports are enhancing their lives" (Hillard, 55).

Meet Brianna Morgan

Age 13

Grade 7, Cornwallis District High School, Canning, Nova Scotia

Brianna is one adolescent who is enjoying the benefits of participating in team sports. She has a 94 percent average, self confidence, and a lot of friends. When talking to Brianna you immediately sense that she likes herself and likes her life right now. What more could a parent of an adolescent ask for?

Brianna has always been interested in physical activity. "When I was younger we lived on a farm and I loved horseback riding, after that I started figure skating and now I teach it." It's only been in the past four years that Brianna started playing team sports and she hasn't looked back since.

"Hockey is my life," explains Brianna. "I love it. I first became involved in hockey four years ago when my best friend invited me to watch her play on a girls' hockey team. It looked like fun and I haven't stopped since. This year I tried out for the rep hockey team in Canning, Nova Scotia, and I was the only girl to make the team. The tryouts were hard but my seven years of figure skating paid off because the coach emphasized skating skills instead of shooting skills, and skating is my strong point. I like playing with the boys because the skating is usually at a higher skill level than in the girls' team. Most of the boys have been playing hockey since they were 5 years old so I have to really challenge myself to keep up to the rest of my team. I also love the competition of playing hockey, I like the adrenaline rush. My teammates on the rep team are great, they may tease me sometimes but they are never mean. Like one day I came out of my change room wearing the wrong color jersey. Everyone had a good laugh but it was all in fun. On the ice they treat me like a regular team member. Sometimes I miss playing on the girls team. Girls have more fun. We yell and cheer each other on. But guys are quieter, they just pat you on the back saying 'good game.' Also, I now have to change in a separate change room when I am playing with the rep team and I feel left out sometimes. I miss all the locker room talk. But I still love playing hockey.

"After high school I want to take physical education at Acadia University and play for their female hockey team. Hopefully by then there will be a strong women's league, so that the Acadia women's team will be playing more games and more people will be coming out to watch them. I went to an exhibition game when the female hockey team was playing and there were only 12 people in the bleachers, not like when the Axemen (the St. Francis Xavier University hockey team) play and the arena is full.

"I enjoy playing in team sports. At school I am on the junior soccer team and I might try out for the senior hockey team next year. I have made a lot of new friends over the past four years playing hockey. It is fun facing off against one of your best friends."

In Canada there is an association to promote women and sports. The Canadian Association for the Advancement of Women and Sport (CAAWS), works with the Sport and Active Living Community to "remember girls and women: To remember that they play, that they win medals, that they coach kids, that they raise money, that they spend money, that they care about recreation and sport." CAAWS works to put girls and women in the sport and active living picture of this country (CAAWS, 1997). Visit the CAAWS home page at infoweb.magi.com/~wmnsport/

Bibliography

Hillard, Wendy. "The Trickle Down Effect." *Women's Sport + Fitness*, 18 (1996) 55.

McConnell, Jane. "Aiming Higher." *Women's Sport + Fitness*, 16 (1994) 15.

CAHPED. "Gender Equity Through Physical Education." Action Bulletin. Summer 1996. Available at infoweb.magi.com/~wmnsport/ (24 Mar. 1997).

RINGETTE

Ringette is a Canadian game that was first introduced in 1963 in North Bay, Ontario. It was to be a winter team sport played on ice with skates for girls as an alternative, somewhere between figure skating and ice hockey. The sport, still primarily for girls, allows players to compete at all levels of physical activity using their strength, intellect, and spirit to obtain measurable results. The game provides a number of opportunities for players to develop their skills on and off the ice to compete and make new friends. Children can start playing ringette as young as 5 as long as there is enough interest to warrant creating a team. There are nine official age classifications ranging from 7 and under to 30 and over, so anyone can play.

The players use a straight stick to pass, carry, and shoot a rubber ring. The objective is to control the ring while moving it down the ice to score goals in the opposing team's net. The game is played by two teams of 9 to 18 players with six on the ice at once. Ringette consists of two 15 or 20 minute stop time periods. The game promotes team play and the development of strong motor skills. For ten years, ringette was played only in Ontario and Quebec but now the sport is played in all ten provinces and the Northwest Territories. This growth has continued internationally with the formation of associations in the USA, Finland, Sweden, Estonia, and France. Yet according to Jill Clarke, Chair of the Ringette Canada National Player Development Committee, ringette is an under-represented sport that does not receive the recognition and media attention it deserves. Ringette allows women and girls the opportunity to play in a sport that promotes fair play and healthy competition. It is one of Canada's success stories.

Meet Tina Ciapero: A Ringette Player

Kingsport, Nova Scotia
Age: 15
Grade: 9 Cornwallis District High School
Interests: Ringette, Choir and Reading

Why do you like to play ringette, Tina?
I like ringette because it is not as competitive as hockey. The team likes to win and a medal is nice but people who play ringette know that it is just a game. I like the noncompetitive aspect of the game.

Why not play hockey?
It is hard to play hockey because everyone starts so young in hockey like age five, so if you want to start at age nine it is too late because everyone else on the team has been playing for years. My mom heard about ringette from a friend she worked with and I decided to try it out. I have a good group of friends on the ringette team, and it helps that we all go to the same high school, so I knew most of the players before I started playing.

Which do you enjoy more, team sports or individual sports?
I like playing a team sport because you can learn from someone else that has more experience and who has been playing longer.

How many hours a week do you play ringette?
Ringette takes up about 3 hours each weekend. I like that though because I like to keep busy and if I wasn't playing ringette I would probably be doing chores for my mom. Playing in tournaments takes up a lot of my weekends because most of our games are played in Halifax. There are only two teams in the valley: one in Canning and one in Berwick, so this means a lot of travel with gas and meal expenses. I did not bother to try out for the Provincial team because it is based in Halifax and it would mean practicing in the city. This is probably my last year playing ringette. I like the sport but it is expensive. The registration fee is $300.00 and now the equipment is expensive too. We even have to buy special masks now that are specially made for ringette to prevent the stick from being able to fit through. So next year I think I will take up swim-

ming. I have a friend on the Triton swim team and she really likes it.

For more information about the sport of ringette visit www.ringette.ca.

Book Reviews

Korman, Gordon. *The Chicken Doesn't Skate*. Scholastic Press. 197 pages (hardcover). ISBN 1-0-590-85300-7

Gordon Korman gave us the world's most amazing drummer (Bugs Potter) and the greatest natural athlete (Rudy Miller), so it's no surprise he's managed to create a story about a legendary teacher's pet. Henrietta the hen is but a chick when she's introduced to Mrs. Baggio's grade six science class, but quickly becomes a sensation. She is deemed the mascot, or more accurately, the good luck charm, of the South Middle School's Rangers who are subsequently on their hottest hockey winning streak ever. It's also through her that young lovers Lynette and Joey can put aside their differences and find romantic common ground. She's even established a sort of love–hate relationship with aspiring horror writer Zachary Gustafson who has traumatically slammed into a sick kind of writer's block where every story he's working on has to do with chickens!

However, to Henrietta's keeper, Milo Neal (son of world renowned scientist Victor Neal), Henrietta is a mere specimen in his science fair project; one link in the food chain.

Unfortunately for Milo, Henrietta has become so popular to South Middle School that he fears there'll be a price on his head if anyone ever finds out his secret plans to polishing off the final step in his experiment.

With only one friend (the neurotic, chicken-envious Zachary) on his side, can Milo get away with reclaiming the Rangers' valuable mascot? Can he get Joey and Lynette to relinquish their love bird? Will Milo manage to complete his food chain assignment and win his famous father's favour?

Korman has written many funnier books than this one. *The Chicken Doesn't Skate* won't stand up to the side-splitting humour of its predecessors like *Losing Joe's Place, The Zucchini Warriors,* or *I Want to Go Home!*

Nonetheless, *The Chicken Doesn't Skate* has an intriguing fashion of storytelling in the way it allows the reader to pore over the personal thoughts of all its central characters. Korman allows us to pry into the gory details of Zachary Gustafson's horror stories. We have access to Milo's coldly calculated, but troubled, experiment notes. And, we are sometimes immersed in the personal psychology delivered by the chicken's most caring guardian, Kelly Marie Ginsberg.

The changing first person narrative is matched by another appealing factor to Korman's book: a lot of the story centres around the games of the Rangers hockey team. Hockey lovers will be enthralled by action sequences relayed by the Rangers' team captain, Adam Lurie. Many will sympathize with his superstitious desperation that demands Henrietta be on the bench for all of the Rangers' games.

Korman, having played hockey since the age of seven, shines in his deft insight to the sport. It's this touch that will win him a new breed of readers.

MacGregor, Roy. Three Screech Owls Hockey Adventures: *Mystery at Lake Placid, The Night They Stole the Stanley Cup,* and *The Screech Owl's Northern Adventure*. ISBN 0-7710-5625

Holy smokes, there's a *girl* on the Screech Owls hockey team! Actually two girls hold positions on the Screech Owls hockey team in the first book (*Mystery at Lake Placid*). Sareen Goupa, the back-up goalie, and Sarah Cuthbertson, team captain, are welcome elements to a genre that typically leaves out good female characters. Cuthbertson isn't just any namby-pamby hockey player either; in addition to her athletic finesse on the ice, she has her wits about her too. Travis Lindsay, the team's assistant captain and central protagonist in MacGregor's fiction, shares a reminiscence in *Mystery at Lake Placid* when the Screech Owls are first written up by the *Toronto Star*. In the story, the reporter writes up Sarah as someone who is too pretty and genteel for the game of hockey. He asks her if she is bothered by the fact that women represent more than 50 percent of the general population, but only make up 10 percent of the Screech Owls. Travis can't help but smile when he recalls Sarah's immediate response, putting the reporter in his place:

"'Why would it?' Sarah [had] answered, 'I've been in on more than 50 percent of the goals.'"

MacGregor will win over many readers because he doesn't let up on cramming lots of hockey action sequences into his books. In the first three Screech Owl adventures, the author has an aptitude for pushing all the right buttons by mixing mystery and action with snowmobile mishaps, run-ins with real-life NHL personalities, and brushes with the law.

Also appealing is the central character's appreciation for the aesthetic aspects of hockey arenas. Travis Lindsay's sentiments resurface in each book whenever he steps onto the ice before a Screech Owls game and traces fresh lines in the new clear surface.

It's the familiar details in the tradition of a good adventure series that make readers feel welcome. The story environment and MacGregor makes use of such details. Just as the Hardy Boys "kicked their motorcycles to life," or Jupiter (of the Three Investigators) had a tendency to "pinch his lower lip when he got thinking," MacGregor has his own trademarks that strengthen the reader's anticipation and association with certain characters. Wayne Nishikawa (everyone calls him "Nish") will always have a bout of motion sickness, warning, "I'm going to hurl!" Travis, secretly scared of the dark, has a way of rounding the rink corners so that his skate blades "sizzle like bacon." And Muck, the team's coach, doesn't last a hundred pages without wearing his expression "like bunched up tape."

The first book of the series acts as a builder for the subsequent Screech Owls adventures. MacGregor is thorough in outlining the twelve members of the team and explores some serious issues bestirring minor hockey leagues today. The following two books (*The Night They Stole the Stanley Cup* and *The Screech Owl's Northern Adventure*) are much more accessible to readers; the author steps up the pace of his narrative and tempers the heavier issues of overambitious parents and coaching.

Given MacGregor's career as a sports authority for the Southam news service, his literature carries an authentic and convincing tone that further engages the reader. Just as I am sure there would be a gaping hole in my childhood if it weren't for the likes of Enid Blyton and Frank W. Dixon, ten years from now current readers of the Screech Owls series will say there would have been a hole in their childhoods if it hadn't been for Roy MacGregor.

Lynch, Chris. *Iceman*. HarperCollins. 181 pages (paperback). ISBN 0-06-447114-4

Iceman stands apart from other hockey books with its macabre protagonist who practices exceptional violence in his approach to playing hockey.

Eric crushes, bashes, and punches his way through wins and losses, game after game. Even in practices, he doesn't cease shedding blood. As a result, the hard-hearted hero is dubbed "Iceman" by his fellow bruised and gashed team mates.

Eric is unable to find a suitable role model in his father (a manic depressive hockey fanatic) who is enthralled by his son's aggressive and brutal playing style. He can't trust his mother who is a retired nun bible-thumper. That only leaves Duane, Eric's older brother, who has absolved himself of hockey in order to pursue a career in music. Eric doesn't feel he can tell his brother the sort of pressure he is going through, so he turns to a complete stranger, a grave digger, to escape the real-life horror he faces daily.

Iceman is a gut-stirring read. The story is a remarkable one, delivered with violently gruesome details surrounding hockey fights, realistic conflicts, and family situations. Author Chris Lynch has a fascinating ability to get inside a kid's brain and trick the reader into siding with this 12 year old cold-blooded goon.

Young athletes (especially hockey players) will be mesmerized by the hockey action and will be forced to ask themselves if violence has any place in hockey. Lynch never makes any judgements, instead leaving this issue of violence hanging in the air. Young people having trouble with understanding death may find Eric's attitude of curiosity towards dead things as enlightening. The most disturbing scenes are also the most human, and they serve to represent the internal torment Eric has trouble addressing.

Crutcher, Chris. *Ironman*. Greenwillow Books. 229 pages (paperback). ISBN 0-688-13503-X

There are some books you wish would never end because their characters and stories become so enjoyably engrossing. *Ironman* belongs to this class of literature. Through Beauregard's personal letters to TV talk show host Larry King, interspersed with Chris Crutcher's third person narrative, a rich and troubling story unfolds with an inspiring message.

Crutcher has invented a likeable, undaunted hero in his main character Beauregard Brewster. Beauregard is threatened by the paired oppressive forces of his father and football coach in the small town of Clark Fork. Following a heated interchange with his high school principal, Beauregard is first suspended, then told he can return provided he begins attending the high school's "Anger Management" class, headed by Mr. Nakatani, a friendly enough fellow who comes across like a Japanese cowboy.

In his letters to Larry King, Beauregard confides he feels out of place joining a group of individuals who should really be locked up in a federal pen:

> The Nak Pack. That's what they call it, no kidding, Larry, and if you wanted to put a major crimp in Clark Fork's future crime wave, you'd call an air strike down on their next meeting. Man, I wish they still just paddle your butt when you screw up; you know, let the vice-principal take a few slap shots at your ass to even the ledger. Besides, I manage my anger well enough. I can get a little out of hand at times, but I really don't think I belong in that group.

The thing is, Beauregard's twisted emotions are imposed on him from other elements in his life. He is anything but "irresponsible" or "a quitter," like his father would have him believe. He drives himself through gruelling workouts that take up three hours each day to train and become a real Ironman. Between swimming with the university team at the crack of dawn, running with his mother's sled dogs, and biking his baby brother up and around the hilliest parts of town, it looks like the Big B will have no trouble reaching his aspirations and will excel at the next Yukon Jack Triathalon.

But what lengths will his father take to teach Beauregard a final, demolishing lesson?

Combining humour and intrigue, the author explores the psyche of his protagonist, simultaneously examining the fragmented lives of students in Beauregard's "Anger Management" sessions, and weaves irony and painful experiences into relationships that eventually take the shape of strong friendships. Sure enough, it's from within this motley bunch that Beauregard is able to confront some of the nasty memories embedded in his childhood.

One of the most attractive features of this novel is its descriptive detail outlining the physical changes and awareness obtained from strenuous training sessions. Even the softest, most couch-cushion-indented reader bodies will feel encouraged enough to puff up and jog a few blocks after having read just a few passages from Crutcher's work.

Cars

YA Hotline, Issue No. 59, 1998

AMBER BUTLER, ELSA MAAN, SARAH MCCLARE, DAVID MCDONALD, AND CORY WILLIAMS

RITES OF PASSAGE—EDITORIAL

What are some of the milestones, the rites of passage, that help form young adults? There are the thoughts of dating, falling in love, parties, and sex. There is the expectation of some type of casual work and pocket money (for clothes). Some thought may be given to higher education and careers. However, nothing moves a young adult to as much excitement as the thought of learning how to drive. They start thinking about it when they are a young teen and the years in between are interminable. That thought becomes a passion and is a topic that is discussed frequently with friends. No longer will they have to go through the embarrassing process of having to ask to be dropped off and picked up by one or the other parent. The closer the young person comes to that magical age of six-teen, the need to drive seemingly becomes indistinguishable from the hormonal changes that are occurring at the same time. It is right up there with life-sustaining necessities like air, water, friends, phones, and junk food.

Parents view learning to drive in somewhat of a different manner (Ayers, 177). How can this person, who just yesterday was learning to walk and who today cannot remember to take out the garbage, turn off the television, or close the refrigerator door, be ready to learn to drive? However, after you, as parents, have done your job well preparing them for this milestone, relax. Most sources consulted state that the learning-to-drive process becomes much "easier" when the expectations and "rules of the road" are clearly laid out right at the beginning. Contrary to popular belief, most young drivers are no worse than the average driver. There are individual differences, as with anything. There are sixteen-year-olds who handle a car with skill and confidence; there are eighteen-year-olds who are so immature that it would be irresponsible to allow them to take the wheel of a vehicle (Ginott, 181). Not all teenagers are bad drivers or risk takers. Teenagers drive as they live. If they are mature in other ways, they'll usually act maturely when they are on the road (Kutner, 73). The only thing young people lack is the experience and the only way they can get that is to drive, drive, and drive some more—with boundaries attached. Although it may be sad for parents to see them grow up so soon, it is also a relief to surrender the task of chauffeuring them (Elkind, 186).

Learning to drive symbolizes autonomy and independence for a young person. It is a very concrete way of expressing freedom (Fleming, 92). It is their clearest rite of passage into adulthood (Kutner, 71). A car provides access to the world and the mobility to socialize with friends as well as being a status symbol (Fleming, 93). This excitement may be overshadowed by the necessary, but often overwhelming, sense of responsibility that driving brings. Not much else makes a young person hit the reality wall as quickly as the costs associated with learning to drive, insurance, and operating a vehicle. The goal for adults is to bring teenagers through this rite of passage intact, healthy, and still excited. And there is help. That is what this issue of the hotline is all about.

Works Cited

Ayers, Lauren K. *Teenage Girls: A Parent's Survival Manual.* New York: Crossroad, 1994.

Elkind, David. *Parenting Your Teenager.* New York: Ballantine Books, 1993.

Fleming, Don. *How to Stop the Battle for Your Teenager.* New York: Fireside, 1989.

Ginott, Haim G. *Between Parent & Teenager.* New York: Avon Books, 1969.

Kutner, Lawrence. *Making Sense of Your Teenager.* New York: Avon Books, 1997.

YOUNG DRIVERS OF CANADA

Peter Christianson was 3 years old when he was in a car crash. His young father was killed instantly. Peter's life was saved because, just before the crash, his father pushed him onto the floor of the car. The crash made Peter afraid of driving and afraid to learn how to drive. Once he finally did learn, Peter went on to race cars—taking his life into his hands constantly. During this stage of his life, five of his friends lost their lives in "regular" car accidents on the road.

Peter is now the president of Young Drivers. The people at Young Drivers have been changing and developing their program for 25 years to keep up to date and to be the best possible. The goal is to train drivers for a lifetime of collision-free driving.

This driving program is available in over 100 centers coast to coast in Canada and is starting in several other countries as well. It is a franchise, which is independently owned and operated. As this is the case, there may be some variance in the details of the program, although the basics should remain the same.

The basic program for an automatic car consists of two 60-minute in-car sessions, eleven 45-minute in-car sessions, and 25 hours in the classroom. The cost for this program (at the time of printing) is $479.00 Cdn. plus HST. (Gift certificates are also available.) Students who wish to learn standard shifting can take three additional lessons—to be done in a car the student provides—for an extra fee. A vehicle is available for Drivers License Examination if it is requested. Payment is required at registration but installment programs are available.

Another service offered by Young Drivers is a road test package for those who already know how to drive but who wish to have a review before taking the drivers test. Young Drivers also offer Co-Driver Survival Training. This is a free two-hour course for the designated co-driver for every student enrolled in Young Drivers. Teaching someone to drive is a big challenge and responsibility. The practice driving sessions are tough on everyone's nerves and have ruined more than one relationship. This free course teaches people how to teach. It includes what to do, what to say, what not to say, how to instill defensive driving habits, and how not to pass along the bad habits we have.

Young Drivers is a very comprehensive course. Classroom instruction covers driving under adverse conditions, basic car maintenance, what responsibilities are associated with driving, emergency maneuvers, risk perception, and much more. Instruction includes videotapes and workbooks.

The in-car instruction includes head-on and rear crash avoidance, turning maneuvers, parallel and parking lot parking, freeway driving, and much more.

When a Young Drivers course has been completed, the graduate is eligible for licensing at three months instead of the mandatory six months. They may also be entitled to an insurance reduction. To see how these bonuses may benefit you, it is best to contact the nearest Young Drivers Center.

Young Drivers maintains that driving is one of the most enjoyable activities a young person can experience. But it is also one of the most dangerous. Young Drivers wants to give you your license to survive. The program wishes to make sure that every driver knows exactly what he or she is doing in every situation, especially when there isn't much time to think. That in itself makes Young Drivers worth investigating when you are contemplating learning to drive.

Contract for Parents and Teens

1. Breaking the driving laws or abusing a motor vehicle can result in the loss of driving privileges, even if we learn about it from a source other than the police. You never know who may be observing you.

2. You will strive to maintain the grades, conduct and attitude at the same high level as when we granted you driving privileges.

3. No one else should be allowed to drive a vehicle entrusted to you. This means that you may not lend your vehicle to friends.

4. If you are ever in a condition that might render you less than 100% competent behind the wheel of a car, phone us at home or wherever we are. This will not result in loss of driving privileges.

5. You are never to be a passenger in a car in which the driver should not be driving. A call to come and get you will not result in the loss of driving privileges. If you cannot reach us, hire a taxi. We will pay for it and there will be no punishment.

_____

(Signature of Parent)

_____

(Son/Daughter)

[Taken from P.A.S.T., (Parents Against Speeding Teens) website, http://www.pastnh.org/contract.htm, accessed December 5, 1998.]

ALCOHOL AND AUTOMOBILES: A COMBUSTIBLE COMBINATION

Drunk driving. A controversial, difficult subject. When I was first thinking about the angle I would tackle while writing about impaired driving, I had wanted to concentrate on issues such as responsibility and accountability. However, the more I delved into the topic the more muddied the waters became. There are so many issues attached to the topic of impaired driving, far beyond just being responsible for one's actions.

In Nova Scotia it is illegal to consume or possess alcoholic beverages if a person is under the age of 19. Right there we have an issue. If someone under the age of 19 is consuming alcohol they have already committed an offence, never mind additional criminal charges should they decide to drive. And what if a teenager has a drinking problem? Another issue. There are also issues of loss. Grieving families who have lost a dear family member due to an accident caused by impaired driving. Not only do families of victims suffer, but the families of the drivers suffer as well. Issues of grief, anger, forgiveness, and dealing with loss are all securely intertwined with this subject. There is also the pain suffered by the drunk who showed bad judgement by getting behind a steering wheel and causing an accident. So what we end up with are emotional, legal, and responsibility issues. It makes the head spin.

How Serious Is the Problem?

According to the Against Drunk Driving (ADD) organization in Canada, impaired driving causes more deaths, injuries, and destruction than all murderers, muggers, rapists, and robbers combined, thereby making it the largest single criminal cause of death and injury in Canada. ADD claims that over the past 10 years, every 6 hours someone is killed by an impaired driver. Every 20 minutes someone, somewhere in Canada falls victim to an impaired driver and every year over 45% of all traffic fatalities involve alcohol. In 1994, more than 1,700 Canadians died as the result of impaired driving.

Definition

Section 253 of the Criminal Code of Canada defines impaired driving as operating or having the care or control of a motor vehicle, vessel, aircraft, or railway equipment whether it is in motion or not (a) while the person's ability to operate the vehicle is impaired by alcohol or a drug or (b) while the person has consumed alcohol in such a quantity that their blood alcohol concentration is over the legal limit of 80 milligrams per 100 millilitres of blood.

Young Drivers Do Not Have the Highest Impaired Driving Rates

I spoke with Cst. Richard McDonald, a member of the Halifax Regional Police. He said that during his 24 years on the force, he had made many impaired driving arrests, but relatively few of those arrests involved young adults. Since 1994, he has been involved solely with young offender arrests, and noted, again, that there are few impaired driving charges laid against young people. He paid the youth of our municipality a high compliment by stating that he thought that young people were just too smart to drink and drive. This is corroborated by findings made by Statistics Canada. Studies show that although young drivers are often believed to have a high incidence of impaired driving, impaired driving is highest among 20 to 44 year-olds. Arrests for impaired driving dropped dramatically for older Canadians. Another positive note is that in 1996 it was discovered that the number of persons charged with an impaired driving offence had decreased for the thirteenth consecutive year.

[See: http://www.statcan.ca/Daily/English/971117/d971117.htm]

Why Does Alcohol Impair Driving?

Alcohol is a depressant.

1. Alcohol can reduce concentration and may slow reaction time.
2. Alcohol affects vision, objects may become blurred.
3. Alcohol affects perception, judgement, and decision-making skills as well as the ability to co-ordinate them.

From the Ontario Ministry of Transportation, http://www/mto.gov.on.ca/english/safety/drink.htm

How to Spot an Impaired Driver

Impaired drivers often exhibit similar irregularities in their driving patterns. Cst. McDonald stated that if police officers have reason to believe a driver may be impaired, they will make the person pull their vehicle over. Physical observations are then made to further corroborate or eliminate the belief that the person is impaired. Police officers will watch for glossy eyes, breath smelling of alcohol, slurred speech, and heavy sweating. Cst. McDonald also noted that an impaired person will usually be either overly or under co-operative when stopped by the police. Police will ask for registration, driver's license, and insurance card. While the person retrieves these papers, the police officer can observe the driver's physical co-ordination.

In Canada a driver may be asked to exit his/her vehicle and walk to the rear of the car. Cst. McDonald noted that impairment is sometimes easily identified, like the time he stopped a driver and when he stepped out of the car he fell flat on his face. Another sign which usually indicates impairment is the driver using the car to steady him/herself. If the driver bounces off the vehicle they are usually impaired. However, there are times when it is not so easy to determine whether a person is impaired. In these situations the person may be asked to take a roadside A.L.E.R.T. test. The person blows into this screening device which has three lights indicating fail/pass/warn. If the person fails, they are usually asked to take a breathalyser test. If the person passes, they are usually told to drive more carefully (remember, he was pulled over because of erratic driving). A warning means that the person is not over the legal blood alcohol limit but really shouldn't be driving. They are usually asked to park their car and take a taxi home or have a friend drive them to where they are going.

It's interesting to note that Cst. McDonald said that half or three-quarters of all the people he has had to pull over have all said the same thing: "But officer, I only had one or two beers." According to the National Highway Traffic Safety Administration, drivers under the influence of alcohol often display certain characteristics when on the road:

* Making wide turns.
* Weaving, swerving, drifting, or straddling the centre line.
* Almost striking an object or vehicle.
* Driving on the wrong side of the road.
* Driving at a very slow speed.
* Stopping without cause.
* Braking erratically.
* Responding slowly to traffic signals.
* Turning abruptly or illegally.
* Driving after dark with headlights off.

If you are in front of the drunken driver, turn right at the nearest intersection and let him or her pass. If the driver is in front of you, stay a safe distance behind. And if the driver is coming at you, slow down, move to the right, and stop.

Penalties for Young Offenders

Cst. McDonald indicated that young offenders arrested for impaired driving may be given probation and ordered to attend counselling. (A young offender is any person between the ages of 12 and 18 found guilty of a criminal offence.) Payment of a fine may also be included in the sentence. Fines are usually lower for young offenders than for adults as young offenders often do not have their own independent means of paying heavy monetary fines. An adult, convicted on a first offence, may have to pay a fine of not less than three hundred dollars. In comparison, young offenders may be asked to pay the victim surtax as opposed to paying a fine. The young offender's license may also be suspended.

Organizations

Many organizations have formed over the years to help combat drunk driving. The following lists what they do:

* *lobbying for tougher laws to discourage those who might drink and drive.* Fewer impaired drivers on the road would mean fewer crashes and more saved lives.
* *supporting Teenage Outreach/Educational programs.*
* *funding Public Awareness campaigns.* Many people do not understand how dangerous it is to drink and drive. They also may not realize how much they can do to help eliminate the problem. MADD (Mothers Against Drunk Driving) Canada hopes that by helping more people understand that even one drink can impair a person's ability to drive safely there will be fewer drunk drivers on the road.
* *maintaining Victim Assistance programs.* MADD Canada offers support to victims and their families. MADD Canada also helps victims to understand how the justice system works and

what their rights are. ADD was established by an Ontario couple who lost a son in a drunk driving accident. Their son, while riding his bike, was struck by a car driven by a drunk driver. The driver didn't stop. The driver was, however, later apprehended by the police. The mission of the organization is to reduce death and injury caused by impaired drivers through educational means. Membership is made up of teens, volunteers, concerned citizens, and victims of impaired drivers. ADD's national headquarters is based in Brampton, Ontario, Canada, and their mandate is nationwide.

Teen-ADD (Teens Against Drunk Driving) was formed in 1983 by the Board of Directors of ADD to provide a forum for students and teens to discuss and promote the dangers associated with drinking and driving. The goal of the organization is to reduce the tragedies caused by impaired drivers and to educate other students and teenagers through presentations, workshops, and newsletters, and to highlight that people must accept responsibility for their actions.

Teen-ADD has a great homepage for teens [http://www.add.ca/teen_add.htm] and anyone interested in the subject of drunk driving. There are links to the Teen-ADD newsletters and a Teen-ADD Starter Kit (this link has lots of resources and information). There's an excellent and thorough step by step program to setting up a Teen-ADD Chapter which would be also helpful in the creation of any new club. True or False Questions; a Did/Do You Know page; a Fatal Motor Vehicle Collision Summary (Peel Region, Ontario); and a Drinking and Driving Resource List (lots of addresses, etc.) can also be found on the web page.

RADD (Recording Artists, Actors and Athletes Against Drunk Driving), an organization that came into full swing in November 1996, has a mission to reduce the incidents of drinking and driving among young Canadians aged 16 to 34 and to encourage the use of designated drivers. The RADD focus is on making responsible drinking the norm, the expected, and the desirable.

Web Sites

MADD Canada http://www.madd.ca/
ADD Canada http://www.add.ca/
Teen-ADD (*-best bet for teens) http://www.add.ca/teen_add.htm
RADD (*-best bet for teens) http://www.radd.org
BACCHUS, The Alcohol Education Group http://www.bacchus.ca/

(*best bet for teens/site also has great resource list for librarians)

So What Do All Those Acronyms Mean?

BAC: blood alcohol concentration; this refers to the concentration of alcohol in a person's blood
DUI: driving under the influence
DWI: driving while intoxicated

Did You Know?

* Crashes caused by drunk drivers happen more often in summer than winter.
* Over two-thirds of crashes caused by drunk drivers occur on weekends and one-quarter of all crashes happen on Saturday.
* Over 66% of drinking/driving crashes happen between 6 p.m. and 3 a.m.

* Every forty-five minutes in Ontario a driver is involved in an alcohol-related crash.
* Over the past decade, about 90% of all crash-involved drinking drivers were male.

(Statistical Yearbook, 1994, Drinking/Driving Counter-measures Office, Ontario)

Programs

Looking for programming ideas for young adults? How about these:

* A slogan campaign (i.e., Drugs and alcohol, a one-way street. Don't drive on it.) With a really cool prize (maybe a gift certificate from a local movie theatre or record store).
* KISS A PIG Campaign (good for teacher/librarians). This campaign serves as a fundraising activity as well as providing drinking and driving awareness messages to students. The goal is to have students donate pocket change to staff coin boxes containing the Don't Drink and Drive message. The staff member with the highest donation is then required to Kiss A Pig. (Yes a real live pig or some other creature of your choosing.) The fun begins near the end of the campaign when the staff member with the highest donation suddenly realizes they will be the one required to kiss the pig. The person usually starts to stuff a fellow staff member's coin box with change just to get out of having to kiss the pig themselves.
* Take instant photographs of people and then have them fill out a form consisting of three statements which the participant has to complete:
"Drinking and driving is . . . ,"
"When partying I look after myself and friends by . . . ," and
"I would like to remind my friends when partying to . . . ."
Participants' photographs and their responses can be taped to a visible area near an entryway or a busy hallway where passing people can stop, read, and take away a personal message.
* Have an Addictions Jeopardy Game: Teams of students play against each other answering questions about alcohol/drugs and gambling like the game on TV.
* Run a poster contest.
* Have a daily quiz question. Participants can drop off their answers at the library and the first correct answer drawn receives a prize.
* In a school setting, have a candy-gram campaign. Teams deliver gum to all classes during the last period of a chosen day. Inside the gum wrappers are messages about drugs, alcohol, and driving. Ten messages can be for prizes like sub coupons or free drinks.
* Around Christmas, put up a tree and decorate it with pledges signed by young adults who plan not to drink and drive or ride with someone who has been drinking.

SO YOU WANNA BUY A CAR, EH?

"Dad, can I have the car tonight?" has become "Dad, I need a car." Suppose everyone in the family agrees to the fact that the son/daughter needs a car. Now what? Buying a car is not as easy as buying a toothbrush; research is the key.

What Is Research?

The two publications that every prospective Canadian car buyer should look at are *Consumer Reports* and *Lemon Aid*. Each of these publications attempts to ease the strain of buying a used car by elucidating any problems with a particular make or model of vehicle.

Consumer Reports publishes an annual buyer's guide for both used and new cars. Each year they buy cars and subject them to various tests. The accelerator, transmission, braking, ride under normal load, ride under full load, routine handling, noise, emergency handling, driving position, front seating, rear seating, access, climate system, controls, trunk, safety, and reliability are all graded. Each entry for a particular model summarizes the results of this inspection. Each car then undergoes a thorough mechanical inspection which looks at the engine, cooling system, fuel economy, ignition, automatic or manual transmissions, clutch, electrical system, air conditioning, suspension, brakes, exhaust, body/rust, paint/trim, body integrity, and hardware. Each of these categories is given a rating. A shaded circle means that that car performs excellently for that category while a dark circle means that that car performs poorly. *Consumer Reports* lists the results of the tests for seven years in each annual buying guide. The fifteen best and fifteen worst buys are featured in this publication.

Lemon Aid is similar to *Consumer Reports* in that it rates the same criteria except this publication also includes steering and suspension, dealer service, repair costs, maintenance costs, parts availability, and crash safety. This publication also grades cars for the last seven years. Each entry lists an overall rating, price analysis, strengths and weaknesses, safety summary, recalls, secret warranties, service tips, and dealer service bulletins. This publication also gives the used value of the car as well as the original selling price. These values are in Canadian dollars. A nice feature of *Lemon Aid* is that it lists some of the best cars to buy that are older than ten years.

Buyers should look at these guides to gain an understanding of the strengths and weaknesses of various cars. They should then choose a couple of models that they would like to look at more carefully. Things to consider are:

1. Do I want front wheel drive, four wheel drive, all wheel drive, or rear wheel drive?
2. Do I want an import or domestic vehicle?
3. Should I look at a car over ten years old?
4. What type of service is available for this car?
5. Are there parts available?
6. How crash worthy is this vehicle?
7. What are the options?

What about the Internet?

The Internet can be a very useful resource when it comes to researching information on a used car.

Buyers, however, should be aware that many web sites are fronts for salespeople, services that put buyers in touch with salespeople, or information services that charge for the information they provide. One way to avoid these sites, which can be annoying, is rather than searching the Internet under "used cars," search a government site.

Industry Canada, for example, has a great site with reputable links to other used car sites. This site is currently located at http://strategis.ic.gc.ca/SSG/ca00627e.html. It can be reached through Strategis at http://strategis.ic.gc.ca and then clicking on the links "Consumer Information," "Consumer Connection" and then selecting automobiles. This site has links to other sites such as Auto.com, Edmund's Automobile Buyers Guide, and Microsoft Car Point. Note that Australia and the United States offer similar services.

I Want to Buy a Toyota Celica. Now What?

Now that you know what type of car you want to buy, there are other considerations to make.

1. When is the best time to buy a car?
2. Where should I buy this car?

Buy Winter

The best time to buy a car is in the winter. This is the time when there are fewer buyers in the market and the car will reveal its worst characteristics.

That Guy Looks OK

You've got this far. Now you have to deal with the dreaded car salesman. You have a few options.

1. New Car Dealers—These are the most expensive, but they do have many benefits. New car dealers are insured against selling stolen vehicles, they have financing plans, they recondition their vehicles, and they offer a wider choice.

2. Used Car Dealers—These are the guys you really have to watch. They are a little cheaper than new car dealers and some do offer credit. These dealers, however, often operate on a marginal budget and therefore cannot recondition their vehicles and they often do not offer repair facilities. If you do buy from a used car dealer ensure that he/she is licensed and find out where he/she buys his/her cars.

3. Private—This is the cheapest alternative. A few things to remember are:
   * get a written sales receipt.
   * ensure that any liens are reported and paid.
   * check the title of the vehicle—if the title lists an R that means the car has been restored. If the seller agrees to clear a lien personally, get written relinquishment of title from the creditor.
   * ask the seller to show you repair bills and the original contract. If this information is not available, don't buy the car.

4. Government and Commercial Auctions—These are risky, there are no guarantees, and you must pay cash.

Don't Trust That Guy

Some things to watch out for:

1. The dealer refuses to identify the previous owner.
2. The mileage has been turned back.

3. The dealer does not want to declare the full purchase price on the invoice. This is a tax trick—don't fall for it.
4. The sales agent is posing as a private party.
5. The money-back guarantee—usually accompanied by exorbitant handling fees, rental fees, or repair costs.
6. The 50/50 guarantee. If a dealer offers to pay 50% of all repairs for the first year, ensure that you can choose the garage.
7. The "As Is" clause.
8. The odometer has been tampered with—ensure that the mileage is shown on the contract.
9. The vehicle is misrepresented—ensure that the vehicle is inspected by an independent garage. Try not to buy a taxi.
10. The stolen car.

I Like the Red One

Once you have chosen a dealer and a car, it's time to test-drive. Some words of caution: take a friend with you. By this time you will probably be more emotionally involved and you will not be very logical in your thoughts. Some rules:

1. Set a price limit and stick to it—remember taxes and licensing fees.
2. Plan on repairs of about $500.
3. Have your friend conduct the first test drive.
4. Consider price, mechanical condition, body and frame condition, and mileage.

Let's Go for a Spin

When your friend test drives the vehicle, make sure he/she drives it hard. Accelerate hard, brake hard, and corner hard. Drive over smooth and rough sur-faces at high and low speeds. Turn on all accessories to make sure that they work. Turn off the ignition and make sure the "check engine" light works. Hand-wash the car yourself in bright daylight, which should reveal any body faults and eliminate bad surprises. Check to ensure that all the paint on the body matches, look for any waves in the panels, and check for a rusty floor or bent frame.

Looks Clean

The next step is the mechanical inspection. Take the car to a mechanic that you respect and have him/her perform a top-to-bottom mechanical inspection. Ask him/her to do a four-wheel alignment. If he/she is unable to do so, it means the frame is damaged and you'd best find another car.

I'll Take It

If you have made it this far, chances are you have made a good choice and your car won't be a lemon. Things to consider when negotiating a price are:

1. If it sounds too good to be true, it probably is. Be wary of absurdly low prices.
2. Depreciation—New vehicles depreciate 10% as soon as they are driven off the car lot; they depreciate an additional 10–15% each year for the first 4 or 5 years. If a vehicle performed extremely well in the new car market, the depreciation should be lower. Similarly, if the vehicle had a poor reputation, the depreciation should be higher. Finally, if a new model just came out with a lower price the depreciation will be higher. Vehicles with the greatest depreciation are the best used cars for your money.

Congratulations on your new car!

Sources

Canada. Industry Canada. "Consumer Connection."
Available: [Online] http://strategis.ic.gc.ca/
sc_consu/consaffairs/engdoc/oca.html,
December 9, 1998.

Consumer Reports. *Used Car Buying Guide*. 1998.

Edmonston, Phil. *Lemon Aid: Used Car Guide*.
Toronto: Stoddard, 1997.

Henry, Len. "Do Your Homework Before Buying a
Used Vehicle." *The Montreal Gazette*. June 27,
1998: G8.

Menzies, David. "Second Hand Values: A Buyer
Guide to Auto Depreciation." *The Financial Post
Magazine*. May 1998: 43–46.

LEARNING ABOUT INSURANCE

Before cars, horses and carriages were the main mode of transportation. Back in 1898 when the first automobile insurance policy was purchased in the United States, there were barely 100 cars on the streets and the main concern then for both insurers and auto drivers was any injury those noisy new machines might do to horses. Since then, the number of automobiles operating daily on roads, streets, and highways has increased dramatically, and, so, therefore has the amount of accidents. Not only do automobile owners and drivers have to worry about accidents, they also have concerns about theft and vandalism. The safeguard against such horrible things is insurance.

Insurance. The very word may make some people cringe and envision their hard-earned money sprouting wings and flying off to places unknown. I looked up the meaning of the word in *Webster's New World Dictionary* and found that insurance is defined as (1) an insuring or being insured against loss; a system of protection against loss in which a number of individuals agree to pay certain sums (premiums) periodically for a guarantee that they will be compensated under stipulated conditions for any specified loss by fire, accident, death, etc., and (2) a contract guaranteeing such protection. Whew! Sounds like good stuff to have. Especially if you are a beginning driver. *Traffic Safety Facts 1997* compiled by the U.S. Department of Transportation, National Highway Traffic Safety Administration, stated the following:

* In 1997, 16 to 24 year olds represented 23 percent of all traffic fatalities, compared with 8 percent for ages 1 to 24, 44 percent for ages 25 to 54, and 25 percent for ages 55 and over.

* On a per population basis, drivers under the age of 25 had the highest rate of involvement in fatal crashes of any age group.

* Motor vehicle crashes are the leading cause of death for 15 to 20 year olds (based on 1994 figures, which are the latest mortality data currently available from the National Center for Health Statistics). In 1997, 3,336 drivers 15 to 20 years old were killed, and an additional 365,000 were injured, in motor vehicle crashes.

* In 1997, 14 percent (7,885) of all the drivers involved in fatal crashes (56,602) were young drivers 15 to 20 years old, and 17 percent (2,001,000) of all the drivers involved in police-reported crashes (12,066,000) were young drivers.

* Almost one-third (312) of the 15 to 20 year old drivers involved in fatal crashes who had an invalid operator's license at the time of the crash also had a previous license suspension or revocation. For the same age group, almost 30 percent of the drivers who were

killed in motor vehicle crashes during 1997 had been drinking.

* In 1997, the estimated economic cost of police-reported crashes involving drivers between 15 and 20 years old was $31.9 billion.

Do these tragic statistics affect insurance rates? Yes, they do. Young adults and their parents are frustrated by the high premiums they must pay in order to exercise the privilege of driving. Some parents leave it to the young adult's discretion: you can drive if you pay the premiums. However, until these tragic statistics begin to improve, teenage drivers are seen as a risk and therefore must pay higher premiums for insurance than adults over the age of 25.

Insurance works by spreading financial risk among large numbers of people. You pay a premium to an insurance company for the right to share in funds set aside to pay loss or damage costs in certain pre-defined circumstances.

Insurance does not have to be complicated, but young drivers should do a bit of homework before speaking with an agent. Terminology is bound to be new and can be confusing. Familiarity with the terms will result in better understanding of the policy and that is important given that if they own a car it will probably be their most expensive asset.

After learning some of the terminology, it would be a good idea to prepare some questions before speaking with an agent. Some questions young adults frequently ask of insurance agents are:

Do I have to buy insurance?
What determines how much I am charged for my policy?
What is a deductible?
Why does where I live affect my rates?
Why do some cars cost more to insure than others?
Can I be added on to my parents' auto insurance?
How often will I have to renew my policy?
Will my rates go up if I get into an accident or get a ticket?
How can I lower my insurance rates?
What is not covered under my auto policy?
Is my car covered if someone borrows it? What about the driver?
Does my insurance cover me if I borrow someone else's car?

Answers are going to vary between provinces, states, and countries. For example, a young adult may be living in Nova Scotia but planning to attend a university in Ontario. If a move is planned from one province to another, it would be a good idea to investigate the insurance requirements for your car before leaving home. A good insurance representative will be able to answer all your questions.

YOUR ACCIDENT CHECKLIST

Don't move your car. Unless it causes a hazard, you can better prove your claim if police can note the exact position of the cars when they crashed.

Call an ambulance if anyone is hurt. Clear the area if you smell or see leaking gasoline; then call the fire department.

Call the police. You may need a police report for your claim.

Admit nothing. Say nothing about who's at fault. Stray comments can work against you in court or the claims process.

Jot down all details. While your memory is fresh, note how the accident happened.

Get personal data. Note the license plate, year and make of all cars involved; other drivers' names, license numbers, addresses and phone numbers, insurance agents' company and policy number; names and addresses of witnesses. See: http://www.badgermutual.com/fyi%20auto.htm

On a lighter note, and just to prove that maybe insurance agencies do have a sense of humour, here are a few statements that were supposedly pulled from actual insurance claims:

* Coming home I drove into the wrong house and collided with a tree I don't have.
* An invisible car came out of nowhere, struck my car and vanished.
* My car was legally parked as it backed into another vehicle.
* I was thrown from my car as it left the road. I was later found in a ditch by some stray cows.

Whether they're true or not, they're still fun. For more insurance odd but true claims see: http://www.insurance-canada.ca/consumerinfo/real10.htm

Sources Consulted

FAQs—By New Drivers About Auto Insurance. (1998). [Online] Available http://www.allstate.com/faqs5.html. [6 December 1998]

The Consumer's Independent Guide to Auto Insurance. (1998). [Online] Available http://www.iiaa.iix.com/autoguid.htm. [6 December 1998]

Traffic Safety Facts, 1997. (1998). [Online] Available http://www.nhtsa.dot.gov/people/ncsa/ovr-facts.html#youth [6 December 1998]

REPAIR AND MAINTENANCE

Trouble-Free Driving

It is important for everyone to know how to operate a car efficiently, safely, and economically. However, the average driver is not a mechanic and new teen drivers will be especially unfamiliar with the workings of their cars. Young people can ensure economic and trouble-free driving by keeping their vehicle in good repair and by detecting vehicle malfunctions early. One of the most important sources of information is the car owner's manual. Libraries usually have a good selection of car manuals.

Preventive Maintenance

Young drivers need to be familiar with the different systems of the automobile to help them to detect things that can go wrong with the car. It is important to know the condition of the battery, antifreeze, tires, oil, windshield washer solvent, and brakes. Important systems to understand are: fuel systems, exhaust system, engine oil system, cooling system, electrical system, brake system, tires, and safety systems.

Emergency Equipment

If your car is maintained properly you should be able to avoid breakdowns but in the event the car is disabled it is recommended that young drivers have the following equipment on hand: First aid kit, flashlight, fire extinguisher, screwdriver, pliers, a cloth, tire gauge, jack, wheel wrench, flares, pencil and paper, blanket, ice scraper, gloves, booster cables, shovel, traction treads, and sand or salt.

The Garage

When taking the car to the garage it's important to describe as accurately as possible the problem without telling the garage the solution. It's a good idea to have the garage phone you with an estimate of cost. This discourages any unnecessary work. If you think you have been charged for parts that haven't actually been replaced, ask for the old parts. The following should be performed twice a year:

* Engine tune-up
* Rotation of tires
* Check antifreeze
* Check brakes

Resources

Automotive service technician. Ottawa: Supply and Services Canada, 1996.

Car care: A complete guide to operation, maintenance & troubleshooting. [videorecording]: Las Vegas: Action Inc., c1992. 3 videocassettes.

Cerullo, Bob. *What's wrong with my car?* New York: Plume, 1993.

Fariello, Sal. *Mugged by Mr. Badwrench: An insider's guide to surviving the shark-infested waters of buying, maintaining, and repairing your car*. 1st ed. New York: St. Martin's Press, 1991.

Gaston, Jim. *The green machine: Drive a safe, thrifty & environmentally friendly car*. Durham, N.C.: CoNation Publications, 1995.

Magliozzi, Tom. *Car talk: With Click and Clack, the Tappet Brothers*. New York: Dell Publishing, 1991.

Ramsey, Dan. *The complete idiot's guide to trouble-free car care*. New York: Alpha Books, 1996.

Schwaller, Anthony E. *Motor automotive technology*. 2nd ed. Albany, N.Y.: Delmar Publishers, 1993.

Car Repair Web Sites

Bob Hewitt's Autorepair Page. Has information on car accessories, batteries, alternators, belts, audio, brakes, clutches, recommendations, and books: http://www.MisterFixit.com/

Autopedia, an online car repair encyclopedia: http://www.autopedia.com/

Cartalk. Advice on choosing a mechanic and also used car information: http://cartalk.cars.com/

WesTech Automotive Excellence. Automotive technical solutions: http://www.westauto.com/

Autoshop Online. Answers to automotive, repair, maintenance, and operation questions: http://www.autoshop-online.com/

Bibliography

How to drive: A driver's textbook. Ottawa, Canada: Canadian Automobile Association, 1989.

Car Plots: Book Reviews

Wieler, Diana. *Drive*. Toronto: Groundwood Books, 1998.

Drive by Diana Wieler is a novel about growing up. Cars take a backseat in the lives of Jens (18) and Daniel (16) Friesen; two brothers who are just starting to get to know one another and themselves.

The story begins with Jens, a high school dropout, working at a used car lot in Winnipeg. He was told by the owner that he had "the drive" to make a good salesman. When he was offered a job, he grabbed it and moved out of his parents' home in rural Manitoba into a small bachelor apartment in Winnipeg.

Daniel, a wannabe jazz star, comes to Jens in Winnipeg looking for help. He desperately needs money to pay back money he owes his agent for tapes that he produced. The story continues with Jens and Daniel taking a truck from the used car lot and heading back to their parents.

Neither Jens nor his brother discuss their problems with their parents. Instead, Jens decides that he and his brother can sell the tapes by going on a road trip, which they disguise as a camping trip. Jens is a master at marketing and the two boys do quite well. During the course of their road tour the two young men learn more about themselves and each other than they ever thought possible.

Drive is a well-written account of two teenagers becoming acquainted with adult life. Wieler somehow seems to know what it feels like to be a young man and portrays that knowledge onto paper with flawless fluidity. This novel is a real page-turner and should be a welcome addition to any young adult's bookshelf. Although the protagonists are male and the problems are stereotypically male, this book would probably be enjoyed by both young men and young women. Some of the content suggests that this book is best suited for teens between 16 and 19.

Paulsen, Gary. *The Car*. San Diego: Harcourt Brace & Company, 1994. 180 p.

This is the story of a 14 year old male, Terry, who is abandoned by both parents without the other's knowledge. He decides to leave school, build a car from the kit that was given to his father and is still sitting in boxes in the garage, take the money he has saved and head out west to visit an uncle he vaguely remembers. He teaches himself to drive and heads out. He quickly meets up with a hitchhiker who introduces him to a war buddy of his and the three of them set out and end up exploring America and getting into some adventures that could not have been predicted.

Gary Paulsen has written other books for young adults and has several Newbery Honor books to his credit. He also has written several books for adults. The author is pictured on the back cover with his car, which happens to be the exact model the young protagonist creates. The book is available in paperback and it has a bright and eye-catching cover.

However, "The Car" is an unimaginative title for a book that starts out like a read of a car kit instruction book. Putting the car together, with all the associated jargon, takes only a little amount of space. This section of the book glosses over several other facts—like the 14 year old has been abandoned by his parents, leaves school, gets involved with a hitchhiker who is homosexual—and "memories" are introduced with no context and that is confusing. After this mixed start, the book quickly evolves to include opinions on the Vietnam War from a couple of war veterans and American history. Time, in this book, is not realistic.

While I can see where this book would have appeal for the young adult audience—and it does cater to a male audience, which is refreshing—several notes of caution came to mind while I was reading this book. The protagonist is a 14 year old who decides to drive across the country with no license and illegal plates. The plates issue gets resolved but the license never does. The 14 year old is labeled as a "natural" driver. Details of his driving are more in tune with race driving and yet they are portrayed as street driving skills. There are also scenes of extreme violence (point blank killing with guns and hands) both in the memories from Vietnam and in response to stimuli while on their trip across the country. I do not think that these were treated or resolved in the detail needed to explain this behaviour. It is especially these two aspects that may be offensive and the pros and cons should be seriously considered before deciding if this book fits into your collection.

Hobbs, Valerie. *How Far Would You Have Gotten If I Hadn't Called You Back?* New York: Orchard Books, 1995.

This is the story of Bronwyn Lewis, a 16 year old girl who is forced to move from her beloved New Jersey home to Ojala, California. Bronwyn finds that in California all her peers look perfect—perfect hair, perfect teeth, and no one does any homework. This sounds more like a science fiction novel than a romance. In this strange new land, Bronwyn feels nothing but anger and loneliness as she attempts to learn a new set of social rules and develop new friendships. She believes that her ticket to acceptance is to own a car. Her parents open a restaurant in this new town, to try to make a living. Bronwyn waits tables and saves money to buy her first car—a '46 Ford which she fondly names Silver after Roy Rogers' horse.

Bronwyn has two talents: She is an excellent driver and a gifted pianist, neither of which she puts to much good use. She sneaks out at night to drive her car and hang out with the other kids. How she manages to sneak out so much I couldn't figure out. You see, she sleeps in the attic of her home with her parents and younger brother. Sleeping quarters are sectioned off with sheets hung from the ceiling. For those of you who might sympathize with me, wasn't it hard enough sneaking in and out with parents sleeping in a *different* room down the hall? A minor point, but one I thought I'd mention.

Bronwyn's relationship with her father is strained due to his attempted suicide and alcohol abuse and her anger at having to leave New Jersey because of these things. The title of the book refers to a joke her father would play with her. If she was leaving the room he would call her back only to say to her, "How far would you have gotten if I hadn't called you back?" Throughout the book there are many times that Bronwyn would have loved to have left and never returned, however she stays and somehow triumphs in the end.

Set in 1950, much of the story centers around teenagers hanging out at the local take-out. It's there that Bronwyn meets J.C., the local bad boy. In traditional style, she is torn between an honest "nice boy" and the typical "bad boy." The "nice boy" is Will, and his character is simply odd and disappointing. The irony is that because of Bronwyn's decision not to "call Will back" after their final meeting, he travels much farther away than she expected.

This novel is aimed at a female audience. There is too much mention of clothes and makeup to hold any teenage male reader's attention. The story is interesting and worth a read, but anyone seeking car-based entertainment may lose interest. There are some car metaphors scattered throughout, and several car races, but they are few and far between and lost among the frills and puffs of other story lines and Aqua Net hair spray. Grades 8–12.

King, Stephen. *Christine.* **New York: Viking, 1983. 562 p.**

This is a novel the average teenager would truly love; that is, they will if they are a fan of graphic violence in their reading. Stephen King's *Christine* is the tale of a young man's love affair with a car. Not just any car, but a classic, a 1958 Plymouth Fury. As one would expect from this master of modern horror, the book is not about drive-ins, restoring old cars in the backyard, or road trips. This is about a murderous sports car on the rampage, haunted by the spirit of its former owner. Christine, the car, causes her former owner to commit suicide, and the ex-owner's corpse checks in from chapter to chapter in various stages of decomposition, a device employed successfully by King in *Pet Sematary.*

There are many things that would interest the teenager in this novel. Besides the violence, which delights the teen almost as much as it offends his/her parents, there is a familiar high school setting with the cast of average boys and girls, cool kids, and nerds. There is, as well, the archetypal boys and cars obsession. It is this normality and familiarity that makes the macabre elements of the novel seem so much more gruesome and demonic. King draws the readers in with his crisp, descriptive prose to a world not much different than their own, except maybe that the teenaged characters are far more articulate than those in real life. Once the author has gained the reader's trust with his believable story then things start happening and boy, things start happening!

Stephen King's *Christine* is as a fine a novel as he has ever produced, and he has penned some superb works. I would highly recommend this book to be on the shelf wherever young adults are found. Be warned about the violence and evil though; do not let anyone read this unaware. The cover art, however, should warn the meek away.

Voigt, Cynthia. *Izzy, Willy-Nilly.* **New York: Atheneum, 1986. 258 p.**

Izzy Lingard was a happy teenager; she was pretty, popular, and a cheerleader. When Marco, a senior and a football player, invites Izzy to a party, Izzy agrees even though she doesn't really like him. At the party Marco drinks a lot of beer. When it's time for Izzy to go home, Tony, another senior whom Izzy likes, offers her a lift. But Izzy feels that if she came with Marco she should leave with Marco. Once in the car Marco has trouble driving. In fact he drives down the middle of the road. Soon he is swerving all over the road and before Izzy has time to react the car veers off the road towards an elm tree. The car crashes into the tree and for several hours Izzy lays unconcious, her right leg badly damaged. The doctor says, "Isobel, I'm afraid we're going to have to take it off." Now everything has changed. Izzy has to learn how to live life as an amputee; everything she has taken for granted has to be relearned. With the support of her friend Roseamund, Izzy finds ways to cope with her new life.

"I Remember . . ."

Generally all drivers have stories to tell about when they were learning how to drive—or teaching someone else how to drive. So we thought we would survey a small sample of friends and family for their experiences and thereby give you the benefit of their wisdom. Now when the driving teacher says that you are the first person this has ever happened to, you can show them that indeed you are not. We are also sure that if you do your own survey, you will find many more unique experiences and many more similarities. Enjoy.

We had just had work done on the car so that everything would be in order for my first driving experience. While trying to dim the high beams (the button for this was then on the floor), I pulled on the steering wheel and quickly found it in my lap. The mechanic had forgotten to replace the nut when they were adding the steering fluid. Luckily I was in a parking lot and not going fast—everything turned out well. (Female, 47 years old)

All my lessons came at 5:30 on cold, dark winter mornings. That is when my brother had hockey practice and my father decided he wanted to share the torture. (Female, 24 years old)

I learned to drive in a large city. I had just received my license when I was asked to pick up some take-out food downtown on a busy Friday night. I was excited to do this until I found out that the only car available to me was a stick shift—which I hadn't learned to drive yet. I went jerking downtown in second gear much to the annoyance of the other drivers and my parents (the food was cold by the time I got it home). (Male, 19 years old)

On the way home from my driver's test—which I passed—we had a flat tire. Although my husband was in the car, he made me get out to change the tire. We got many looks. (Female, 42 years old)

Don't ever take out an angry teenager. I had a teenager pull out from a parking space into busy traffic without looking because she had just waved to her boyfriend and he ignored her. Luckily all we got were honks. (Female driving instructor, 36 years old)

I kept putting off learning to drive because I knew that I would then have to chauffeur my family around to everything as I would be the only one who either knew how to drive or had a valid license. I finally got my license when I was 25. (Male, 30 years old)

I was the only girl in the family. My father did not think it important for the girl to learn how to drive. My brothers all learned but they, too, did not want to teach me. I finally learned when I was 23 and after I had my first child. Although my brothers were not willing to teach me, they were willing to babysit my child so that I had the time to take lessons. (Female, 45 years old)

I was so scared when I went to take my driver's license that I had no spit in my mouth. I remember that clearly although it was a long time ago. I got my license the first time I tried the test. When we were finished, I put on the hand brake and broke the line—I was so nervous. (Female, 73 years old)

I was teaching a foreign student. She was very good. We practiced the examination route so much that I was confident that she would pass the test with no problems. When I saw her in tears, I was alarmed. She was so scared that she often misunderstood the examiner and turned left when she should have turned right, kept going when she was asked to park. It was a shame because she was a really good driver. (Male instructor, 54 years old)

I never learned to drive. My husband was trying to teach me but the first time I was behind the wheel of the car I ended up in the ditch while trying to get out of the driveway. I never tried again. (Female, 86 years old)

I was only fifteen at the time—and knew I shouldn't be driving but one night I thought I would try out the family car up and down the driveway. It worked great until I panicked when I saw approaching headlights and stepped on the gas instead of the brake and ended up on the nicely manicured lawn. I had to do some explaining the next morning when my parents saw the tire marks across their lawn. (Male 31, years old)

Witchcraft

YA Hotline, Issue No. 61, 1998

BETH CLINTON, KAREN HUTCHENS, JEFF MERCER, PATRICIA OAKLEY, NATHALIE RICHARD, AND TAMARA WETERINGS

HELLO WITCHCRAFT!

Witches have fascinated people for thousands of years. Storytellers have been telling tales of magic and witchcraft even before the invention of writing. Witches are featured in ancient legends, folk tales, stage drama (from slapstick comedies to opera), children's stories, science fiction, fantasy and classical literature. Their popularity has not decreased: you will find them flourishing in popular culture—movies, computer games, the new age movement, fashion, talk shows, stores, and witchcraft paraphernalia.

There are many reasons why witchcraft is an appealing subject for teenagers. The haunting, and in some cases, taboo aspect of it draws teens hungry for group activities cloaked in secrecy and mystery. It is important that parents, educators, and librarians not judge these activities and interests without informing themselves. To this end, we have included many resources as well as facts and our own research to draw attention to witchcraft's ancient, varied application. Hopefully, in the process, some of the negative witch stereotypes and myths will be dispelled.

Our bibliographies of "Witch" materials—fiction and non-fiction—will provide ample suggestions for YA reading whether for pleasure, interest, or school projects. Our other aim is to give librarians or educators an idea of the wealth of entertaining and educational "witch" resources available for booktalks, displays, and programming.

Fact or Fiction

The belief in witchcraft began 300 years ago.

Fiction. People began to believe in witchcraft around 1100 AD.

Witchcraft was viewed as an immense threat to civilization.

Fact. "Many contemporary observers looked upon manifest witchcraft as quantitatively and qualitatively the single greatest threat to Christian European civilization" (Kors and Peters, 5).

Witches always wore tall pointy black hats.

Fiction. Medieval artwork illustrates witches wearing various types of scarves or hats. Victorian fairytales contained drawing of witches wearing the pointy hats.

Witches can be female or male.

Fact. Many people have assumed that witches were female and warlocks were male. However, warlocks are different from witches.

Wiccans only celebrate Halloween.

Fiction. They have eight festivals called Sabbats that correlate with nature. For example the first days of winter, spring, summer, and fall.

Only old women were accused of witchcraft.

Fiction. All kinds of people were killed because they were believed to be witches. Clergy, lawyers, rich people, and poor people were killed in large quantities.

One of the strongest indicators that someone was a witch was the "devil's mark."

Fact. There does not seem to be an exact description of the mark. It has been described as pea-shaped or long and narrow. A needle was inserted in the mark and if the person did not feel any pain and no blood appeared, then the judge and the prosecutors declared this person a witch. The person would be tortured until a confession was given.

Witchcraft was a crime that was seen as equal to other capital crimes.

Fiction. People thought that it was such a horrible crime that often people accused of witchcraft did not get a fair day in court.

Witchcraft is an evil practice of worshipping the devil.

Fiction. Witchcraft or Wicca is a religion that uses magic. The concept of a devil does not exist in Wicca. Wiccans are not anti-religious. They promote doing good deeds. They believe that whatever you do comes back to you threefold.

Witches use magic wands.

Fact. Witches use wands to direct energy when healing people.

The concept of witches and witchcraft strongly evolved from fear of the devil.

Fact. Theologians and philosophers perceived the devil as having immense powers with which to harm mankind.

The people who charged other people with witchcraft did not suffer any repercussions.

Fiction. "In traditional Germanic and English law a private individual unable to prove his charge of witchcraft suffered the penalty reserved for the witch" (Kors and Peters, 14).

Sources Consulted

Cunningham, S. *The truth about witchcraft today*. St. Paul, MN: Llewellyn, 1997.

Kors, A.C. and Peters, E. (Eds.) *Witchcraft in Europe 1100–1700*. Philadelphia: University of Pennsylvania Press, 1972.

Powell, S. (1998). The witch's hat. [Online]. The witching hours. Available: http://shanmonster.bla-bla.com/witch/index.html

Sidky, H. *Witchcraft, lycanthropy, drugs and disease: An anthropological study of the European witch-hunts.* New York: Peter Lang, 1997.

Witches' league for public awareness. Salem, MA: Witches' League for Public Awareness, 1986.

WICCA AND WITCHCRAFT

What Are Wicca and Witchcraft?

Though Wicca and witchcraft are often used interchangeably and are intrinsically related, they do not quite mean the same thing. Simply put, in modern terms, Wicca is the religion, and witchcraft is the practice of that religion. Wicca actually evolved from witchcraft however, making this topic complex and difficult to define. Most dictionaries do not even list Wicca, making it very difficult to find a standardized, generally accepted definition. The only dictionary I could find that even attempted to define Wicca was *The New Shorter Oxford Dictionary on Historical Principles.* Even the *Encyclopedia of Religion* did not have Wicca listed. The Oxford simply defined Wicca as "the practices and religious cult of modern witchcraft." This definition is much too concise to encompass everything Wicca represents. Kirpatric et al. summed it

up best in a 1986 study when their research concluded that "Wicca, the Craft of the Wise, is an 'Earth religion' with an animistic and polytheistic worship of nature, often with an androgynous pantheism. This religion lacks bureaucratic rationality and possesses, instead, magical rituals to re-enchant the social world. No members identify with Satanism, and most are followers of Margaret Murray, Gerald Gardner, or recent feminist witches like Starhawk or Z. Budapest. They view themselves as representatives of the religion of pre-Christian Europe. All Wiccans worship a goddess in some form." Witchcraft tends to be defined in a negative light in many dictionaries. The Oxford's definition is fairly standard, and it defines witchcraft as "the practices of a witch or witches, especially the use of magic or sorcery; the exercise of supernatural power supposed to be possessed by a person in league with the devil or evil spirit." This is without a doubt the popular view of witchcraft, and as Kirpatrick's research has proved, it is an erroneous one in the modern context of Wicca.

Schools of Thought

Since 1880, witchcraft has been subject to four major schools of thought. *The Encyclopedia of Religion* defines them as follows: "The first, rooted in classical 19th century liberalism, perceived witchcraft as an invention of superstitious and greedy ecclesiastics eager to prosecute witches in order to augment their power and wealth. The second school, that of Margaret Murray, argued that witchcraft represented the survival of the old pagan religion of pre-Christian Europe." The encyclopedia states that Murray's theory was short lived, lasting from the 1920s to the 1950s, but, as stated above, today's practitioners of this religion are still followers of Murray. The encyclopedia goes on to say, "The third school emphasizes the social history of witchcraft, seeking to analyze the patterns of witch accusations in Europe much as anthropologists have done for other societies. The fourth school emphasizes the evolution of the idea of witchcraft from elements gradually assembled over the centuries." According to the encyclopedia, most scholars currently belong to one or the other of the last two schools. Wicca, however, is such a new phenomenon that scholars have not yet formulated mainstream schools of thought on the topic. In fact, Wicca has only appeared in the latter half of the 20th century, and as such, not much research has been done.

Research Trends and Relationship to Other Disciplines

Researchers are now becoming more interested in the neopagan movement of Wicca as a serious field of study. The early 20th century studies mostly focused on witchcraft in the middle ages. Scholars have picked up the study of the neopagan Wiccan community initiated in the 1970s by Marcello Truzzi and Gordon J. Melton. The trends today seem to focus on feminist perspectives of the medieval witch persecutions, the political activism of Wiccans, the issue of feminist spirituality, and the place of males in such a female-oriented religious movement.

Wicca has attracted the interest of many disciplines. Although Wicca has been studied as a spiritual experience, it has not been studied much under the umbrella of the field of religion. It is interesting to note that the few studies that have been conducted in the field of religion tend to be qualitative rather than quantitative in nature. The leading field of study for Wicca has been anthropology, and other fields such as psychology, sociology, parapsychology, women's studies, men's studies, history, and philosophy have also produced theses and empirical studies. Although there are still studies focusing on the historical perspective of the witch craze being published, the focus is slowly moving toward studying the phenomenon of Wicca as a neopagan faith. As such, scholars are starting to take interest in the topic of female divinity and the cult of the Goddess as a new area of historical study. Recent dissertation titles such as "Beyond Obedience: Lessons about the Mass Violence of Ordinary People through an Examination of European Witch-Hunting" and "Common Elements of Structure in Magic, Witchcraft and Analytically Oriented Psychotherapy" give an idea of the range of studies being done on this topic.

Sources Consulted

Brown, Lesley. *The New Shorter Oxford English Dictionary on Historical Principles*. Thumb index ed. Oxford: Clarendon Press, 1993.

Eliade, Mircea. *An Encyclopedia of Religion*. New York, London: Macmillan, Collier Macmillan, 1987.

Kirpatrick, R. George, et al. "An Empirical Study of Wiccan Religion in Postindustrial Society." *Free Inquiry in Creative Sociology* 14(1986): 33–38.

THE APPEAL OF WITCHCRAFT TO TEENAGERS

Witches, like many teenagers, are a largely misunderstood bunch. However, the truth is that most modern day witches are ordinary, well-educated, middle-class people.

They are not psychotically deluded, devil worshiping, or desirous of joining or forming a cult. What appeals to most people involved in witchcraft is that it is a meaningful activity full of community and positive messages. However, there is a myriad of reasons why witches and covens attract a teen following.

Although T. M. Luhrmann, a social anthropologist, studied witchcraft's appeal to a segment of the British middle class, her observations seem especially relevant when applied to teenagers. One of the reasons Luhrmann cites for joining a coven is the opportunity to play— to use the imagination and to role-play. The coven offers a well-defined, separate context in which teenagers can act out fantasies of an alternative world. Luhrmann finds an "increased capacity for play a great resource, and indeed through play there are real psychotherapeutic benefits" (13). Luhrmann points out that whether or not magical rituals alter physical reality is not an issue. What Wicca offers is a critique of what is presented as true. It is an alternative to modern ideals of rationality (Luhrmann, 13). For teenagers, Wicca provides a framework for questioning beliefs and value systems and also allows them to experiment with different identities. The ambivalence towards what is "true" and what magic can do may appeal to teens that feel ambivalent towards many aspects of the adult world.

Witchcraft's close relationship to imagination and fantasy is something that many teens feel comfortable with and enjoy; Wicca can be a creative outlet or a form of escape from the intensity of "growing up." The popular Young Adult genres, Fantasy and Science Fiction, are closely related to this function. Luhrmann describes witchcraft as "a secretive otherworld, and more than other magical practices it is rich in symbolic, special terms" (48). Wicca involves a move into an alternate reality and can be seen as a sophisticated extension of a child's easy entry into fantasy/play worlds. Wiccans often draw on a utopian vision of a paradisical past—perhaps there is an element of yearning for something lost.

Luhrmann also stresses that witchcraft offers an alternative, utopian idealism. Contemporary Wicca is linked to the "New Age" movement that grew out of the counter-culture of the sixties. During that time, "New Age" was a variant to the mainstream and embraced everything from holistic medicine to anti-nuclear politics. In the sense that some Wiccans are feminist and/or advocates of environmental awareness, Wicca is issue oriented, which speaks to many teens.

Another feature of the "New Age" movement (under which Wicca falls) is the central place of festivals and gatherings. Part of the festival experience is about getting together with friends, burning incense, and listening to music. This is not exclusively a Wiccan activity—teens all across North America love gatherings or "get-togethers." Part of the strong appeal of Wicca is the sense of community it provides. Although each coven has its own well-defined practices, the Wiccan community is diverse and loosely interconnected. This brings us to one of the paradoxes of Wicca. Although it is about community and rituals, it is also about moving away from what is accepted in the mainstream. There are aspects of conformity, but also non-conformity. This paradox must appeal to teens: teenagers are group oriented and yet, on the other hand, they are rebelling against conformity and trying to eke out an identity for themselves.

Wicca's community aspect is related to the idea that witchcraft is an ancient nature-religion in which everything is interconnected. Members of covens consider themselves part of a "family" and the central concept of Mother Earth in Wicca sets the tone for a caring and tolerant environment. Although not all covens are feminist, there are some that have a feminist emphasis. While covens are run by women called high priestesses, most covens welcome men, who are also referred to as witches.

There are many different covens, varying in style and custom. The feminist coven is only one of many different types. However, it is obvious why feminists would embrace Wicca and make it their own. Feminist covens usually initiate only women, and they emphasize the matriarchal aspects of Wiccan spirituality. They often focus on the reawak-

ening of powers and capabilities that they believe have been suppressed by patriarchal societies. Another characteristic of feminist covens is their political orientation. A positive relationship to the body and an intuitive and passionate way of being are part of the feminist's approach to witchcraft. A return to a matriarchal society where there is no split between the mind and body is a typical feminist Wiccan desire; interconnectivity is stressed and expressed by viewing spirituality and politics as one. Margot Adler in her book, *Drawing Down the Moon*, explains that feminist Wiccans are interested in creating "a society and culture that would be meaningful" (178). Once again, for teens this type of emphasis would be appealing. More importantly, the idea of empowerment may be particularly attractive to the female teen Wiccan. Adler points out that witchcraft is one of the few "New Age" religions in which women can participate on an equal footing with men (207). Nevertheless, feminist or non-feminist, Wicca aims to empower and hence may appeal to male or female teenagers: "Witch after all, is an extraordinary symbol—independent, anti-establishment, strong, and proud" (Adler, 183).

Sources Consulted

Adler, Margot. *Drawing Down the Moon*. Boston: Beacon Press, 1986.

Luhrmann, T.M. *Persuasions of the Witch's Craft*. Cambridge: Harvard University Press, 1989.

POPULAR CULTURE'S OBSESSION WITH WITCHES

This issue of the *Hotline* is dealing with the subject of witches and witchcraft. Specifically, we are looking at the fascination that young adults have with this subject. In investigating this, however, we must first step back from the world of the young adult, and examine the larger issue of popular culture's obsession with spell-casters.

Elsewhere in this issue we will discuss the subject of witches in folklore and the like, which has been around ever since humanity began. This article will deal more specifically with modern culture, especially that of the twentieth century.

Witches have been seen in all facets of modern popular culture. Stories have been written about witches since the advent of literary fiction. Fantasy novels often include witchcraft, magic, and the practitioners thereof. Two modern examples include C. S. Lewis' *The Chronicles of Narnia* series, and some of the *Conan the Barbarian* novels. The witches in these examples are (or tend to be) evil, but this is not always the case. Comic books have also included witches, as both supporting and main characters. For instance, Harvey Comics and Archie Comics have each had a series with a witch as the protagonist: Harvey presented Wendy the good little witch, and Archie had Sabrina, the Teenage Witch. Both of these characters were on the side of goodness.

Witchcraft has remained a fascination of the general public over the years, and this interest has evolved with the advent of new technologies. Once motion picture came of age, witches entered that medium as well. Naturally, the fairy tale witches were prominent, such as those in Disney's *Snow White and the Seven Dwarfs* and *Sleeping Beauty*. Live action films also followed this trend of adapting literature to the big screen. Therefore, they too included their share of witches, the most notable being Glinda the Good Witch and the Wicked Witch of the West from *The Wizard of Oz*, adapted from Frank L. Baum's books of the same name. Another film that featured witchcraft, *Bell, Book and Candle* (1958), and was based on a play by John van Druten.

Shortly thereafter, television became the visual medium of choice for recreation, and witches moved onto the small screen. The example that comes to mind is the successful 1960s series *Bewitched*.

Society's interest in witches and witchcraft seems to ebb and flow. In the first half of the century, up to and including the sixties, interest was relatively high. However, except for some fantasy/horror films, interest dropped during the 1970s, 1980s (one notable exception; *The Witches of Eastwick* starring Jack Nicholson, Cher, Susan Sarandon, and Michelle Pfeiffer), and even the 1990s. That is, up until now. In the last few years, the supernatural and paranormal worlds have once again enthralled popular culture's consciousness, and witches are at the forefront to this new wave of interest. In 1996, *The Craft* became a blockbuster hit (a movie about a coven of teenage witches). Most recently, *Practical Magic* has begun to reap similar success as a movie about two sisters who are also witches. A movie version of *Bewitched* is currently in production. *Sabrina, the Teenage Witch* is presently a very popular television series. It is a situational comedy based on the character of the same name from Archie Comics. Another TV series, *Charmed*, has just debuted and is also doing quite well. This program revolves around the lives of three sisters who have just inherited their unearthly powers. A third popular television series that has a spell-casting character is *Buffy the Vampire Slayer* (the character is among the supporting cast). Two other television programs that have feature witches and/or witchcraft in some episodes are *The X-Files* and *Millennium*. Even large corporations are using witches to sell their products. Cover Girl, the cosmetics giant, is advertising its new "Bewitch, Bejewel, Bedazzle" line with spokespersons acting as witches in the advertisements.

A daytime talk show, *The View*, recently had some Wiccans (followers of contemporary witchcraft) perform a few ritual ceremonies on one episode, which leads to another side to this story. The actual practice of witchcraft, or Wicca, has become more commonplace and acceptable in today's society. Modern-day witches no longer have to hide themselves from prying eyes; they may practice their craft openly and generally without fear of persecution. Therefore, the popularization of witchcraft in popular entertainment has helped increase the acceptance of the practice of Wicca. This new acceptance of actual witchcraft has also opened the door for greater use of witches and their craft in the entertainment industry.

From folklore, to Shakespeare, to literary fiction, to Hollywood: popular culture's interest in witchcraft has always been around. Is it any wonder that young adults, who are trying to find out about themselves and their places in modern society, are as fascinated by the subject as everyone else?

VIEWS OF AN EVERYDAY WITCH

What are the opinions of witches with respect to their beliefs, practices, and the way others sees

them? Vanessa Smith, owner of Little Mysteries Bookstore (Halifax, Nova Scotia) and a witch, agreed to do an interview to shed some light on witchcraft and Wicca. Her store contains a cornucopia of information on witchcraft and pagan religions and serves as the location of many public talks. Over cups of ginger tea and hot chocolate Vanessa discussed what it was like to be an everyday witch as well as her own personal opinions on the appeal of witchcraft to young adults.

What, in your opinion, is a witch?
A witch is a follower of a nature-based pre-Christian European tradition. Wicca is a deity-based religion that is balanced between the God and Goddess. Witches believe in natural forms of magic. There is a distinction between a witch, a druid, and a shaman.

How long have you been involved in witchcraft?
I have been involved in witchcraft for eight years.

What attracted you to witchcraft? Was it other people?
Nobody I knew practiced witchcraft. I became knowledgeable and interested in witchcraft after reading a book of fiction that portrayed everyday witches in a positive light. At the back of this book there was a place one could write to for information on witches. It has been a journey of self-discovery through books.

What about witchcraft spoke to you personally?
I was always interested in environmental and feminist issues. The worship of the Goddess and respect for nature appealed to me.

Have you used library resources to learn more about witchcraft?

I rarely visit libraries, mostly because the books that I want are not available (usually stolen). The local library buys many books from my bookstore.

What is the best thing about being a witch?

I think the best thing about being a witch is the creative process and self-expression. There is no clergy to go through. I can speak to God/ Goddess directly. It is a hands-on type of worship.

What is the worst thing about being a witch?

I dislike the stereotypes and misinformation about witches. I do feel that it is getting better. I feel witchcraft should be seen as a legitimate path to worship and spirituality.

Have you ever experienced any problems personally with being a witch?

I have been lucky. My family has been very supportive. My husband is also a witch. My friends have also been very supportive, even if they are not practitioners themselves. I expected some negativity from a small area when I opened the bookstore, but didn't receive any. Church groups did not protest.

Are you a member of a coven?

Yes, I am a member of a coven. There are five members.

Can you describe a particular type of "witch" personality?

There is no particular personality. People seem to be attracted to witchcraft for different reasons because it has very diverse forms of expression. People interested in feminism and mythology are drawn to witchcraft. People who are spiritual but follow their own path are attracted to it. I do see the trend of more older people becoming involved. The demographics used to be from eighteen to forty year olds, but that has been expanding to include people of up to 60 years of age. Public interest in spiritual things has had a general resurgence and people want to develop a spirituality both inside and outside regular pathways. There is a lot more information on witchcraft, with more books being published and more information on the web. Witches do form in covens and groups but most are solitary practitioners.

What do you think of the modern day portrayal of witches in popular culture?

I think it is in most cases very silly. Modern day witches are typically very boring. They are not as flashy or dramatic as portrayed on television. I would prefer a show such as *Charmed* over books and movies that have witches portrayed as baby snatchers and Satan worshipers.

What about the stereotypes dealing with nudity and drugs—are these accurate?

Nudity and drugs are stereotypes. Sky clad practitioners do use nudity to get closer to earth. They view it as a more natural state. No local groups that I know of practice this. I believe this tenet is not historically accurate. Drugs may be used by a small minority but are not part of the teachings of Wicca. Most groups do not advocate drugs of any kind. In my coven we will serve apple juice at the end of ceremonies.

Why do you think young adults are attracted to witchcraft?

I think a lot of young adults, at least the ones I come across in the store, like witchcraft because it is both strange and weird and to frighten friends and family. Smaller numbers are actually attracted to the spiritual side, in most cases because they don't agree with religious practices that they are being exposed to. They are looking for something else. A young man became involved in witchcraft primarily to scare his parents but is now an honest seeker. I estimate, in my experience, that fifty to sixty percent have passing interests with less than fifty percent having made witchcraft a daily practice.

Do you get a large number of young adults coming to your store?

Yes, there are a fair number of young adults who come into the store. Many come in for talks at the store. Many come in to the store to look at the books.

What do the young adults seem most interested in?

They seem most interest in witchcraft, spell casting, tarot cards, runes (divination stones with symbols). Some are browsers and will come and read about one particular spell.

Do you ever get complaints from parents or groups?

We do have some problems with parents, mostly phone calls. In general the parents want to know what a particular book is about, they want to set their minds at ease. Most are afraid that the books might be encouraging their children to do something bad. Sometimes I will get calls from parents who are very upset and will not accept anything that I have to say. I merely state to them the facts as I see them. Some consider witchcraft pure evil or weird, in which case you cannot do much. Questions and confrontations generally end with a phone call. I will answer questions for parents. Some parents will actually support their children. For example, one young boy comes in with his mother who buys him items to support his spiritual path.

Do you have any advice for young adults? What, if anything, should they be aware of?

Young adults at open meetings or open events should beware of strangers. They should follow the same general safety practices that they would for becoming involved in any type of organization. Be aware of the Wiccan Rede (the basic tenets of Wiccan religion) so that people can't misquote from it. Try to know the background of Wiccans and anyone giving out information. The best advice is to educate themselves. There have been very few cases of problems in this area.

Are there any gender differences between young adults and the practice of witchcraft?

There seems to be slightly more girls than boys interested in witchcraft. Boys are more interested in the spells. The power of the spells and the control aspect appeals to them. Girls seem more interested in the associated ceremonies. The average age is about twelve to thirteen.

Do you have any suggestions or advice for librarians?

I think librarians may want to consult with witches as a knowledgeable resource when purchasing materials on the subject of witchcraft. Some books are better than others, and we will share our expertise.

CENSORSHIP AND WITCHCRAFT

Spells, hexes, charms, the occult and especially witchcraft are words that represent a challenge to censors who want to keep this type of subject matter out of libraries. Books that are accused of promoting witchcraft and occultism (and therefore Satanism) are one of the most popular targets for censors today.

Challenges against particular books tend to focus on materials for younger young adult readers. Some specific example include:

* *Curses, Hexes, and Spells*, by Daniel Cohen
* *A Wrinkle in Time*, by Madeleine L'Engle
* *The Headless Cupid*, by Zilpha Snyder
* *The Figure in the Shadows*, by John Bellairs

In a study on censorship in public libraries in Canada, Alvin Schrader discovered that some censors save time and effort by challenging entire subject areas. Some of the general challenges and the reasons behind them were:

* All books dealing with the occult, because "satanic books damage the minds of youth and could turn people away from Christianity."
* All books on witchcraft, magic and parapsychology, which are "the work of the devil."
* All books on witchcraft and homosexuality, which would "lead young people into a lifestyle that was not normal and damaging."

It's not only books that will come under the censor's watchful eye. In the summer 1996, a lecture program on astrology, numerology, and tarot cards was cancelled in a New Hampshire library. The lectures were part of a young adult summer program aimed at attracting junior and senior high school students to the library. The lectures were cancelled after a local clergywoman organized a campaign against them that included suggestions that the library's budget should be cut if the lectures were not. The clergywoman stated that, "I'm opposed to [the program] because the bible is opposed to them. It's dangerous."

As well, the Internet is not only a hotbed for sexual censorship, but also for information on witchcraft . . . at least in Wisconsin. A 15-year-old student was looking up Internet sites having to do with witchcraft in her school's computer lab. She was told she was not allowed to look at such sites. After she complained to the higher powers (i.e., the principal, the superintendent, and the school board) an Internet policy was drafted that prohibits students from accessing "controversial materials." Although the school board denies the policy is related to the student's complaint, you can be sure that witchcraft sites would fall into the category of controversial.

In spite of problems that may be encountered, these programs can be extremely successful. One librarian recounted how she had a Wiccan give a lecture in the library just before Halloween.

Although the program was aimed at teenagers, many people including librarians and families with small children attended. After the lecture the librarian ordered some Wiccan print materials and they were very popular.

Of course the best way to prepare for and protect against problems and challenges is policy, policy, and policy. Have a collection policy, a program policy, and an Internet policy. Have them in writing and have them endorsed by your library's board or whoever is running the show. With documentation you can show why the books were chosen, why the program was planned, and why there are no restrictions on Internet access. And if the written policy charm does not protect your library, you can always take one of your handy books on witchcraft and cast a spell that will solve all your problems.

Sources Consulted

Foerstel, Herbert N. *Banned in the U.S.A.: A Reference Guide to Book Censorship in Schools and Public Libraries.* Westport, CT: Greenwood Press, 1994.

" 'It's Not in the Cards': NH Library Cancels Tarot, Astrology Programs After Protest." *School Library Journal.* 42 (Oct. 1996), 11–12.

Schrader, Alvin M. *Fear of words: Censorship and the Public Libraries of Canada.* Ottawa: Canadian Library Association, 1995.

"Witchcraft Sites Deemed Off-Limits to Wisconsin Student." *School Library Journal.* 44 (July 1998), 16.

RESOURCES AND INFORMATION

Fiction Books

Donoghue, E. *Kissing the witch: Old tales in new skins.* New York: HarperCollins Juvenile, 1997. A modern re-telling of 13 fairy tales that will appeal to teens.

Grant, R. *In the land of winter.* New York: Avon Books, 1997. A practicing Wiccan loses custody of her daughter and is faced with discrimination.

Lamb, C. *Brigid's charge.* Corte Madera, CA: Bay Island, 1996. Described as a "Quaker-Wiccan historical novel" about a healer who faces persecution after she emigrates to America.

Michaels, B. *Witch.* New York: Berkley Publishing Group, 1996. A woman begins having strange visions after she moves into her new home.

Millhiser, M. *Death of the office witch.* New York: Penguin US, 1995. For the mystery aficionado, this story focuses on the death of a modern witch.

Napoli, D. *The magic circle.* New York: Puffin Books, 1997. A story about the witch from Hansel and Gretel, who was once a healer and has been tricked by the devil into becoming an evil witch.

Pike, C. *The witch's revenge.* New York: Picket, 1996. For younger readers. A group of teens visit the castle of a prominent citizen that one of them believes to be a witch.

Sabrina the teenage witch series. Various titles. Saint Louis, MO: Archway. Sabrina the teenage witch from the TV series has various adventures and problems.

Singer, M. *California Demon*. Westport, CT: Hyperion Press, 1994. For younger readers. A young girl accidentally lets an imp out of his bottle resulting in fast-paced, funny adventures.

Nonfiction Books

Bourne, L. *Witch amongst us: The autobiography of a witch*. London: Robert Hale Ltd, 1995. An English witch discusses her personal experience with witchcraft and the occult.

Buckland, R. *Advance candle magick: More spells and rituals for every purpose*. St. Paul, MN: Llewellyn, 1996. Learn techniques of how to use herbs, stones, visualization, and astrology to improve magick.

Cunningham, S. *The complete book of incense oils and brews*. St. Paul, MN: Llewellyn, 1989. Simple recipes for incense, oils, bath salts, sachets, and ointments among other things.

Cunningham, S. *Wicca: A guide for the solitary practitioners*. St. Paul, MN: Llewellyn, 1988. Directed toward people who are interested in practicing Wicca but do not have contact with other practitioners.

Dunwich, G. *Wicca love spells: How to attract a lover, make a former lover return to you . . . and much, much more*. Secaucus, NJ: Carol Publishing Group, 1996. This book covers almost every aspect of love magic, ancient and modern.

Glass-Koentop, P. *The magic in stones*. St. Paul, MN: Llewellyn, 1989. Basic approaches to studying runestones, understanding, finding and casting runestones.

Hunter, J. *21st Century Wicca: A young witch's guide to living the magical life*. Secaucus, NJ: Carol Publishing Group, 1997. A modern approach to practicing Wicca, it covers history and it includes a section on being a teenage witch.

Moorey, T. *Witchcraft: A beginner's guide*. London: Hodder and Stoughton, 1999. A book for people who are drawn to magical and mystical topics or for people wondering about natural sources.

Ravenwolf, S. *Teen witch: Wicca for a new generation*. St. Paul, MN: Llewellyn, 1998. A handbook that covers the true meaning of being a witch and the basics of practicing the Wiccan religion.

Ravenwolf, S. *To stir a magick cauldron: A witch's guide to casting and conjuring*. St. Paul, MN: Llewellyn, 1995. Contains more advanced spells and information than the books for beginners.

Ravenwolf, S. *To ride a silver broomstick: New generation witchcraft*. St. Paul, MN: Llewellyn, 1993. This is a good book for beginners that contains lots of useful information.

Television

Bewitched. Columbia TriStar Television. 1964–1972.

Charmed. Spelling Television. 1998-.

Sabrina, the Teenage Witch. Hallmark Home Entertainment. 1996-.

Motion Pictures

Bell, Book and Candle. Dir. Richard Quine. RCA, 1958.

Conan the Barbarian. Dir. John Milius. Universal Pictures, 1981.

Craft, The. Dir. Andrew Fleming. Columbia Pictures, 1996.

Crucible, The. Dir. Nicholas Hytner. 20th Century Fox Film Corporation, 1996.

Four Rooms. Dir. Allison Anders. Miramax Films, 1995. Note: first segment only.

Hocus Pocus. Dir. Kenny Ortega. Walt Disney Home video, 1993.

I Married A Witch. Dir. Rene Clair. United Artists, 1942.

Matthew Hopkins: Witchfinder General. Dir. Michael Reeves. America International Pictures, 1968.

Rosemary's Baby. Dir. Roman Polanski. Paramount Pictures, 1968.

Suspiria. Dir. Dario Argento. 20th Century Fox Film Corporation, 1977.

Teen Witch. Dir. Dorian Walker. Trans World Entertainment, 1989.

Witches, The. Dir. Nicolas Roeg. Warner Bros., 1990.

Witches of Eastwick, The. Dir. George Miller. Warner Bros., 1987.

Wizard of Oz, The. Dir. Victor Fleming. Warner Bros., 1939.

Web Sites: The Virtual Cauldron

Atho's Pagan Files Collection http://www.pagans. org/~atho/index.html. Huge site with lots of links on modern witchcraft. Includes information on Wicca and pagans in general. Easy to navigate—this page is an excellent starting point for a variety of information for researchers and those interested in paganism and witchcraft in general. Ten stars for the amount and variety of information it contains.

The Salem Witch Trials http://www.gprep.org/ ~mikes/salem/mainindex.html. This site contains information on the Salem witch trials. The page is easy to navigate and is well laid out. The site includes a chronology of accusations.

Teenage Witchcraft http://www.witchvox.com/ xteen.html. This section of Witch's Voice is designed for the unique needs of the teen witches of the world. It features writings of the modern teenage witch and gives the teen pagan point of view.

Witchcraft Craze History http://www.geocities.com/ athens/2962/witch.html. This site contains a variety of interesting links to the subject of the witchcraft craze, such as timelines of witchcraft and people killed because they were thought to be witches.

Witches of the World http://www.witchvox.com/ xwotw.htm. This is part of the Witch's Voice Network. It includes Witches, Wiccans and Pagans around the world, as well as information about festivals, events, circles, pagan spiritual gatherings and the latest on TV, radio and the Web. It is an excellent resource for contact information.

Witches' League for Public Awareness http://www. celticcrow.com/. Homepage of the *Witches' League for Public Awareness*, this site contains a wide variety of information about witchcraft and earth religions. It includes interesting topics, such as the portrayal of witches in the media and craft community resource page. In addition, it provides a feedback forum. This page is easy to navigate. It loads quickly because it does not have a huge quantity of graphics. A nice feature is that it includes a section on the news of the day concerning witchcraft.

Witch's Brew http://www.witchs-brew.com/wbrew. html. This is a very interactive web site. It is excellent for terminology and is searchable. It also includes back issues of the Witch's Brew Journal, a newsletter designed to bring the Pagan/Wiccan community closer together. There is a commercial element to this page, but it is a good source for someone who is interested in buying merchandise.

The Witch's Voice Network; News and Education http://www.witchvox.com/xbasics.html. Enter a virtual cauldron of the latest information on modern day witchcraft and the activities of the neo-pagan global community. The Witch's Voice has over 600 crafted pages of information including pages that may be reprinted for people dealing with censorship. The page is updated on a daily basis. Ten extremely large stars!

Witch's Voice School Report on Witchcraft http://www.witchvox.com/basics/school_reports. html. This page, another branch of the Witch's Voice Network, offers answers to questions and extensive web links to help anyone researching the topic of pagans and witchcraft.

Witches' Web http://www.witchesweb.com. The Witches' Web is a Pagan news, education and networking web site. It also includes a popular message and chat board, "The Witches' Web Forum," for exchanging ideas and/or chatting with other witches and pagans from around the world.

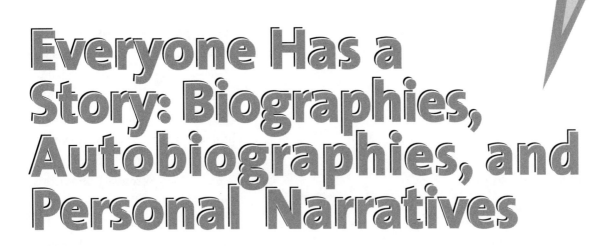

Everyone Has a Story: Story: Biographies, Autobiographies, and Personal Narratives

YA Hotline, Issue No. 62, 1999

TANYA BOUDREAU, KELLY DUNNE, VANESSA MENOR, PATRICIA STACHIW, AND CAROLYN WHALEN

WHO WE ARE

Our goal with this *Hotline* was to bring to our readers' attention some of the important resources available to librarians when choosing collections. Our theme was "Everyone Has a Story," and we tried to illustrate this by including some interviews with real teens that wanted to show their stories. All of us have a story to tell that is as personal as our fingerprints; it is who we are. The powerful, the famous, and those of us just trying to get through life, all have something to learn from each other's story. We tried to show different stories from various people—some famous and some unknown to many. We also tried to make the point that one must be careful when recommending biographical works for teens. The importance of truth in biographies and autobiographies may seem obvious, but creative license does take over in many works—such as the case with our own biographical sketches! We all must take responsibility for what we read and work to discern fact from fiction in these works. When we recommend YA resources, we must remind teens of this responsibility to not take everything at face value and be open to different interpretations from different sources and voices.

EVALUATING BIOGRAPHIES AND AUTOBIOGRAPHIES

Most sources insist that we should evaluate biographies and autobiographies much as we would any novel or non-fiction resources. I would add that in the case of YA biographical stories, respect for historical truth and engaging character portrayals must be at the forefront of the author's intentions. Something that must also be evaluated and that is highly subjective is the "worthiness" of the subject; we must examine and judge if our libraries should include "unauthorized" biographies of artists undergoing their fifteen minutes of fame or works by authors with perhaps a personal ax to grind. Many books fall short of the barest of expectations and it is up to librarians to choose those works that best tell the story of the people and places of interest to teens. In addition, while we may not want to tie up our resources with "The Unauthorized Biography of Katie Homes of *Dawson's Creek,*" it cannot be denied that these are the most popular of the recreational-reading biographies. In this case, it is our job to separate the outlandish and the malicious from the well intentioned and factual. The following are some characteristics of good biographies and autobiographies for young adults outlined by Arthea Reed in *Reaching Adolescents:*

Length of Material: Length should be manageable and should not feel like a history text.

Hero: The hero should be real and realistic. A biographer should choose as his or her subject someone who is not necessarily rich or powerful, but who has impacted our world in some way—either for good or bad. The biography should show that history comes from real lives and show how these lives have made an impact on current times. Characters must be believable and this means they must be fallible. Not even the youngest of teens will believe a rendering that is without failure or unpleasantness. The more believable a character is, the more apt a child is to read and obtain information from the biography.

Secondary Characters: Should be real and realistic, but may be fictionalized to some extent. Secondary characters must be believable as far as mannerisms and actions go, but as for historical accuracy, this is usually set aside in the interest of developing the main character and moving the story along. Such characters often act as foils for the main character.

Storyline: Should be *historically accurate.* Storyline should be *readable.* The story should be engaging and suspenseful and follow a storyline not unlike that in fiction.

The story should *relate to the needs and interest of the readers.* Teens will simply not read a biography or autobiography outside of classroom assignments if the character is not of interest and the story holds no poignancy or relevancy for the reader.

Point of View: The best biographies and autobiographies written with a teen audience in mind will be written from the point of view of the young hero or subject of the work.

Setting: The setting of the story must be as familiar to the author as his or her own backyard; a convincing depiction of the subject's surroundings adds to the story and understanding of the character.

Theme: Reed concludes that the best biographies and autobiographies will demonstrate that history and the study of the people that made it is interesting and fun.

Work Cited

Reed, Arthea. *Reaching Adolescents.* New York: Merrill, 1994: 210–215.

YOUNG ADULT AUTOBIOGRAPHIES THAT EVERY LIBRARY SHOULD OWN

Alicea, Gil C. *The Air Down Here: True Tales from a South Bronx Boyhood.* Chronicle Publishers, 1990. ISBN 0811810488.

Gil Alicea was 16 years old when he wrote these 115 short autobiographical essays. Proud of his family and of his Puerto Rican heritage, he shares his views of his neighbors' problems: drugs, violence, street gangs, and the police. He also points out the New York Board of Education's misrepresentation of kids from the Bronx in a piece about schools: "It makes me feel that a lot of people judge us before we start. . . . Why can't we start like everybody else?" Gil's reflections on his experiences with his family, at school, and among his friends are those of a young man filled with hope for his future and joy in his present. Illustrated with black-and-white photos taken by Gil, this is an authentic and truthful self-portrait. Kids in urban neighborhoods

may recognize themselves, but teens wanting to know more about their urban peers will also enjoy the book. In addition, the format may attract reluctant readers.

Anonymous. *Go Ask Alice.* Aladdin Books, 1998 (rev. ed.). ISBN 0689817851.

The torture and hell of adolescence has rarely been captured as clearly as it is in this classic diary by an anonymous, drug-addicted teen. Lonely and awkward "Anonymous" swings madly between optimism and despair. When one of her new friends spikes her drink with LSD, this diarist begins a frightening journey into darkness. The drugs take the edge off her loneliness and self-hate, but they also turn her life into a nightmare of highs and lows. Although there is still some question as to whether this diary is real or fictional, there is no question that it has made a profound impact on millions of readers in the more than 25 years it has been in print. Despite a few dated references to hippies and some expired slang, *Go Ask Alice* still offers a jolting chronicle of a teenager's life spinning out of control.

Bitton-Jackson, Livia. *I Have Lived a Thousand Years: Growing Up in the Holocaust.* Aladdin Books, 1999. ISBN 0689823959.

In a graphic present-tense narrative, this Holocaust memoir describes what happens to a Jewish girl who is 13 when the Nazis invade Hungary in 1944. She tells of a year of roundups, transports, selections, camps, torture, forced labor, and shootings, then of liberation and the return of a few. Horrifying as her experience is, she does not dwell on the atrocities. There is hope here. Unlike many adult survivor stories, this does not show the victims losing their humanity. The facts need no rhetoric. On every page, they express her intimate experience. After the war, the teenager finds her brother and hears how her father died. She wonders whether she dare enjoy the luxury of being a girl, of "having hair."

Filipovic, Zlata. *Zlata's Diary: A Child's Life in Sarajevo.* Penguin, 1995. ISBN 0140242058.

Zlata Filipovic of Sarajevo began keeping her diary in 1991, just before her eleventh birthday. We immediately sense that Zlata and her family have a deep love for their country, but just as we begin to enjoy Zlata's cheerful disposition, the chaos and terror of war shatter her world. Schools close, socializing becomes too risky, and what was once a cozy home is transformed into a fragile shelter bereft of electricity or water. In spite of great tragedy and deprivation, Zlata keeps making her diary entries, carefully chronicling the claustrophobia, boredom, resignation, anger, despair, and fear war brings. Another birthday passes, and Zlata's observations become even sharper and more searing. The convoys of fleeing citizens remind her of movies she has seen of the Holocaust; she notices that grief and hardship have made her valiant parents haggard and sorrowful. With a precision and vision beyond her years, Zlata writes that the "political situation is stupidity in motion," and more hauntingly, "life in a closed circle continues." Zlata brings Sarajevo home as no news report can.

Frank, Anne. *Anne Frank: The Diary of a Young Girl.* Bantam, 1993. ISBN 0553296981.

A beloved classic since its initial publication in 1947, this insightful journal is a fitting memorial to the gifted Jewish teenager who died at Bergen-

Belsen, Germany, in 1945. Born in 1929, Anne Frank received a blank diary on her 13th birthday, just weeks before she and her family went into hiding in Nazi-occupied Amsterdam. The diary's universal appeal stems from its riveting blend of the grubby particulars of life during wartime (scant, bad food; shabby out-grown clothes that can't be replaced; constant fear of discovery) and candid discussion of emotions familiar to every adolescent. Yet Frank was no ordinary teen: the later entries reveal a sense of compassion and a spiritual depth remarkable in a girl barely 15.

Jiang, Ji-Li. *Red Scarf Girl: A Memoir of the Cultural Revolution.* Harper Trophy, 1998. ISBN 0064462080.

Ji-Li has written a compelling memoir that reveals her gradual disillusionment with what she had been taught to believe about the Chinese communist government. She was a young teenager at the height of the fervor, when children rose up against their parents, students against teachers, and neighbor against neighbor in an orgy of doublespeak, name-calling, and worse. A highly successful student, Ji-Li's life begins to unravel during the Cultural Revolution when her family wants her to turn down a chance to be trained by the government as a gymnast. Self-centered at first, the effects that propaganda has upon the lives of people she respects—including her own family—expand her concerns beyond her own. A unique yet universal coming-of-age story.

Keller, Helen. *The Story of My Life.* Buccaneer Books, 2000 (rev. ed.). ISBN 0899665098.

Helen Keller's triumph over her blindness and deafness has become one of the most inspiring and well-known stories of our time. Here is her famous autobiography, a book that captures her early years and her struggle to communicate and become educated. Rendered deaf and blind at 19 months by scarlet fever, she learned to read (in several languages) and even speak, eventually graduating with honors from Radcliffe College in 1904, where as a student she wrote *The Story of My Life.* That she accomplished all of this in an age when few women attended college and the disabled were often relegated to the background is remarkable. An active and effective suffragist, pacifist, and socialist she lectured on behalf of disabled people everywhere. She also helped start several foundations that continue to improve the lives of the deaf and blind around the world.

Lobel, Anita. *No Pretty Pictures: A Child at War.* Camelot Books, 2000. ISBN 0380732858.

Nominated for a 1998 National Book Award for Young People's Literature, *No Pretty Pictures: A Child at War* is Anita Lobel's gripping memoir of surviving the Holocaust. Lobel spent from ages 5 to 10 hiding from the Nazis, protecting her younger brother, being captured and marched from camp to camp, and surviving completely dehumanizing conditions. A terrifying story by any measure, Lobel's memoir is all the more haunting as told from the first person, child's-eye view. Her girlhood voice tells it like it is, without irony or even complete understanding, but with matter-of-fact honest and astonishing attention to detail. Indeed, and appropriately, there are no pretty pictures here, and adults

choosing to share this story with younger readers should make themselves readily available for explanations and comforting words. This is a story that must be told, from the shocking beginning when a young girl watches the Nazis march into Krakow, to the final words of Lobel's epilogue: "My life has been good. I want more."

Sparks, Beatrice (Ed.) and James Jennings. *Almost Lost: The True Story of an Anonymous Teenager's Life on the Streets.* Avon, 1996. ISBN 038078341X.

The true story of a suicidal teenage boy discusses the events that led to his leaving home, his attempts to survive on the streets, his desperation to escape a brutal gang, and his fight with self-hatred. Dr. Beatrice Sparks deals with a tough social issue faced by thousands of teens, parents, educators, police, and others: teenage gangs. Sam, 14, comes to Dr. Sparks in an attempt to leave behind his gang life. Helping Sam to recall his troubled past, Dr. Sparks examines the disturbing incidents that lead him to leave home and begin his life as part of a street gang.

Haley, Alex with Malcolm X. *The Autobiography of Malcolm X.* African American Images, 1989. ISBN 0345350685.

Malcolm X's memoir belongs on the small shelf of great autobiographies. The reasons are many: the honesty with which he recounts his transformation from a bitter, self-destructive criminal into an articulate political activist, the continued relevance of his militant analysis of racism, and his emphasis on self-respect and self-help for African Americans. *The Autobiography of Malcolm X* defines a journey from ignorance and despair to knowledge and spiritual awakening. When Malcolm tells coauthor Alex Haley, "People don't realize how a man's whole life can be changed by one book," he voices the central belief underpinning every attempt to set down a personal story as an example for others. If there was any one man who articulated the anger, the struggle, and the beliefs of African Americans in the 1960s, that man was Malcolm X.

YOUNG ADULT BIOGRAPHIES THAT EVERY LIBRARY SHOULD OWN

Blassingame, Wyatt. *The Look-It-Up Book of Presidents*. Random House, 2001. ISBN 0394968395.

An inexpensive, high-quality reference book that children have turned to for more than 20 years now contains a completely revised chapter on Bill Clinton, plus a brand-new chapter on the winner of the 1996 presidential election! Middle-graders can find out the answers to such questions as: When and why was the White House set on fire? Which president appears on the $5,000 bill? And who served only one month in office? All 42 presidents are arranged chronologically with short biographical sketches, exciting you-are-there action photos, cartoons, and campaign memorabilia. It is American history in a nutshell.

Chipman, Dawn, et al. *Cool Women: The Reference*. Girl Press, 1998. ISBN 0965975401.

The roster of female role models in *Cool Women* is extremely eclectic, spanning history and national boundaries to include Cleopatra and Amelia Earhart. Mexican freedom fighters stand side by side with Soviet WWII fighter pilots, Mother Jones, and Rosie the Riveter. Author Pam Nelson places emphasis on women who overcame their own fears to go beyond society's expectations and succeed on their own terms. *Cool Women* also introduces many young readers to women about whom they might otherwise not learn until adulthood, such as Dorothy Parker, Janet Flanner, and Jane Goodall. The eye-catching design and friendly writing style (Josephine Baker's "to-do list" includes "Become toast of Paris") will keep girls' attention and hopefully inspire them to check out some of the references provided. *Cool Women* was nominated by the American Library Association as one of the Best Books for Young Adults of 1998.

Faber, Doris and Edith P. Mayo (Eds.). *Smithsonian Book of the First Ladies*. Henry Holt, 1996. ISBN 0805017518.

From Martha Washington to Hillary Rodham Clinton, with a foreword by Clinton herself, the *Smithsonian Book of the First Ladies* briefly examines the lives of each woman who has occupied the White House by the side of the president. Three-to-four-page biographies, with accompanying photos or illustration, focus on each woman's significant life events, particularly as they related to the presidency. Although these biographies are traditional in nature, Mayo, curator of the Smithsonian First Ladies exhibition, does not shirk mention of controversies, such as FDR's love affairs or Betty Ford's alcoholism. Interspersed within the biographies are brief vignettes on such topics as temperance, suffrage, campaigning, and education, all as they relate to women. *Smithsonian Book of the First Ladies* shows that these women are a lot more than just the wives to the presidents. Complete with bibliography and index, this collective biography will support initial, cursory research into the women of the White House.

Gottlieb, Agnes Hooper et al. *1,000 Years, 1,000 People: Ranking the Men and Women Who Shaped the Millennium.* **Kodansha Press, 1998. ISBN 1568362536.**

This fascinating compilation of the 1,000 most important, influential, and intriguing figures of this past millennium ranks the top ones and profiles each with a brief biography and a discussion of his or her importance in history.

Krystal, Barbara. *100 Artists Who Shaped World History.* **Bluewood Press, 1997. ISBN 0912517263.**

In this book you will find the answers to questions about 100 different artists who played a significant role in the development of painting, sculpture, and photography. Read the capsule biographies to learn how each artist discovered his or her own innovative style and the struggles they faced in their personal and professional lives. *100 Artists Who Shaped World History* is organized chronologically and provides the reader with the essential facts and information in a concise and entertaining fashion.

Lewis, Barbara A. *Kids with Courage: True Stories about Young People Making a Difference.* **Free Spirit Press, 1992. ISBN 0915793393.**

Meet 18 remarkable kids with the courage to speak out, fight back, come to the rescue, and stand up for their beliefs. Relates the stories of kids who made a difference in their neighborhood, community, or the world by helping in such areas as crime, life saving, and the environment. As fun to read as fiction, these exciting true stories prove that anyone, at any age, in any life circumstance, can make a real difference in the world.

Northrup, Mary. *American Computer Pioneers (Collective Biographies).* **Enslow Press, 1998. ISBN 0766010538.**

In 10 brief chapters, this Collective Biographies entry does more than offer nice insights into the people who revolutionized technology in the twentieth century. The book gives a succinct, chronological overview of computer technology's evolution from the punch card system to the ease of Internet travel thanks to Netscape software. It traces the computer's transformation from a huge, tediously slow machine to today's speedy microchips and software that do everything from conducting a census to creating visual effects for movies. Each biography smoothly blends personal background and professional achievement. Although most of the subjects are stereotypical technical wizards, others, like the colorfully witty "Amazing" Grace Hooper (developer of COBOL) and jaw-droppingly brilliant An Wang (inventor of the word processor), are fascinatingly original characters. The book consistently implies that risk-taking and hard work result in financial success, but using creative energy and contributing to society are even more rewarding.

Sanford, William R., Ron Knapp, and Carl R. Green. *American Generals of World War II (Collective Biographies).* **Enslow Press, 1998. ISBN 0766010244.**

When Dwight Eisenhower suffered a football injury at West Point, the army almost did not offer him a commission when he graduated, out of fear that he might not be physically active enough. General Patton kept calling out orders to his troops when he was wounded and bleeding on the ground during tank warfare in World War I. General Matthew Ridgeway jumped out of planes right along with the paratroopers he commanded. Seven other famous generals share the spotlight in this brief, engaging collective biography from the Enslow series—Henry Arnold, Omar Bradley, Curtis LeMay,

Douglas MacArthur, George Marshall, Holland Smith, and Joseph Stilwell. The text flows well, highlighting interesting personalities and covering aspects of the war in an accessible fashion. The selections include seven or eight pages of text each, along with well-chosen, average-quality black-and-white photos. Readers interested in World War II and military biography will enjoy this title, and students needing information on the war will find it helpful.

Young, Perry Deane and Duberman, Martin (Eds.). *Lesbians and Gays and Sports.* Chelsea House, 1996. ISBN 0791026116.

Part of the Issues in Lesbian and Gay Life series, this volume touches on a broad range of topics. The many forms in which prejudice surrounding the issue of sexual orientation can become manifest in professional and amateur sports are discussed sympathetically. In addition to a look at the closeted world of professional football and the macho mystique, the author dedicates a chapter each to baseball, tennis, and the Olympics. The obligatory biographies—Kopay, Tilden, King, Navratilova, etc.—are here, as is a tribute to Tom Waddell, the "father" of the Gay Games, and there is a particularly insightful discussion of the "L" word, and the crippling effect it has had on women's athletics is not good. At times, the book has a bitter edge, and at others, it seems to be more about the valor of coming out than about heroics on the playing field. Nevertheless, this is important information for young people to have, especially young gay and lesbian athletes.

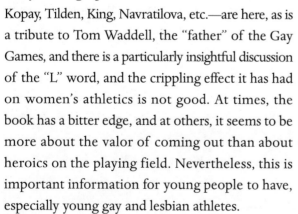

Yount, Lisa. *Asian-American Scientists (American Profiles Series).* Facts on File, 1998. ISBN 0816037566.

In this entry in the American Profiles series, Yount dispels stereotypes with this upbeat and accessible biographical collection of 12 Asian-American scientists. Readers meet computer scientist Tsutomu Shimomura, who hunts down lawbreakers on the information superhighway; Time's 1996 "Man of the Year," David Ho, whose research on AIDS and new drug treatments seems to have eliminated HIV from the blood of infected patients; Paul Ching-wu Chu, "superconductivity's superstar"; Har Gobind Khorana, who created the first artificial genes; and more. The biographies, each accompanied by a list of further reading and a chronology, offer glimpses not only of the diverse career paths of 12 individuals, but lucid descriptions of their fields of interest, research, and prospects for the future. A big plus here is that each profile, which ranges from seven to nine pages in length, is enhanced by a chronology and a "further reading list" for those students who want more.

I WANT TO BE SOMEONE . . . NOW YOU CAN!!

John Palmer notes that "the genre of autobiography has long been dominated by authors who hold some sort of power. Benjamin Franklin was a leading politician in colonial and early post-colonial America, a member of that society's power structure. Even today, traditional print autobiographies come from revered business leaders, superstar professional athletes, military heroes, religious leaders and others who, in one way or another, are a part of the ruling elite." (From *Brave New Self: Autobiographies in Cyberspace* by John P. Palmer http://cctr.umkc.edu/user/jpppalmer/hps.htm.)

Well, not anymore. Now anybody can be a somebody. Welcome to the era of the personal web page, where anybody can have a shot at his or her fifteen minutes of fame. If you believe your life is worth sharing with others, grab a piece of bandwidth and go crazy. The Internet is your oyster. You have a place to express your views, write fiction, and most importantly, let everyone who visits your site know that you are a special person. Give them your history (go ahead, tell them where you were born); express your feeling about the present (political views?); and share your hopes and dreams for the future (when I grow up I want to be a . . .). Why should you do this? Because you are special, just like everyone else.

Self-Help Books for Teens

Canfield, Jack, Mark Victor Hansen, and Kimberly Kirberger. *Chicken Soup for the Teenage Soul*. Deerfield Beach, Florida: Health Communications, 1997.

This book is one of the popular *Chicken Soup for the Soul* series. It contains stories, poems, and cartoons that address problems which relate specifically to things that trouble teenagers. All kinds of topics are covered from dating and relationships to drunk driving and suicide. The book appeals to teenagers because most of it is written by teens and has a very easy-to-read format. It is a guide for the teenager through a difficult period in their life. *Chicken Soup for the Teenage Soul* is sad and funny and can be enjoyed by adults as well, especially those who live with a teen.

Highly recommended for those who like *Chicken Soup for the Teenage Soul* are *Chicken Soup for the Teenage Soul II* and the others in the series. Visit http://teenagechickensoup.com/ for great teen links and other titles that you may enjoy and http://www.inspirationalstories.com/index.html for Afterhours Inspirational Stories.

Levenkron, Steven. *Cutting: Understanding and Overcoming Self-Mutilation*. New York: W.W. Norton, 1998.

Filled with real stories from people who self harm, this book is highly accessible and readable. The sad and disturbing practice of self-injury is handled honestly and optimistically. Using personal narratives, Levenkron educates the reader as well as offering encouragement throughout. I had no idea how prevalent this problem was until I read this book and visited the web sites.

Dr. Lynn Ponton reviewed the book in *The New England Journal of Medicine*, March 11, 1999, Vol. 340, No. 10, and her recommendation was that the book was very useful to educate the reader about the subject.

One site, http://www.cyber-psych.com/selfinjury.html has good links (especially one excellent true story of a teen overcoming self injury) and http://www.drizzle.com/!llama/books.html gives a very comprehensive list of related titles. Also visit http://www.gurze.com/index.htm for more information on the book.

Drill, Esther, Heather McDonald, and Rebecca Odes. *Deal with It: A Whole New Approach to Your Body, Brain, and Life as a GURL*. New York: Simon & Schuster, 1999.

Provides information, guidance and gives the reader options for dealing with issues that concern girls, from relationships to dealing with how your body is changing. The book addresses issues in a straightforward and often humorous way, letting young women know that there are options and solutions to problems and they are not alone with their problems.

Especially interesting and encouraging are the excerpts from conversations with real girls on the gURL web site, which can be seen at http://www.gurl.com/.

Adderholdt-Elliott, Miriam and Jan Goldberg. *Perfectionism: What's Bad about Being Too Good?* **(revised and updated edition). Minneapolis: Free Spirit Publishing, 1999.**

With pressure to perform and succeed so important in society today, perfectionism is a problem for many teenagers. This book clearly explains the distinction between normal, healthy ambition and when to recognize that perfectionism is a problem and should be dealt with. The causes and possible consequences are explored.

The book explains why some people become perfectionists, what perfectionism does to the mind and body, and why girls are especially prone to perfectionism. Also included are biographical sketches of famous perfectionists and risk takers, and youth who share their thoughts and feelings on being perfectionists.

Fuyo Gaskins, Pearl. *What Are You?: Voices of Mixed-Race Young People.* **New York: Henry Holt & Company, 1999.**

Forty-five young adults give their thoughts on what it means to be "mixed-race" and how this affects them personally. The teens speak about themselves and what is important to them. Learn more about the book and the author at http://whatareyou.com/ and the Mixed-Race Links at http://www.mavin.net/links_mixed.html provide links to sites with wonderful information. In a *Booklist* review, May 15, 1999, Hazel Rochman calls this a "landmark book." Indeed it is. A group that has been largely forgotten has found a voice.

Motley Kalergis, Mary. *Seen and Heard: Teenagers Talk About Their Lives.* **New York: Stewart, Tabor & Chang, 1998.**

Mary Motley Kalergis interviewed and photographed 51 young adults who spoke openly about family, friends, school, and work. We get their feelings—fears, hopes, and dreams—in the first-person stories from young people. They talk about what is and what they hope to achieve. Teens can feel assured from these stories that they are not alone with their feelings and concerns. To learn more about the book and the author visit http://www.sugarda.com/seenandheard.html.

"Rarely are adolescents captured with such depth: It is as if we are peering past their physical attributes into their souls." From a review by Patricia Hersch, *USA Today,* October 22, 1998.

Allison, Anthony. *Hear These Voices: Youth at the Edge of the Millennium.* **New York: Dutton Books, 1999.**

Hear These Voices: Youth at the Edge of the Millennium delves into the lives of fifteen youths who are living in a world of drugs, violence, political unrest, and disease. These teens are trying to rise above their circumstances and make a better life for themselves. Through interviews and photographs we learn about these teens who have so little, live in such awful circumstances, and yet have hope and the wish for a better future.

For an excellent review, visit http://www.ala. org/booklist/v95/youth/ja1/55alliso.html.

Hersch, Patricia. *A Tribe Apart: A Journey into the Heart of American Adolescence.* New York: Fawcett Columbine, 1998.

Excellent portraits of ordinary teens. The author spent three years of intense observation, research, and conversations with eight teenagers living in her hometown of Reston, Virginia. Her conclusion: teens may not be a different species, but they are certainly different. Hersch feels that adults abandon today's youth and they are left out there, alone and "a tribe apart."

WHOSE STORY IS IT ANYWAY? THE NEED TO BALANCE HISTORICAL TRUTH WITH AUTHOR INTERPRETATION

As librarians, we are encouraged when a young person wants to learn more about an historical figure or when they are intrigued with an heroic personality of the present. We believe that, as with a good novel, young adults can learn much about the world around them and become familiar with another culture or mind-set when they chose to read a biography or autobiography of a person who interests them or of someone they admire and can look up to. Teachers and other educators do a great service to their students when they complement a history or a social studies lesson with a biography of an individual that illustrates and brings to life the story of that period in time or that serves to give another side to the "official" text-book rendition of the incident. We are heartened when a student returns a book, whether it is non-fiction or fiction, and says, "You know, I learned a lot from this book." However, what exactly did they learn from reading this book? How responsible is the author (and the librarian or teacher who recommends the book) for the historical accuracy of the contents of the story?

In the case of non-fiction resources, authors must research their topic and have a clear grasp and understanding of their subject in order to present the most informed and accurate work possible. It is the responsibility of publishers, reviewers, and librarians to select those works that demonstrate significant research and validity and to demand only the highest quality of writing and research for their YA audience. But, in the case of biographies, autobiographies, and historical fiction, the balance between authenticity and fact on the one hand and interpretation and creative license on the other makes for challenges and sometime controversies in the matter of selecting reading material for YAs.

Everybody loves a good story, especially a story about someone we "know" like Elizabeth I, Terry Fox, or Geri Halliwell, formerly of the Spice Girls. To be as a "fly on the wall" in a room with our favorite music artist when that first record deal was won, or when Elizabeth was deciding the fate of her cousin queen is a great thrill and we rely on the author to not only draw the scene for us in an exciting and engaging way, but also to make it believable.

We want to be transported to this time and to be with these characters. We want to be convinced that Elizabeth would have said this, or that Scary Spice would have said that, and that Alexander Graham Bell would have done this in response to Mabel's frustrations. In order for the author to create, or more properly re-create, the world of his or her real-life characters he or she must do two things: (1) research the time and place; and (2) "responsibly imagine" and interpret the characters' words, mannerisms, and actions.

It is of great importance that authors spend much time researching the period in which they will be involved and be able to set the characters' speech, actions, and mannerisms in the historical context of the era. Nothing makes for a more unreadable story than a menagerie of characters slipping in and out of modern and period speech; a series of historical "goofs" such as inaccurate dates or political references; or the glossing over of such important elements like the technology, food, clothing, and even smells of the time. YAs are not ignorant of history and deserve to be offered the best of what the author can realistically portray of the time. Teens can know the difference between a good memoir, biography, autobiography, or fictionalized history and a poorly written one by using the "been there" test. A good work will promote the response: "I felt that I had really been there!," while a bad one will leave the reader, at best dissatisfied with the genre and at worst, misinformed and misled. It is the duty of librarians and teachers to promote those works that leave a favorable impression in the minds of YAs and highlight these works in our book talks, book displays, and in our advisory lists.

The second responsibility of authors in creating an engaging work of this genre is harder to define and more open to interpretation and controversy. How far can an author go when he or she is trying to re-create the dialogue and actions of an historical figure and to what degree is the author bound to be accountable for the accuracy of the work? As my title asks, "Whose story is it anyway?," one can ask whether the story of Napoleon "belongs" to the author who interprets Napoleon's life in a compelling and believable way, or can it really only belong to history and Napoleon himself—his secrets and motives locked away forever and his writings and documented actions solely the property of historians and archivists. Successful biographers borrow from both viewpoints and complement historical truths, as we know them, with the best of their imagination to portray a well-developed and believable character, capturing the emotional truth of person and place.

No biographer can always know exactly what happened or what was said, and in the case of biographies of figures long lost to historians and scribes, one may never know what were the thoughts of fascinating figures like Genghis Khan, Cleopatra, or Rasputin. All that is left to us in many cases are scanty and unverifiable accounts by persons who may never have known them, or luckily, some surviving writings of the person that may not be accurate portrayals of their true intentions or feelings. The author has no choice but to fill in the picture of their subject with a mixture of popular "lore" that has accompanied our collective understanding of these historical people through the years and a measure of "responsibly imagining" what these people, given the historical context, would have done or said. I borrowed the phrase "responsibly imagining" from Kathryn Lasky who was quoted in an article by Nina Lindsay in which she investigates the potential problems associated with the success of popular historical series like Dear America and American Dreams (Lindsay, 34–35). In it, she warns that authors must balance historical truth with necessary creative license, especially in YA literature when impressionable minds may take what is offered as the only version of the truth. Some of what is being offered seems designed to be misleading, as in the case of the Dear America books where the novel is in the form of a diary, complete with bookmarks, and the true author is not given credit on the front cover. Albeit most of us are willing to suspend our disbelief, and some of us get more out of the work by believing in this "diary"; however, many young readers are dismayed to eventually learn that the work was "fake" or fictionalized and, worse than that, some never understand that the work is fiction and may be getting a distorted view of history. (See the following article *Whose Truth Is It? Recent Controversies . . .*)

To be a responsible author, one must use his or her imagination judiciously in the case of YA biographies, autobiographies, and memoirs. It is perfectly permissible in the absence of historical documentation to use one's imagination to shed light of understanding on a character's actions or motives; indeed without use of creative license, many works of biography would never be written for sheer lack of primary source materials. In this case, the authors are reclaiming their subject from the obscurity of history or distance and treating it, to some extent, as a character of their own imagination. Lindsay quotes Kathryn Lasky, author of *Elizabeth I: Red Rose of the House of Tudor*, and her point illustrates the role of the biographer or historical fiction author: "Although historians may say that Elizabeth was always strong, they do not know for sure. They never will and this is why it is so much fun to write a fictional diary for a real princess. I could, based on what I found, try to responsibly imagine the loneliness, the fears, and the joys of a princess" (Lindsay, 35). Biographers, whether they write fictionalized or factually-based accounts, must meld and find balance between the views of historians and of their own creative consciences, which allows them to be true to their own artistic interpretations, but at the same time, respects and does not deny historical evidence. To ignore either would result in a book that lacks both artistic merit and leaves readers cold, and misinformed. As librarians, if we are to fulfill the goal of learning and greater understanding, it is our responsibility to insist on some respect for history from the authors who claim to give "truthful" accounts of personages in biographies and historical fiction. Although all truth is mutable, whether it is historical truth or emotional truth, we cannot allow our teen readers to be misled or given only one viewpoint of history and of the people who shaped it.

Work Cited

Lindsay, Nina. "Repackaging the Past." *School Library Journal* 45 (July 1999): 34–35.

WHOSE TRUTH IS IT? RECENT CONTROVERSIES IN YA BIOGRAPHIES AND HISTORICAL FICTION

The notion of inserting fictional characters into biographies or into seemingly otherwise accurate historical works is not new and has recently been high-lighted in several well-acclaimed adult works. Included in this list are *Dutch: A Memoir of Ronald Reagan* and Wayne Johnston's *The Colony of Unrequited Dreams*. Some YA books using the same device have recently come under attack for misleading YAs and portraying the lives and experiences of certain groups of people in a dubious and less than authentic fashion. The best known of this type is Ann Rinaldi's *My Heart Is on the Ground: The Diary of Nannie Little Rose, a Sioux Girl, Carlisle Indian School, Pennsylvania, 1880* of the Dear America series. Rinaldi has been accused of misrepresenting the hardships imposed on Natives in residential schools and criticized for an inaccurate portrayal of Native Americans. I don't want to rehash the criticisms of the text, but I would like to suggest that the best way to correct an imbalance or a bias in a work is to collect others that refute or counter-balance the point of view expressed in the offending work. One work that does this is *Where Courage Is Like a Wild Horse: The World of an Indian Orphanage*. It is the memoir of Sharon Skolnick and this book, among others, can serve to balance the viewpoints and opinions of disparate groups who all have something to contribute. Nevertheless, whether that something is what we think our teens should be reading is open for debate.

Online Resources

★ ★ ★ ★   Excellent site with plenty of information

★ ★ ★   Site has flaws but still pretty good

★ ★   May be interesting or useful to some

★   Not great but we feel it is still worth a look

General Web Sites

Biography http://www.biography.com/
    "The Web's Best Bios"! ★ ★ ★ ★

The Michigan Electronic Library (MEL) http://mel.lib.mi.us/reference/REF-biog.gtml

Another great site that has links galore. One link, Find-a-Grave, is particularly interesting at http://www.findagrave.com/ ★ ★ ★ ★

Author Web Sites

Author Biography and Autobiography—Kay E. Vandergrift http://www.scils.rutgers.edu/special/kay/authorbios.html

Bibliography of works by and about authors of interest to YAs. ★ ★ ★

Vandergrift's Biography and Autobiography Page—Kay E. Vandergrift http://www.scils.rutgers.edu/special/kay/biography.html

Bibliography of critical materials about the writing of biographies and autobiographies. ★ ★ ★

Learning about the author and illustrator pages—Kay E. Vandergrift http://www.scils.rutgers.edu/special/kay/author.html

Hundreds of links to online biographical information about children's and YA authors. Incredibly comprehensive. Lots of information for book reports and "about the author" assignments. ★ ★ ★ ★ +

Canadian Web Sites

Great Canadian Scientists http://www.science.ca/css/gcs/home.html

Interesting site that is also on CD-ROM and available in book form. ★ ★ ★

Canadian Museum of Flight http://www.canadian-flight.org/

This web-museum of flight is a great site. It looks good and has plenty of excellent information. Check out the Aviation History link for "some excellent biographies of a few legends of Canadian aviation." ★ ★ ★ ★

Heroes of Lore and Yore: Canadian Heroes in Fact and Fiction—National Library of Canada http://www.nlc-bnc.ca/heroes/index.html

Of great interest for all ages. Provides biographical sketches as well as links and bibliographies of suggested readings. ★ ★ ★ ★

Web Sites Especially for Teens

Anne Frank House http://www.annefrank.nl/

A very interesting site that provides information about Anne Frank herself, her diary, and the house where she hid away during the war. ★ ★ ★

Schoolwork: Biographical Resources http://www.schoolwork.org/biography.html

Online resources to help with school assignments on famous people. Interesting site: Notable Citizens of Planet Earth. ★ ★ ★

Multnomah County Public Library Homework Centre http://www.multnomah.lib.or.us/lib/homework/biohc.html

Many interesting sub-divisions and links, for example: Trappers, Fur Traders, Frontiers & Mountain Men. Good homework resource. ★ ★ ★ ★

Miscellaneous Web Sites

Turn-of-the-Century Child: Examine Their Faces http://NuevaSchool.org/~debbie/library/cur/20/turn.html

A very interesting site—take some time at this one to look around. A great educational tool and a lot of fun as well. ★ ★ ★ ★

Reader's Choice Biographical Bookshelves http://www.thegrid.net/dakaiser/books/bio/

Bibliographies and reviews of recommended biographies grouped by theme; not necessarily intended for YAs. ★ ★ ★

Biographies That Highlight Universal Human Values http://www.dalton.org/libraries/fairrosa/lists/biographies.html

Interesting concept for grouping of themes. Includes citation and brief abstracts. ★ ★ ★

Multiculturalism

YA Hotline, Issue No. 64, 2000

NADINE D'ENTREMONT, RACHEL KELLY, JOY MASSELINK, AND JOANIE SEBASTIAN

MULTICULTURAL PROGRAMMING FOR YOUNG ADULTS: MAKING IT WORK IN YOUR LIBRARY

Introduction: The Need for Multicultural Programming

Together with culturally diverse collections, multicultural programming allows the library to take a proactive role in teaching tolerance and fighting prejudice, in preparing young adults for life in the global community, and in celebrating artistry and diversity (Harrington, 12). At a deeper level, this type of programming can also offer the young adult a perspective that reaches beyond egocentrism, encouraging adolescents to assume roles in the larger world. In another sense, and depending on the type of programming done, it also offers a potential forum for multicultural young adults to voice frustrations and concerns about being a member of a minority group.

With population experts predicting that one third of the young adults served in libraries will be from minority groups by the year 2014, multiculturalism in the public library—in the form of both collections and programming—becomes more of a right than an option (Harrington, 14). In this way, multicultural programming is advantageous to libraries, so that library users, regardless of cultural background, will become library advocates as well as users. Decisions made by libraries control the cultural images experienced by YAs in the library: collection decisions determine the literature and media that reaches teenagers, while programming decisions determine what communities' needs are being addressed by the library. It is thus important that the library's day-to-day practices make cultural communities feel invited by making informed decisions regarding both collections and programming.

Barriers to Multicultural Programming

Different patron age groups require different approaches to multicultural programming, and this fact is particularly true when it comes to teenagers. Indeed, according to Tracey Jones, Branch Manager and Youth Services Librarian at the Halifax North Library in Halifax, Nova Scotia, multicultural programming for young adults is often difficult. This is true for three main reasons: First of all, as with any type of programming, teens are busy—what you offer has to be enticing enough to compete with school, extra-curricular activities, jobs, sports, and any variety of other activities that might comprise a teen's to-do list. Second, at a time in the teenager's life where one of the main struggles centers on determining an identity representative of who he or she truly is, adolescents in the midst of this struggle often turn aside from their own culture, making it difficult to do programming that is overtly multicultural. Third, often teens are more interested in the web or the latest yo-yo expert than multicultural issues—the key is to find out what the young adults want.

Getting Started: Tips and Planning for Multicultural Programming

Keeping such barriers in mind then, how do you get started with multicultural programming at your library? Before even beginning with this type of programming, it is important to assess how committed your library and you yourself as the librarian are in carrying out multicultural services. In order to be successful, multicultural programming truly needs to be an integral part of library service. This means that it is both important and necessary to include multicultural programming throughout the year. One-shot, isolated activities tend only to indicate that certain cultures are separate from the mainstream, perpetuating stereotypes and prejudices (Harrington, 21). Isolated programs also have the potential to have librarians evaluate their programs by superficial measures: Did we have an activity for Multicultural Day? Hence, if your library is not committed to multicultural programming in whatever form or fashion from the beginning, it is likely that it will result in a superficial effort and eventually fizzle out all together.

If your library is, however, committed to promoting multiculturalism and, more specifically, multicultural programming, you have the tools necessary to proceed. The first step: a community analysis. Your library should gather information on the communities it serves. This can be accomplished via surveys, interviews, and focus groups with teens themselves, which ask about interests, barriers that prevent youth from attending programs, and possible programming ideas. If you have a Youth Advisory Board, this is also an opportune time to involve members and obtain a teen perspective. When teens are actively involved in library programming, the library belongs to them and they will be more likely to support it and its programs. Parents and community leaders can also be solicited for information regarding teen interests and programming.

At this point, librarians can also contact local organizations to inquire about their multicultural programs. Exploring programs offered by these organizations will not only avoid duplication, but can allow the library to more effectively organize its own programming and/or participate in a community program that is already established. To demonstrate the library's availability and support, your library might also wish to send representatives to community events emphasizing a multicultural flavor.

In order to keep fresh and expand upon multicultural services offered by your library, you should also keep up-to-date on the literature discussing this topic and encourage your staff to do so as well. You can also find ideas by attending conferences, networking, and getting involved in listservs and professional discussions on multicultural programming.

Multicultural Programming Ideas

Once you have your community analysis in hand and have begun community networking, you and your Youth Advisory Board, if your library has one (this is a good opportunity to establish one if you don't have a Board up and running!), are ready to begin brainstorming for possible programming ideas. This endeavor is often one that is individual to the community being served. Nevertheless, some possible programming ideas include:

Booktalks: By promoting multicultural literature alongside mainstream literature, the booktalking librarian can bring a multicultural perspective which enlarges upon the typical canon of YA literature.

Media sessions discussing how different cultural groups are recognized in the media (books, magazines, music, television or movies): As noted by Tracey Jones at Halifax North Library, providing a forum for young adults to talk is an important and generally well received aspect of successful programming. Consider having sessions which allow for lots of discussion.

Movie nights: A typical movie night can be easily made multicultural by featuring multicultural media stars such as Denzel Washington as Malcolm X. Consider also showing documentary type movies; you'll be surprised at how receptive teens are to these. Also, allow for mingling (bring food!) and casual discussion after the movie or documentary.

Guest speakers: Local performers, educators, student groups, and community leaders can be brought in to present and discuss issues, or just to do fun activities.

Popular topics: You can capitalize on a popular topic by making it multicultural. In this way, multicultural programming is made unobtrusive, overcoming the identity barrier discussed above. For instance, a topic such as body art—currently popular among teens—can be made to have a multicultural flavor by discussing the significance of body decorations in other cultures, such as Mehndi or henna tattoos for instance, and the art of make-up and hairstyles of several cultures. The principle of capitalizing on a popular topic and combining it with a multicultural flavor can be applied to many other topics. Give it a try!

Promotion and Marketing

Once you have established a few programming ideas, it is essential to market these. The key to marketing any type of activity or program to young adults is repeat saturation. Remember, teens are busy with several competing interests, so don't be afraid to have several announcements of programs, multicultural or otherwise, broadcast over the radio and via school PA systems, as well as marketing through advertisements in newsletters and posters. Another effective public relations mechanism is to adapt techniques used by businesses to reach culturally diverse markets. Learn how to use images familiar to specific cultural groups you hope to reach. With such marketing, your library will convey a message about its willingness to serve cultural groups in the community.

Evaluation

Evaluation is essential to determine the success of your programs (Harrington, 111). Did they effectively meet the needs/wants of the community? Were a variety of culturally diverse programs offered? Were programs representative of the culture in question? Did they reinforce or break down stereotypes? Was the activity presented within its cultural context? Did programs offered reinforce the split between "them" and "us," or were they successful in connecting participants as members of the larger human family?

These types of questions and others relating specifically to multicultural programs offered by your library should be asked via interviews, surveys, and/or focus groups and results analyzed to determine the success of the program and what changes might be done to improve upon it.

Conclusion

There is no exact formula to follow when doing multicultural programming. The most successful programs will, however, come from those libraries familiar with their community, considerate of different cultures and accompanying cultural perspectives, and enthusiastic about the possibility of introducing young adults to cultural literatures and different ways of thinking.

Work Cited

Harrington, J. N. *Multiculturalism in Library Programming for Children.* Chicago: American Library Association, 1994.

BUILDING A MULTICULTURAL BOOK COLLECTION FOR YOUNG ADULTS: SOURCES TO CONSULT

What sources should you consult for quality multicultural collection building for a young adult collection? In fact, it is often somewhat difficult to locate books with a multicultural focus. Even more difficult to locate are *young adult* books with a multicultural focus. As a good place to start, some journals regularly review multicultural materials for young adults. These include:

American Libraries
Booklist
Bulletin of the Center for Children's Books
Catholic Library Journal
Horn Book
Kirkus Reviews
Library Journal
MultiCultural Review
School Library Journal
Voice of Youth Advocates (VOYA)

Although the majority of these reviewing sources do not contain a section specific to multicultural materials per se, they often provide a number of reviews relating to multicultural material for teenagers under the larger sections of "Fiction" or "Nonfiction." Since it is likely that you will already be using many of these sources for other types of reviews, you can also check them out for reviews to build your multicultural YA collection.

In addition to reviews found in journals, you might wish to consult other sources that are more specific to multiculturalism. These include detailed annotated bibliographies, guides and sourcebooks, articles coupled with annotated lists of multicultural books, and websites that provide lists of multicultural materials. Because such sources are so specific, they are a great source to use when building or adding to this type of collection. To help you when building your YA multicultural collection, listed below are several of these collection development tools coupled with a brief description of each.

Annotated Bibliographies

Christenbury, L., ed. *Books for You: An Annotated Booklist for Senior High Students*. Illinois: National Council of Teachers of English, 1995.

Although this bibliography discusses books relating to a wide variety of topics, an entire chapter is specifically devoted to the theme of multiculturalism. In this chapter, more than 150 titles and annotations with a multicultural focus appear. Annotations include full bibliographic information, a summary of the book, and a statement of awards the book has won. Also included in this source are author, subject, and title indexes. A truly terrific source for multicultural collection building.

Kruse, G. M. and Horning, K. T. *Multicultural Literature for Children and Young Adults: A Selected Listing of Books by and about People of Color, Volume One: 1980–1990*. Wisconsin: Cooperative Children's Book Center.

Kruse, G. M., Horning, K. T., and Shliesman, M. *Multicultural Literature for Children and Young Adults: A Selected Listing of Books by and about People of Color, Volume Two: 1991–1996*. Wisconsin: Cooperative Children's Book Center, 1997.

Together, these volumes represent a selection of children's and young adult books with a multicultural focus, published in Canada and the United States between 1980 and 1996. In these volumes, "multicultural" refers to people of color, including Africans, Afro-Caribbeans, African-Americans, American Indians, Asians, Asian Americans, Asian Pacific Peoples, and Latinos. An entire chapter is devoted to annotations of fiction for young adults. An author/title index is also included. Quite a comprehensive and useful source, particularly for libraries serving such multicultural areas.

Miller-Lachmann, L. *Our Family, Our Friends, Our World: An Annotated Guide to Significant Multicultural Books for Children and Teenagers*. New Jersey: Reed Reference Publishing, 1992.

This bibliography lists 1,038 multicultural books for children and teenagers published between 1970 and 1991. Each chapter includes an introductory section, a map of the region being highlighted, and an annotated list of books for youth from preschool to grade 12. The bibliography is also indexed by author, title/series, and subject. With almost half of the bibliography devoted to young adults and the book's detailed annotations, this is a comprehensive source to consult for collection building.

Totten, H. L. *Culturally Diverse Library Collections for Youth.* **New York: Neal-Schuman, 1996.**

Aimed specifically at librarians serving a young adult population, this annotated bibliography includes annotations for print and video collections written both for and about African Americans, Native Americans, Asian Americans, and Hispanic Americans. The bibliography is divided into five sections: four sections representing the specific ethnic groups and the last section providing annotations on multiethnic items. Materials within each section are further subdivided by genre: biographies, literature, folklore and poetry; young adult fiction; reference and critical works; and nonfiction. Author, title and subject indexes are included. Quite a comprehensive source for collection building.

Sourcebooks and Guides to Multicultural Resources

Kutzer, M. D. *Writers of Multicultural Fiction for Young Adults: A Bio-Critical Sourcebook.* **Westport, Conn.: Greenwood Press, 1996.**

An excellent reference book and collection development tool, Kutzer's compilation contains 51 alphabetically arranged entries about authors of multicultural literature for young adults. Within each entry is a biographical introduction to the author, an overview of his or her major works, a section on the critical reception of his or her works, a bibliography of the author's writings, and a selected critical bibliography. Also included in this volume is a selected bibliography of 68 works covering the theme of multicultural literature. The first part of this bibliography provides general studies, while the sections following are divided into specific cultural groups.

Muse, D., ed. *The New Press Guide to Multicultural Resources for Young Readers.* **New York: New Press, 1997.**

Although much of this source concentrates on multicultural literature and educational resources for children, a section of the guide is also devoted to young adult materials, including critical and detailed reviews of items such as novels, poetry, anthologies, and biographies. Included also is an index of authors, illustrators, titles, and ethnicities. With a third of the 1,000 reviews devoted to young adult materials, the guide is a good place to start for multicultural collection building.

Rochman, H. *Against Borders: Promoting Books for a Multicultural World.* **Chicago: American Library Association, 1993.**

In this excellent annotated bibliography, Rochman includes fiction, nonfiction, and videos for students from grades six to twelve. Part I, "Themes: Journeys Across Cultures," explores multiculturalism in a broad sense and discusses criteria for the inclusion of materials. Part II, "Resources: Going Global," is divided into three sections: Racial Oppression, Ethnic USA, and The Widening World—and it is in these sections that the annotations are placed. Included also are indices to Part I of the book as well as an author/title index. Useful to librarians not only for collection development, this source will also come in handy for multicultural programming.

Annotated Lists within Articles

Ericson, B. O. "At Home with Multicultural Adolescent Literature." *ALAN Review* **23 (1) (1995): 44–46.**

Included in this article are 24 brief annotations of current fiction for young adults that focus on the role of the home in cultures of the United States.

This is a good source to consult when adding to an already existing multicultural collection.

Hayn, J., and Sherrill, D. "Female Protagonists in Multicultural Young Adult Literature: Sources and Strategies." *ALAN Review* 24 (1) (1996): 43–46.

In addition to providing the rationale and assumptions for providing an awareness of literature featuring female protagonists or authors in a variety of multicultural contexts, Hayn and Sherrill provide annotations of 10 contemporary young adult novels with multicultural heroines.

McDonald, J. "A Multicultural Literature Bibliography." *ALAN Review* 23 (3) (1996): 13–15. Full text of this article can also be found online at: http:// scholar.lib.vt.edu/ejournals/ALAN/ spring96/toc.html

This article presents 40 items of a multicultural nature for young adults. Included are works of fiction, nonfiction, drama, short stories, and poetry which have won awards or which have been recommended by reviewers. A short bibliography, but nevertheless what is included in it is useful.

Stover, L. "A New Year's Resolution: Breaking Boundaries." *English Journal* 85 (1) (1996): 86–90.

This article includes reviews for 39 books for young adults which bring forth issues such as cultural awareness and cultural differences. Also a short, but quite useful, bibliography.

Web Sites

Although the majority of websites found on multiculturalism are simply lists—and not annotated bib-

liographies—of multicultural materials, such sites are useful if you are looking for extremely current material or if you do not have access to many of the print resources listed above. Here are just a few sites that offer a variety of culturally diverse materials for young adults:

Central Rappahannock Regional Library. (1999). *Planet CCRL: The Teens Page: A Multicultural Bibliography.* 6 December 1999. Available at: http://www.crrl.org/ teens/multi_bib.htm

This selective bibliography provides 21 annotations for young adult multicultural books. These are further subdivided according to three cultural regions: Asia, South America, and Africa. A nice feature is the labels indicating age appropriateness; however, this is a short and very selective bibliography, most useful when searching for books on the three indicated regions.

Ericson, B. (1995). *At Home with Multicultural Adolescent Literature.* 7 December 1999. Available at: http:// borg.lib.vt.edu/ejournals/ALAN/fall95/Ericson.html

This annotated list of multicultural books for YAs is available in the print *ALAN Review* (see previous page), but can also be conveniently accessed at this site.

Goldenberg, A. (1995). *Annotated Bibliography of Children's Literature Focusing on Latino People, History and Culture.* 7 December 1999. Available at: http:// latino.sscnet.ucla.edu/Latino_Bibliography.html

Lists children's literature and resources for teachers and librarians, as well as materials for young adults. Annotations include age appropriateness and a brief summary of the book. A great source to consult when collecting Latino materials.

Kaupp, P. A. (1999). *A Critical Bibliography of North American Indians for K–12.* **7 December 1999. Available at: http://nmnhwww.si.edu/anthro/outreach/Indbibl/bibliogr.html**

A comprehensive source, this bibliography of North American Indians for K–12 provides brief, yet useful annotations. Each item is furthermore labeled for age appropriateness. Supported and made possible by the Anthropology Outreach Office at the Smithsonian Institution's National Museum of Natural History, this is a highly authoritative site and one that is extremely useful when searching for YA materials relating to North American Indians.

Mele, J. (1996). *Multicultural Book Reviews for K–12 Educators.* **7 December 1999. Available at: http://www.isomedia.com/homes/jmele/homepage.html**

Although intended for educators, this site may also be useful for librarians collecting multicultural items. Reviews are brief and can be submitted by anyone. Age appropriateness is also indicated as is overall quality of the book as deemed by the reviewer.

MULTICULTURALISM IN TEEN MAGAZINES

Let us begin with a role-playing exercise: You are a visitor from the far-off planet Pluteen, allowed 15 minutes on Earth to gather information on adolescents. Unfortunately, you've landed in a junior high school on a Friday at 3:30 pm, and the place is deserted. Because your inflexible leader will not allow you to change locations without prior warning, you must make the most of materials at hand.

While you do collect some potentially useful material (a stray basketball; a Sugar Ray CD; a Tommy Jeans sweatshirt), you have almost given up hope of determining what earthling adolescents look like when, finally, you come across a stack of magazines read by teens, carelessly tossed in the corner of a classroom. There are a few fashion magazines (say, *YM*, *Twist*, and *Seventeen*), a music magazine (perhaps *Teen Machine*), a video game magazine (maybe *NextGen*) and a sports magazine (*Hockey Digest*: we are somewhere in Canada). Elated, you accumulate all the information you can about what typical teenagers look like, in order to create a report for your leader. Although you make a number of notes, your first observation is that earthling teenagers are mostly Caucasians.

The problem with many teen magazines, of course, goes far beyond the lack of representation of people from different cultures. The visitor from Pluteen will report to her leader that teens on Earth are thin, well-dressed, and perfectly groomed. These upper-middle-class creatures are especially interested in the opposite sex, celebrities, sports, music, clothes, hairstyles, video games, clothes, celebrities, clothes, celebrities, clothes . . . and so on.

Those who have worked with young adults here on Earth, of course, know that many teenagers are in fact attracted to publications that cover the above topics. According to the October 18, 1999 edition of Newsweek, the most popular magazines among the 12–15 age group in the United States are *Gamepro*; *Nintendo Power*; *Electronic Gaming Monthly*; *Sports Illustrated for Kids*; and *Sport* (for boys), and *Teen Beat*; *Superteen*; *Teen*; *All About You*; and *Twist* (for girls). Comments recently made on PUBYAC (a listserv devoted to the discussion of library services for children and young adults) echo these findings: librarians who responded to a question on popular teen magazines stated that favorite titles include *GamePro*, *Nintendo Power*, *Teen*, *Seventeen*, *Electronic Gaming Monthly*, and *Slam* (a basketball magazine).

Yet there is a need for teen publications that go beyond *Teen*- and *GamePro*-type coverage, whether by offering a non-Eurocentric perspective on topics such as looks and leisure, or by reporting on supplementary topics such as current events and social problems. One may comment, of course, that the content of magazines popular among teens is no different from the content of any other magazine: in most mainstream publications, as in society as a whole, certain ethnic groups have far more exposure and power than do other groups. In magazines for young adults, however, it is especially crucial that culturally diverse individuals be represented so as to provide positive role models for youth of various cultures.

Magazines Directed at Specific Cultural Groups

It is important for anyone working with teens, especially in multiethnic communities, to be aware of publications that are written for particular cultural groups. While the following list provides a (small) sample of what's "out there" for all ages, the magazines that interest you will likely depend on the makeup of your community.

Black Beat: As one 16-year-old put it, "If you love R&B and rap music, then Black Beat is the magazine for you" (SmartGirl Magazine Reviews).

Essence: African-American culture and celebrities; described by the manufacturer as a magazine for "the African-American woman who is looking for a rich source of useful, provocative information. . . . Each issue covers such topics as health, career, contemporary living, and family concerns as well as fashion, beauty, and fitness" (http://www.essence.com/).

People en Espanol: Like the title says—*People* magazine in Spanish.

Latina: Beauty, health, and lifestyle, from a Latin American perspective (www.latina.com).

Al Jadeeda: A weekly magazine covering a wide range of topics, including cinema, culture, the arts, fiction, science, and ecology.

Aramco World: News and commentary from Arab and Muslim worlds.

A. Magazine: Established in 1990 for English-speaking Asian Americans.

Cross-Cultural Magazines

Other magazines do not focus on any specific cultural groups, but do make an effort to include articles that relate to individuals from a variety of backgrounds.

Girl: Still a beauty and fashion magazine where everyone is beautiful, but where beautiful is also multicultural.

"Fashion for every body. Beauty for every face" (http://www.girlzine.com/).

HUES: HUES, or Hear Us Emerging Sisters, was founded in 1992 by three 19-year-old women as a "forum where women of all cultures, sizes and identities could share their experiences, insights and recipes for power" (www.hues.net).

Reluctant Hero: This Canadian publication, which is completely ad-free, is written by teen volunteers assisted by adult editors. Content is varied, but often includes articles on topics such as growing up outside the dominant culture in Canada, or trips to other countries.

Teen People: According to magazine editor Christina Ferrari, "We believe that teenage girls are eager to see a wider range of body types and ethnicities in their magazines" (Brody).

Teen Voices: Editor and founder Alison Amoroso explains the philosophy behind this teen magazine: "[W]e keep to our mission of always presenting girls with different racial backgrounds, so that no one will feel that the magazine is not for them" (Tanenbaum).

The Road Ahead

While the magazines listed here do not represent a total turnaround in publications for young adults, they do indicate that a more multicultural future for teen magazines may not be far off. Most of the periodicals listed here, of course, are geared specifically to young women. If, as the *Newsweek* statistics indicate, teen boys prefer periodicals about sports and video games (which are undoubtedly read by teen girls, too), one may wonder about the cultural images represented there. Sports magazines, in particular, reflect cultural divisions within professional sports, which in turn reflect different cultural and socioeconomic patterns in society as a whole. As more and more youth grow up with multicultural perspectives, however, there might be hope for greater diversity in the world of young adult magazines overall, as well as in the world outside of teen magazines, too.

Works Cited

Brody, Barbara. "'Mode' Creators Offer 'Girl' as Answer for Teens." *Advertising Age* 69.24 (June 15, 1998): 36+.

"Newsstands Bare of Intelligent Magazines for Teens." *Canadian Press Newswire*, January 4, 1996.

PUBYAC listserv. October 12–15, 1999.

SmartGirl Magazine Reviews. Available online: http://www.smartgirl.com/pages/magazines.html.

Tanenbaum, Leora. "What Girls Read." Online essay: http://www.tunxis.commnet.edu/tctc/faculty/gotowka/psywomen/readings/whatgirlsread.html.

MULTICULTURAL MOVIES: USING FILMS TO ENGAGE YAS IN CULTURAL DISCUSSION

In "Growing Up, Reaching Out: Multiculturalism through Young Adult Literature and Films," Gretchen Schwarz builds on Hazel Rochman's thematic approach to structuring young adult book promotion, and suggests ways that themes such as "the costs of racism" and "caught between cultures" (41) can form the basis of multicultural units in the classroom. Specifically, Schwarz recommends ways that teachers can construct units that make use of not only books but also films to introduce multicultural topics. She writes: "Multicultural units across the curriculum . . . can draw on a rich, largely untapped resource for the multicultural classroom: feature films, both American and foreign. Multimedia approaches increase student engagement" (41).

The use of films is also an excellent way to engage young adults in library programs. Using Schwarz's model for organizing multicultural units in the classroom, I will examine how public libraries can make films the starting point for young adult involvement in both local and global cultural communities.

Even in this electronic age, films are able to affect teenagers in a way that few other media can: movies are immediate and powerful (Foster, 14). Although most teenagers watch movies for entertainment, the stories that unfold on screen also provide adolescents with information on any number of real-life topics. Indeed, when it comes to social interaction and societal issues, many adolescents probably get more information from movies than they do from books, or even from the Internet. Further, unlike other popular forms of YA entertainment, such as video games or web sites, films are ideally suited to be enjoyed by a number of individuals at once, and thus are perfect for sparking group discussion on potentially sensitive cultural issues.

How to Use Films Effectively

Tracey Jones, Branch Manager and Youth Services Librarian of the Halifax North Memorial Public Library in Halifax, Nova Scotia, affirms that movies,

particularly those that explore issues that are already important in adolescents' lives, can comprise a strong starting point for young adult programming in a multicultural community. Even in mono-cultural environments, however, films may be used to help young adults transcend their individual concerns and examine larger questions that may be socially, geographically, or historically removed from their daily lives (Schwarz, 40).

While a film program will likely be more successful if the person in charge of designing it customizes movie selections to best suit the interests of the YAs for which it is intended, here are a couple of suggestions that might be employed to explore multicultural themes.

Movie: Malcolm X (1992)

At Halifax's North Branch Library, the viewing of this Spike Lee film was a popular event. With Denzel Washington playing Malcolm X, this movie follows the famous civil-rights leader on the streets, in prison, in religion, and in politics.

Related Resources

* *I Know Why the Caged Bird Sings* by Maya Angelou (Bantam Books, 1983): An autobiographical account of Angelou's rocky road through personal tragedies and racial politics, told in exquisitely poetic language.
* *Black Ice* by Lorene Cary (Vintage Books, 1992): Another perceptive autobiographical work, this one about the author's attempts to be a success but not a sellout at a prestigious private school.
* *Freedom's Children: Young Civil Rights Activists Tell Their Own Stories,* edited by Ellen Levine

(Harper, 1995): This collection tells the stories of African American children and young adults involved in the civil-rights movement.

Movie: Smoke Signals (1998)

This 1998 release, which was the first feature film entirely made by a Native American crew, features characters who seem altogether human and believable. Two young men from an Idaho reservation, Victor and Thomas, travel to Phoenix to retrieve the ashes of Victor's father—and work through the legacies they have gained from past generations along the way.

Related Resources

* *The Lone Ranger and Tonto Fistfight in Heaven* by Sherman Alexie (HarperPerennial Library, 1994): The collection of short stories which inspired *Smoke Signals* deals with both tradition and the present on the Spokane Indian Reservation.
* *Rising Voices: Writings of Young Native Americans* by Arlene B. Hirschfelder, Beverly R. Singer (Ivy Books, 1992): Young adults write essays and poems on identity, community, and a plethora of other issues relating to growing up Native American.
* *Bone Dance* by Martha Brooks (Bantam Books, 1999): This American Library Association "Best Book for Young Adults" introduces readers to city girl Alexandra Sinclair and prairie boy Lonny LaFreniere, who are connected through a tract of land, past sorrows, and a Native heritage.

It might not be wise to make use of too many resources at a film session. Instead, one might opt to introduce related materials in a kind of mini booktalk format, so that participants will be aware of related materials, but not feel overwhelmed by too many sources of information. Resources may instead be arranged in a library display that promotes the issue under consideration as well as the library's movie programming efforts.

Also, instead of designing film discussion programs around one specific cultural group, YA librarians and educators may find that using the thematic organization advocated by Rochman and Schwarz will provoke more valuable YA discussion of cultural, racial, or ethnic issues. That is, using a theme-based approach can help highlight that cultural conflict (as well as cultural concord) is not specific to any groups or location, but rather a widespread phenomenon that deserves the attention of all cultural groups. The overarching topic one uses to begin discussion need not even be focussed explicitly on racial issues; instead, one may structure debate around broader issues such as "freedom" or "identity, unity, and individuality."

Some Challenges

Sparking Interest   Some of the difficulties that may arise in the process of developing a YA program based on film are the very same problems that may occur in any attempt at youth programming. One important factor is appeal to YAs. In the classroom, of course, teachers face the task of increasing students' interest in the topic at hand. In a library, however, the challenge may be first of all to bring in young adults, if comparable activities are not already a part of the library's YA services, or if no YA services exist at all. As Tracey Jones of the Halifax North Memorial Public Library explains, teens will not necessarily be interested in a program with a specifically cultural focus, even if popular movies are involved. Although it is true that "[m]ulticultural stories can offer the young adult a perspective that expands beyond familiar personal interests to the lives and problems of those marginalized in our own society, to the experiences and issues of young people in other parts of the world, to past human struggles that influence the present" (Schwarz, 40), one cannot take for granted the success of a program simply because it attempts to broaden perspectives or spark valuable cultural or cross-cultural discussion.

As with all library programming, Jones stresses the value of speaking with community members before commencing any particular activity. In her own experiences in her community, Jones found that even young adults who were not open to explicitly culture-based sessions were indeed interested in movie sessions that engaged them in discussions of topics, such as the media or celebrities, that were of greater interest to them. These topics could be related to multiculturalism in discussions of issues such as representation of cultural groups in the media.

Careful Preparation   Eileen Oliver describes an instance where a lack of classroom planning on multicultural issues led to an unfavorable and uncomfortable situation:

> Last year in a nearby high school, a very unpleasant situation occurred as a result of what I will call "multicultural backlash." In the English department's zeal to infuse its curriculum with diverse literature, an unfortunate scenario was created that all of us interested in teaching multicultural literature should recognize. It seems that one of the instructors introduced a Toni Morrison excerpt with very little in the way of curricular planning beyond the significance of symbolism and language choice.
>
> What occurred, then, was a misrepresentation of "the message" that students were to receive. Not only did the European American students misinterpret the text, but also, according to the half dozen students of color in the class, the instructor was ill-equipped to handle the discussion and those in the minority felt victimized. As a result, feelings were hurt, accusations were made, and no one found the experience a positive one in any way. (57)

In the design of any session that will address cultural concerns, then, it is even more important than usual to plan, plan, plan. In fact, it would do well to seek the help of qualified partners such as social workers or multicultural coordinators. Best of all, if possible, one could contact members of different cultural communities directly. Even if one lives in a relatively homogeneous region, it helps to consult various cultural organizations, many of which are accessible via the web.

Licensing Issues   Tracey Jones was careful to explain that, even when the beginnings of a thriving YA movie program is in place, it is not always simple to keep the project going. In particular, licensing problems may present obstacles to a successful undertaking: a library, since it is a public facility, cannot show a movie for which it does not have public performance rights.

Since obtaining public performance rights is not always feasible for cash-strapped public libraries, another option is to consult with the department of education, for a list of video resources available for educational purposes. One should not simply assume that YAs will only be interested in Hollywood-style feature films. At Halifax's North Branch Library, for example, the showing of the National Film Board's *Speak It! From The Heart of Black Nova Scotia* proved to be a well-received and thought-provoking event, since the film deals with a very local issue: the experiences of Black students in a predominantly white school environment. Of course, not all educational documentaries are equally valuable; it is important to screen any film before presenting it to YAs, in order to judge whether it is simply too out-of-date or otherwise unsuited for serious consideration by young adults.

Conclusion: Go Ahead and Do It!

Although there may seem to be many things that can go wrong with YA movie programs, there are many more things that can go right! Don't be afraid to ask young adults about the films they are interested in, and try to work those into an entertaining yet enlightening video session. Remember, movies provide an effective means of engaging teens, whatever their culture.

Works Cited

Foster, Harold M. "Film and the Young Adult Novel." *The ALAN Review* 21.3 (Spring 1994): 14–17.

Oliver, Eileen I. "Taking Responsibility for What We Teach." *The ALAN Review* 25.3 (Spring 1998): 57–60.

Schwarz, Gretchen. "Growing Up, Reaching Out: Multiculturalism through Young Adult Literature and Films." *The ALAN Review* 22.3 (Spring 1995): 40–42.

Wright, Alaina. *Multicultural Education Resource List.* N.p.: Department of Education and Culture [Nova Scotia]: 1996

WORLD MUSIC: GATEWAY TO THE GLOBE

Right about now you may be asking yourself, "So what is world music anyway?" World Music, to put it plainly, is exactly what it sounds like. It is music from around the world. It is sounds and instruments that reflect varied geographic areas. World music combines the structure and elements fundamental to all music with instruments and vocals that reflect the society or culture that created them. The concept of World Music is little more than a decade old. "The name was dreamed up in 1987 by the heads of a number of small London-based record labels who found their releases for African, Latin American and other international artists were not finding rack space because record stores had no obvious place to put them. And so the world music tag was hit upon, initially as a month-long marketing campaign to impress on the music shops, the critics and the buyers that here were sounds worth listening to" (Ellingham, Introduction). The term World Music stuck, and is still used a decade later, along with new terms like Roots Music, International Music, and Global Music.

As far as we know, every culture celebrates some form of music. It is a fundamental part of life that brings us joy and fulfillment. It is fused with our culture and represents who we are. Even though the interpretation of music varies from culture to culture, and even within our own culture from generation to generation, it is a global tradition full of splendour and vitality. Imagine a world without music. It is almost impossible, if not painful, to contemplate. Think about all the important roles music plays in our lives. We use music as background noise, we use music to sell products, we use music to keep us company and sometimes, to comfort us. Music is an instrument of religion, spirituality, entertainment, and pleasure.

Thanks to improvements in technology in recent decades we are now able to hear music, not only from our own culture, but around the globe. Listening to music from other cultures gives us an insight into life in other parts of the world. The wonderful thing about music is that it is universal. We may not all speak the same language, but we all share a love of music and we all share similar elements within our music. Music is composed of melody, harmony, and rhythm, combined with musical instruments and vocals, whether it is created in Ecuador or India.

World Music is ever evolving to include progressive music within individual cultures and a fusion of music between cultures. "Music-cultures, especially today, are dynamic rather than static; they are constantly changing in response to inside and outside pressures. It would be wrong to think of a music-culture as something isolated and stable, impenetrable and uninfluenced by the outside world. A conglomeration of music-cultures is taking place all over the world" (Titon, 13). This conglomeration of music-cultures combined with traditional and progressive music from within individual cultures creates a wide array of World Music to choose from. Not only is World Music available, but resources surrounding the World Music topic are plentiful, including web sites, books, magazines, and compilation CDs. All of these items make it easier for the new listener to discover and enjoy music from around the globe.

Traditionally the content of music in libraries and in the school curriculum has been based on a single culture. Thanks to increased interest and technological improvements we now have an abundance of music to choose from, to enjoy, learn from, and share with young adults.

World Music can be incorporated into the library on its own, or in conjunction with other multicultural programming. On its own, World Music can be highlighted by creating displays about radio shows or artists. These displays can be supported with quality World Music CDs and reference materials. As part of your overall multicultural programming World Music can be used as a complement to programming involving multicultural films, guest speakers, book talks, and holiday celebrations or shows. There are a variety of sources to choose from when exploring World Music. The following information lists a number of resources to start with when building a World Music collection.

Works Cited

Ellingham, Mark, ed. *World Music: The Rough Guide.* 2nd ed. London: Penguin Books, 1999.

Titon, Jeff Todd, ed. *Worlds of Music: An Introduction to the Music of the World's Peoples.* New York: Schirmer Books, 1996.

World Music: Resources

Compact Discs

Songs from around the World. Rhino Records
All Over the Map. Uni / Rounder

The Best of Global Celebration. Ellipsis Arts
The Rough Guide Music Sampler. World Music Network
World Playground. Putumayo World Music

Web Sites

World Music Charts Europe, http://www.welt-musik.de/charts/main.htm

International Music Archives, http://www.eyeneer.com/World/index.html. *An educational resource providing information about music from around the world*

New Native, http://www.wcpworld.com/native/sounds.htm. *World Café Production's page about traditional music in world cultures and the evolution of music from around the world. Links to record labels and traditional and contemporary world music sites*

Books

Ellingham, Mark, ed. *World Music: The Rough Guide.* 2nd ed. London: Penguin Books, 1999.

May, Elizabeth, ed. *Music of Many Cultures: An Introduction.* Los Angeles: University of California Press, 1983.

Nettl, Bruno, ed. *Excursions in World Music.* New York: Prentice Hall, 1996.

Titon, Jeff Todd, ed. *Worlds of Music: An Introduction to the Music of the World's Peoples.* New York: Schirmer Books, 1996.

SEASONAL CELEBRATIONS: A LIST OF HOLIDAYS CELEBRATED AROUND THE GLOBE IN SPRING, SUMMER, FALL, AND WINTER

Spring
Easter—March or April
Passover—Begins between March 27th and April 4th

Earth Day—April 22nd
South African Freedom Day—April 27th
Mother's Day—May
Buddha's Birthday—May
Children's Day—May 5th
Cinco de Mayo—May 5th

Summer
Father's Day—June
Summer Solstice (Northern Hemisphere)—June 21st through June 22nd
Winter Solstice (Southern Hemisphere)—June 21st through June 22nd
Canada Day—July 1st
American Independence Day—July 4th
Bastille Day—July 14th
Prophet Mohamed's Birthday—August

Fall
Rosh ha-Shanah—September/October
Yom Kippur—September/October
Respect for the Aged Day: Japan—September 5th
Mexican Independence Day—September 16th
Halloween—October 31st
All Saints Day—November 1st
Day of the Dead—November 1st
Traditions Day: Argentina—November 10th
Hanukkah—Falls between November 25th and December 26th

Winter
St. Nicholas Day—December 5th
Winter Solstice—December 22nd
Winter Solstice (Northern Hemisphere)—December 21st through 22nd
Summer Solstice (Southern Hemisphere)—December 21st through 22nd

Christmas—December 25th

Boxing Day—December 26th

Kwanza—December 26th through January 1st

New Year's Day—January 1

Chinese New Year—Late January/February

Valentine's Day—February 14th

Ramadan—Because it occurs at the start of the ninth month of the Islamic calendar, Ramadan moves throughout the years, occurring within each season over time.

HOLIDAYS AND FESTIVALS AROUND THE WORLD

Every day varied celebrations take place around the world. These celebrations are grounded in folklore, religion, thoughtful reflection, or celebratory commemoration. To exemplify the number and variety of celebrations and holidays that take place across the globe daily, we will look at one day of the year, May 5, and consider the diverse celebrations that take place on this day alone. Some suggestions for incorporating diverse holidays and festivals into your library's programming will follow a quick look at four distinct holidays that fall on May 5th each year.

May 5th: A Day in the Year of Celebration— Cinco de Mayo: Mexico

Cinco de Mayo is a national holiday in Mexico celebrating the battle of Puebla that took place on May 5, 1862. In this battle, an unlikely group of outnumbered soldiers and peasants were victorious over invading French forces. Although the battle on Cinco de Mayo was only a minor setback for the French troops, it gave the Mexicans the confidence that they needed to persist until their eventual victory over the French on April 2, 1867. Today *Cinco de Mayo* is primarily a regional holiday celebrated in the state of Puebla in Mexico, but it is also celebrated in other parts of Mexico and in North American cities with significant Mexican populations. The Cinco de Mayo celebration includes parades, parties, speeches and festivities.

Dutch Liberation Day: The Netherlands

Dutch Liberation Day commemorates the day on which Nazi forces were driven out of Holland by the Allies in 1945. Holland had been occupied by Nazi forces since 1940. Many Dutch cities hold military parades and special concerts on this day. A special commemorative service is held in Amsterdam's Dam Square each year.

Kodomo-no-Hi /Children's Day: Japan

Children's Day originated as Boy's Day in the ninth century. The holiday became Children's Day in 1948 and is a national holiday celebrated throughout Japan on the fifth day of the fifth month of each year. The holiday is observed with large family picnics and parties. It is a day on which to celebrate the good health and happiness of children. Families take part in the tradition by hanging *koinobor* (wind socks shaped like carps) from flagpoles outside of their houses. Generally, only families with boys partake in the *koinobori* tradition. Girls have their own special day which is celebrated on the third day of the third month (March 3rd) of each year. Children's Day is part of *Hakata Dontaku* (Golden Week) in Japan.

Hakata Dontaku/Golden Week: Japan

Hakata Dontaku, or Golden Week, is the largest festival in Japan. Golden Week includes Children's Day, Constitution Day, and Holiday for a Nation. "The festival originated in the *Morumachi* Period (1333–1568) as a procession of the merchants of Hakata, an old section of Fukuoka City, paying their new year visit to the *daimyo*, or feudal lord. The festival's highlight is a three-hour parade with legendary gods on horseback, floats and musicians playing samisens (a three-stringed instrument similar to a guitar), flutes and drums" (Carlson, 131).

Napoleon's Day: France

Napoleon was "one of the most celebrated individuals in European history and still has many admirers. Napoleon is best known for the zeal with which he pursued the military expansion of France and for his reforms, which left a lasting mark on the judicial, financial, administrative, and educational institutions of not only France, but much of western Europe" (Carlson, 218). Napoleon died on May 5th, 1821, at the age of 51. His remains were taken to Paris for a grand funeral. In Paris, he was entombed under the gold-plated dome of the Church of Saint-Louis. On May fifth of each year his enthusiasts congregate at the site of his tomb to take part in a commemorative ceremony.

HOLIDAYS AND FESTIVALS IN YA PROGRAMMING

It is evident that each day of the year provides great cause for celebration, but how does one incorporate this into library programming? The number of holidays on each day of the year yields an opportunity to examine and celebrate one particular culture or to incorporate a number of worldwide holidays into a celebration of cultural diversity. If one single holiday is focused on, it could be used in conjunction with other multicultural programming. For example, the Japanese holiday *Kodomo-no-Hi* could be commemorated by giving craft lessons in origami, sampling traditional Japanese food, and providing entertainment. Or it could simply be an overall celebration of the joys of youth; something that may very well be appreciated by YAs who are so often incorrectly targeted as troublemakers or nuisances in public places. The librarian could also take this opportunity to book talk several books involving Japanese themes. This opportunity should also be embraced as a way to explore several aspects of this particular culture. The holiday of *Kodomo-no-Hi* could be incorporated into other library programmes involving films, music, and other resources in Japanese culture.

World holidays and celebrations could also be used to promote an international day of celebration. Young adults from the local community could be invited to share their traditional foods, music, and dress. Each individual could bring an item representing his or her culture. The day would be a celebration of all cultures, with a variety of music, possibly guest speakers, and tradition dancers or dance lessons. Naturally, all of these events could be combined with cross-cultural book displays and book talks.

Some Precautions to Consider

When planning holiday programming take care to find out the true background and current traditions for each holiday. An example of a holiday that has grown and changed from its inception is *Cinco de Mayo*. *Cinco de Mayo* began as a relatively small regional holiday, but has developed into a significant North American holiday, due partly to commercial interests in the United States. As an author on the Kidlink Multicultural Calendar states, "You will find though that in Mexico and amongst many Mexican nationals this celebration is not half as important as the 16 de septembre celebration of independence. We have in the U.S. changed the significance of the day" (Berthoin-Hernandez). Avoiding misinterpretation of the significance of holidays could be accomplished by communicating with local community or social organizations and, if possible, by asking YAs of varied cultural backgrounds to assist in programming.

Also take care to avoid the exclusion of other cultures by celebrating individual holidays of particular cultural or ethnic groups. In order to avoid feelings of alienation consider having an international day on which to celebrate various world-wide celebrations.

As with any YA programming, there is also the challenge of appealing to YAs. A good start for an international celebration is to talk to young adults and find out what cultures they are interested in before planning begins. Perhaps they are interested in sharing some traditions from their own culture. If so, get them involved by asking them to assist in the planning of holiday festivities or an international day.

Works Cited

Berthoin-Hernandez, D. *Cinco de Mayo—Mexico: A Page from the KIDPROJ Multi-Cultural Calendar* http://www.kidlink.org/KIDPROJ/MCC/mcc0317.html.

Carlson, Barbara, and Sue Thompson, eds. *Holidays, Festivals, and Celebrations of the World Dictionary.* Detroit: Omnigraphics, 1994.

For Your Consideration

The holidays noted in this article, as well as those in the Seasonal Celebrations list, are by no means exhaustive. They are a beginning point; an enticement into the world of holidays and celebrations. To expand this list of holidays and enjoy all there is to learn about the celebrations of the world, please consult the resources listed below.

Angell, Carole S. *Celebrations Around the World.* Golden: Fulcrum Publishing, 1996.

A daybook of holidays and celebrations around the world www.earthcalendar.net

Holidays around the world for grades K–12 http://falcon.jmu.edu/~ramseyil/holidays.htm

An exhaustive monthly list of international holidays http://www.rubicon.com/passport/holidays/199905.htm

Valuing Our Differences: Celebrating Diversity. A calendar of holidays from the University of Kansas http://www3.kumc.edu/diversity/

Kidlink Multicultural Calendar http://www.kidlink.org/KIDPROJ/MCC/

Earth Calendar: Searchable by date, country and religion http://earthcalendar.webjump.com/

Official List of Bank Holidays www.national-holidays.com/

Annual Calendar of Japanese Holidays http://www.jinjapan.org/kidsweb/calendar/calandar.html

CONNECTING WITH OTHER CULTURES THROUGH MULTICULTURAL ORGANIZATIONS

In the Local Community

Every community has different organizations, agencies, and associations that may provide reliable multicultural information. To get in touch with these organizations, a good place to start is the local department of education. In Nova Scotia, for example, the Department of Education and Culture publishes guides such as *Community Resources for Multicultural/Anti-Racism Education* to help teachers contact relevant organizations and develop culturally sensitive curricula. Organizations listed in this guide include the African Canadian Education Project (ACEP), the Arab Canadian Association of the Atlantic Provinces, the Armenian Cultural Association of the Atlantic Provinces (ACA-AP), the Atlantic Jewish Council, the Atlantic Multicultural Council, the Confederacy of Mainland Micmacs (CMM), the Fédération Acadienne de la Nouvelle-Écosse (FANE), the Indo-Canadian Association of Nova Scotia, the Metropolitan Immigrant Settlement Association, and the Nova Scotia Gambia Association, to name but a few.

Of course, multicultural organizations and associations often do not have branches in small rural areas. There is no reason, however, why interested teens in rural communities may not contact province-, state-, or even nation-wide organizations to obtain information on a specific cultural topic, or perhaps even to begin a local branch. Many cultural organizations even have distinct youth branches. The Fédération Acadienne de la Nouvelle-Écosse (the Acadian Federation of Nova Scotia), for example, oversees the Conseil Jeunesse Provincial, a provincial youth advisory board for francophone young adults in Nova Scotia.

Remember that many cultural associations may be valuable as providers of not only helpful print resources but also reliable Internet information. In addition, some cultural organizations may volunteer guest speakers or performers for educational programs. Make contacts with multicultural associations in your part of the world!

On the World Wide Web

The Internet is an invaluable resource for introducing YAs to cultural organizations, both large and small, throughout the rest of the world. Here are just a few web sites that may be of interest to young and old alike. While not all organizations listed are multicultural groups per se, they all promote cultural pluralism and awareness.

International Links

Global Youth Village (An exciting—albeit pricey—summer program where youth can gain skills on development issues, prejudice, peace building, and community action.)

http://www.legacyintl.org/gyvhome.htm

InfoNation (An easy-to-use database that allows you to view the most up-to-date data for the Member States of the United Nations.)

http://www.un.org/Pubs/CyberSchoolBus/infonation/e_infonation.htm

The Multicultural Pavilion ("Resources and Dialogues for Educators, Students, and Activists")

http://curry.edschool.Virginia.edu/go/multicultural/

New Internationalist (From the print magazine of the same name, a guide to world issues. See especially the "Teaching Global Issues" section.)

http://www.oneworld.org/ni/index4.html

One World (Disseminating development information to promote global understanding.)

http://www.oneworld.org

United Nations Web Site
    http://www.un.org

UN CyberSchoolBus (Promoting education about international issues and the United Nations.)
    http://www.un.org/Pubs/CyberSchoolBus/index.html

UNESCO (United Nations Educational, Scientific and Cultural Organization)
    http://www.unesco.org/

Youth in Action Network (Connect with students from around the world to discuss important issues; although a public forum, users must register.)
    http://www.mightymedia.com/act/

Youth against Racism (Teaching people effective means of combating racism.)
    http://WWW.EDnet.NS.Ca/educ/school-pages/yar/

Other Places to Find Resources (Links to Links)

Multicultural Organizations from DiversitySearch.com
    http://www.diversitysearch.com/multicultural.html

Multicultural Organization Links from the Multicultural Pavilion
    http://curry.edschool.Virginia.edu/go/multicultural/sites/orgsites.html

Multicultural Association of Nova Scotia Links
    http://www.mans.ns.ca/links.html

Book Reviews

Richter, H. P. *I Was There*. New York: Holt, Rinehart and Winston, 1972.

Hitler has risen to power and children throughout Germany are joining the Hitler Youth movement. Eight years old in 1933, the narrator is fascinated by the power of the older boys in the movement, especially his friend Heinz, and is eager to join. When the narrator joins as a *Pimpf*—the youngest members of the Hitler Youth—Heinz mentors and kindly watches over him. Gunther, another friend of the narrator, is not so enthusiastic about joining the movement however. In fact, in 1935 at only ten years old, Gunther's opposition to the principles upheld by the Hitler Youth and Nazism as a whole is strong.

Gunther is finally forced to participate in the movement only because of pressures put on him by his family, friends and the Reich itself. But, even so, Gunther refuses to torment the Jewish people, and he never comes to believe in the Hitler Youth movement. Even Heinz, although the leader of his Hitler Youth unit, questions life and practices under Nazi rule, as does the narrator.

From 1933 to 1943, together the boys experience frenzied Hitler parades, badge selling, tormenting (and refusing to torment) Jews, preliminary training, and, finally, firsthand experience with war itself. Weaving together these experiences with complex characters struggling for truth, *I Was There* gives an autobiographical account of shared experience under Nazi rule. It provides an authoritative and intimate glimpse into the response of young German people to Nazism during this period and offers an honest and compelling read to young adult readers of any culture. Highly recommended.

Paterson, Katherine. *Of Nightingales That Weep.* New York: Harper & Row, 1974.

Dwelling in a world of royalty and honor, Takiko, the daughter of a samurai, never weeps. When her warrior father is killed however, Takiko finds this a difficult rule to follow, especially after her mother marries an ugly country potter. Eager to escape her country dwelling and return to royalty, Takiko goes to work at the Japanese imperial court. Her talent on the musical instrument called the koto is quickly discovered, as is her beauty, by a handsome young man, Hideo, who is also an enemy spy. As war breaks out between two warrior clans—the Heike, of which Takiko is part, and the Genji, of which Hideo is part—Takiko flees the court and embarks upon a struggle between loyalty to her people and love for Hideo. In a story of self-discovery and loyalty, Takiko discovers that her choice is ultimately tied to her samurai honor. Rich in culture and history as well as all absorbing, this book is highly recommended for any young adult.

Carlson, Lori M. *Cool Salsa: Bilingual Poems on Growing Up Latino in the United States.* New York: Henry Holt, 1994.

This profound collection of poems by 29 Latin American poets brings to life the vivid details of growing up Latino in the United States. These poems resonate with the difficulty of grasping two cultures and two languages at once and of attempting to fit into two worlds. The editor, Lori M. Carlson, brings together poems of struggle, celebration, and pride; poems that deliver emotional conflict, sweet reminiscence, and true emotions of joy and strife; of family and independence. An excellent introduction by Carlos Hijuelos and skilful translations are just two of the noteworthy aspects of this book of poems. The poets themselves (as E. J. Vega's poem shows) bring to life vivid images of the tastes, sounds, smells, and surroundings of Latin American life.

> According to my sketch,
> Rows of lemon & mango
> Trees frame the courtyard
> Of Grandfather's stone
> And clapboard home;
> The shadow of a palomino
> Gallops on the lip
> Of the horizon.

This compilation generously includes both Spanish and English versions of each poem. This feature reflects how the poets are expressing themselves with two sides of their spirit. This is a joy for the reader of both Spanish and English as we are able to simultaneously experience both cultures and follow the poets as they shift back and forth between American and Latino life.

Miklowitz, Gloria D. *The War Between the Classes.* New York: Laurel Leaf, 1985.

Only when their roles are reversed and the colour of their armband determines their social class did the students in Mr. Otero's social studies start to become aware of the prejudices and discriminatory practices that are so evident for ethnic-minorities every day. For the most part, minority students get higher social status armbands while the white, rich kids become the underprivileged class.

Amy is torn apart. As a Japanese-American girl, she is soon one of the most privileged in her class; but her boyfriend Adam is at the bottom of the barrel and the game prohibits their seeing one another. Not only that, but Amy tries to make peace in her family, as her parents do not approve of her non-Japanese sister-in-law. In effort to prove her teacher, peers, and parents wrong, she sets out on a campaign to break down the barriers of discrimination.

This is an excellent book that examines the depth of racism and discrimination in society.

Paton, Alan. *Cry, the Beloved Country.* New York: Charles Scribner's Sons, 1948.

In contrast to the beautiful scenery described in the opening paragraphs, Paton's tragic novel portrays the divisive struggle of Blacks in White-dominated South Africa in the days of apartheid.

Steven Kumalo leaves his serene country home for the city of Johannesburg in search of his son, who left for the city some time ago and has not sent word of his whereabouts. His journey leads him to several new friends and dusty, poor townships until he hears the news that his son was involved in the murder of a white man, the son of a prominent landowner from Kumalo's same region.

The dead man's last written words echo the sentiments of the book: *"We believe in help for the underdog, but we want him to stay under"*; in this light, Kumalo's son can be seen as a victim of circumstance. While his father mourns his son's choices, he takes steps to rebuild after returning home to his luscious rural community in the valley of the Umzimkulu. In this moving novel, Paton explores the historical, social, economic, and institutional divisions that were built in the era of apartheid.

Hirschfelder, Arlene B. and Beverly R. Singer, eds. *Rising Voices: Writings of Young Native Americans.* New York: Ivy Books, 1992.

I am an Indian in a confusing
  world,
In a world that won't let me
  be free.
Oh, how I long for my
  freedom.

These lines from the poem "Longing," written by a

twelfth-grade Choctaw-Chickasaw student in the late 1970s, may perhaps encapsulate the spirit of this collection of poems and essays better than any outsider's review of the work. Indeed, it is only by reading through the 60+ pieces in this anthology that one may begin to perceive the traditions, aspirations, and realities that make up the lives of its young writers. The collection, divided into sections on Identity, Family, Homelands, Ritual and Ceremony, Education, and Harsh Realities, covers everything from oppression to grandfathers, from struggles to chili, with authenticity.

With unclouded observations from Native American youth from the late 19th century to 1990, this book is as suited to the history or social studies classroom as it is to an English curriculum. At times gritty and at times reverential, this work, is above all, always honest.

Appendix

Updated List of Resources

Since the original publication of these issues of the *YA Hotline*, many new resources have become available, most notably electronic ones. This appendix lists some current electronic sources of information to supplement the resources identified in the body of the text.

CHAPTER 1: EATING DISORDERS

My thanks to Heather Hamilton, youth services librarian at the Halifax Regional Library, for her help in preparing this resource list.

The National Eating Disorder Information Centre
http://www.nedic.on.ca/default.html

Canadian information, resources, glossary of eating disorders, Q&A, and more. The site also con-tains a comprehensive list of nonfiction and self-help titles for adults, teens, and children.

Body Positive
http://www.bodypositive.com

A useful site for information and suggestions on building self esteem.

Resources and links related to body image
http://depts.washington.edu/ecttp/nutrition/imageframe2.htm

A U.S. government site for teen body issues and eating disorders. This is an excellent portal to other reliable information sources.

Reading Rants
http://tln.lib.mi.us/~amutch/jen/bones.htm

This is a book list on eating disorders, including detailed reviews.

CHAPTER 2: IS EARTH WOMAN DOOMED?

The InSite

http://www.talkcity.com/theinsite/index.html

This site is a great portal to all kinds of environmental information.

The Scorecard

http://www.scorecard.org

The Scorecard site allows you to enter your zip-code to find out the major polluters in your community (in the continental United States only). This site is maintained by the Environmental Defense Fund.

The Action Center

http://www.actionpa.org

The Activists' Center for Training in Organizing and Networking contains lots of suggestions for environmental action which would be useful in any location.

The David Suzuki Foundation

http://www.davidsuzuki.org

Greenpeace

http://www.greenpeace.org

For those who want to learn more about the original "environmental warriors."

World Wildlife Federation

http://www.wwf.org

This site contains a wealth of information about endangered species worldwide.

CHAPTER 3: SCARED STIFF

All Horror Pages

http://www.geocities.com/Hollywood/Bungalow/7586/home.html

A wealth of up-to-date information on books, movies, television shows, and games, in addition to many links to related sites.

The Cabinet of Dr. Casey

http://members.tripod.com/lestatspage/literature.html

A broad-based investigation of horror in literature, film, theatre, comic books, and games.

Dark Echo

http://www.darkecho.com

Interviews with authors of horror fiction.

Gothic Net

http://www.gothic.net

Interviews, book reviews, and original stories plus lots of links to related sites.

Pathway to Darkness

http://www.pathwaytodarkness.com

A site entirely devoted to vampires.

CHAPTER 4: FEATURING COMICS AND GRAPHIC NOVELS

Marvel Comics Online

http://www.marvel.com/

This site contains a listing of TV shows, a guide to the new comics, and weekly cybercomics.

The Marvel Chronology Project

http://www.chronologyproject.com

The Marvel Chronology Project aims to catalogue every appearance by every Marvel Comics character and put them in chronological order.

Reading Rants

http://tln.lib.mi.us/~amutch/jen/graphic.htm

An annotated list of graphic novels.

Graphic Novels in Libraries Listserv

http://topica/com/lists/GNLIB-L

Of course, anyone with an interest in graphic novels should read Kat Kan's column in *VOYA* for reviews and an ongoing discussion of new trends and old favorites.

CHAPTER 5: IN SEARCH OF SCIENCE FICTION

Out of This World: Canadian Science Fiction and Fantasy

http://www.nlc-bnc.ca/events/sci-fi/esci-fi.htm

This site, published by the National Library of Canada, lists Canadian science fiction resources.

SF Canada

http://www.sfcanada.ca

This site is produced by an association of Canadian writers working in the fields of science fiction, fantasy, and horror.

Prix Aurora Awards

http://www.sentex.net/~dmullin/aurora

This site is produced by the Canadian Science Fiction and Fantasy Association. The Aurora Award is given annually to the best Canadian work of science fiction or fantasy.

CHAPTER 6: TEENS ON THE INFOBAHN

CNET: HTML for Beginners

http://www.cnet.com/

This site provides easy, step-by-step instructions to help you design your own Web page.

Geocities

http://geocities.yahoo.com/home/

This site provides free home pages and easy-to-follow instructions on how to create one.

Homestead

http://www.homestead.com

This is a virtual teen community and offers free Web pages that were built in four minutes.

HTML Goodies

http://htmlgoodies.earthweb.com

This site contains hundreds of tutorials on Web page design.

CHAPTER 7: YOUTH AND ATHLETICS

Fantasy Sports Guide

http://www.fantasysportsguide.com

This site allows you to create your own dream sports team.

Just Sports for Women

http://www.sportsforwomen.com/

This site is devoted to news and features about women in sports. You can participate in discussions or post your questions about women and sports.

Sport! Science

http://www.exploratorium.edu/sports/index.html

This site answers a wide range of questions about sports and science.

Ringette Canada

http://www.ringette.ca

The official Web site for Canadian Ringette.

CHAPTER 8: CARS

Alcohol: The Deadliest Drug

http://library.thinkquest.org/10885

This site, designed by students, aims to promote education about alcohol abuse.

Just One Night

http://www.pbs.org/justone

This site, produced by PBS, investigates drinking and driving, and alcohol and the law.

Kelley Blue Book

http://www.kbb.com

This site lists new and used car prices plus answers to FAQs about buying a car.

National Highway Traffic Safety Association

http://www.nhtsa.dot.gov

This site, maintained by the NHTSA, includes safety tips for safe driving as well as statistics on accidents.

Teen New Drivers Homepage

http://www.teendriving.com

This site was designed by a teen. It includes tips as well as links to other driver information sites.

CHAPTER 9: WITCHCRAFT

Omphalos: The Directory and Search Engine for Witchcraft and Paganism

http://www.omphalos.net/directory/wicca_and_witchcraft

This comprehensive search engine covers authors, covens, and the history and traditions of witchcraft. It is a portal to hundreds of related sites.

About Wicca

http://www.aboutwicca.com

This site provides information about witchcraft, rituals, and spellcasting.

Ghostdragon

http://www.ghostdragon.net

This site provides a compilation of international information about witchcraft.

The Teen Wiccan Page

http://members.xoom.com/YoungWitches

This site is specifically designed for teen witches.

CHAPTER 10: EVERYONE HAS A STORY

Biographical Dictionary

http://www.s9.com/biography

This online dictionary covers more than 28,000 notable men and women who have shaped our world from ancient times to the present day.

Biography-Center

http://www.biography-center.com

A searchable, multilingual biographical directory.

The Biography Maker

http://www.bham.wednet.edu/bio/biomaker.htm

Produced by Bellingham Public Schools, this site will help you convert basic facts into a well-written and lively biography.

Lives, the Biography Resource

http://amillionlives.com

This site provides a collection of thousands of annotated links to biography sites.

Memorable Canadians

http://www.nlc-bnc.ca/8/2/index-e.html

This new Web-based biographical index is available through the National Library of Canada's Web site.

CHAPTER 11: MULTICULTURALISM

McGraw-Hill Multicultural Supersite

http://www.mhhe.com/socscience/education/multi

This site, prepared by Paul Gorski, coordinator at the Student Intercultural Learning Center of the University of Maryland, College Park, focuses on teacher resources for multicultural education.

Multicultural Pavilion

http://curry.edschool.virginia.edu/go/multicultural

Another excellent site created by multicultural educator Paul Gorski.

National Organization for Multicultural Education

http://www.nameorg.org

Canadian Council for Multicultural and Intercultural Education

http://www.ccmie.com

Diversity Database

http://www.inform.umd.edu/EdRes/Topic/Diversity

The University of Maryland's index of multicultural, multiracial, and multigenerational diversity resources.

Tolerance.org

http://www.tolerance.org

This Web site has a special section for teens and children called Planet Tolerance. The Do Something section contains suggestions on how to promote equity at the local, regional, and national levels.

Index

ecology and the environment, 15–31
environmental literature, selection of, 15–16
environmental organizations, 17–18, 22–23; rock music
    and, 18–20
Eva, 69, 70–71

filters (Internet), 82–87

graphic novels, 47–60; manga, 56–58; selection of,
    49–50
gymnasts, 109–11

horror literature, 33–46; anthologies of, 37–38; appeal of,
    36–40; booktalking, 40–41; censorship, 41–46; defined,
    33–35; history of, 33; reference books, 37

Internet, 73–101; access policies, 90–91; censorship, 91–94;
    evaluation, 94–96; filtering, 82–87; parents and, 87–90;
    'zines, 96–98

manga, 56–58
Maus, 50
multicultural: holidays, 190–93; magazines, 182–84;
    movies, 184–88; music, 188–90; organizations,
    193–94; programming, 175–78; Web sites, 194–95
multicultural collection building, 178–82; annotated
    bibliographies, 179–80; annotated lists, 180–81;

review sources, 178–79; sourcebooks, 180; Web sites,
    181–82
multiculturalism, 175–98

North York Public Library (Ontario), 78–82

ringette, 117–19

science fiction, 61–71; defined, 61, 62; feminism and,
    66–70; history of, 62–64; in the classroom, 70–71;
    selection guides, 64–66
self-help books, 167–69
sports, 103–22; nutrition and, 111–15; steroids and, 106–9;
    women and, 115–19
Suzuki, David, 21–22, 30–31

Web sites, creating and maintaining, 74–78
Wicca, 145–47
witchcraft, 143–57; appeal of, 147–48; censorship and, 153–54;
    facts about, 143–44; fiction resources, 154–55; interview
    with a witch, 150–53; motion pictures and, 155–56; non-
    fiction resources, 155; popular culture and, 148–50; tele-
    vision and, 155; Web sites, 156–57; Wicca, 145–47

YA Hotline, history, ix–xi
Young Drivers of Canada, 124–25

'zines on the Web, 96–98

Contributors

Larry Amey taught young adult literature at the School of Library and Information Studies at Dalhousie University and was, for many years, the editor of the *YA Hotline*. He is now retired and living in Australia.

Jill Anderson (issue 58) is an information specialist in Ottawa, Ontario.

Annette Anthony (issue 57) is a librarian at the College of the North Atlantic in St. John's, Newfoundland.

Tanya Boudreau (issue 62) is a youth services librarian in Saskatoon, Saskatchewan.

Amber Butler (Lannon) (issue 59) is a librarian in Vancouver, British Columbia.

Carolyn Carpan (issue 57) is a reference librarian/ assistant professor at Rollins College, Florida.

Elizabeth Clinton (issue 61) is a reference librarian in Grants Pass, Oregon.

Alison Creech (issue 57) is a youth services librarian in the Halifax Regional Library, Halifax, Nova Scotia.

Nadine d'Entremont (issue 64) is a public librarian in Toronto, Ontario.

Kelly Dunne (issue 62) is a records specialist in Toronto, Ontario.

Ilana Ferris (issue 55) is a reference librarian in Eugene, Oregon.

Jacqueline Greenough (issue 58) is a library technician at Georges P. Vanier Junior High School, Fall River, Nova Scotia.

David Hansen (issue 46) is a reference librarian with the Halifax Regional Library, Halifax, Nova Scotia.

Vivian Howard currently teaches classes in young adult literature at Dalhousie University's School of Library and Information Studies. She is also the editor of the *YA Hotline* newsletter.

Catherine Hoyt (issue 53) is a legislative librarian in the northern Canadian territory of Nunavut.

Karen Hutchens (issue 61) is an adult/youth services librarian in Saskatoon, Saskatchewan.

Jacqueline James (issue 55) is a library assistant in Ontario.

Elizabeth Jones (issue 46) is a retired teacher-librarian in Halifax, Nova Scotia.

Rachel Kelly (issue 64) is an assistant public library branch manager in Queens, New York.

Doreen Landry (Metcalfe) (issue 53) is a children's librarian in Leominster, Massachusetts.

Elsa Maan (issue 59) is a teacher-librarian in Nova Scotia.

Sharon MacKinnon (issue 53) lives in Halifax, Nova Scotia.

Joy Masselink (issue 64) is a planning officer in Halifax, Nova Scotia.

Lara McAllister (issue 56) is a librarian at the Bedford Library in Lower Sackville, Nova Scotia.

Sarah McClare (issue 59) is a reference librarian in Lower Sackville, Nova Scotia.

David McDonald (issue 59) is a Medianet application specialist in Halifax, Nova Scotia.

Vanessa Menor (issue 62) is a youth services librarian in Wellington, Florida.

Jeff Mercer (issue 61) is an automation specialist with the Nova Scotia Provincial Library in Halifax.

Cameron Metcalf (issue 58) is a librarian at the Ottawa Hospital in Ottawa, Ontario.

Patricia Oakley (issue 61) is a librarian at the University of New Brunswick.

Rhonda O'Neill (issue 57) is a courthouse librarian at the Nunavut Court of Justice in Iqaluit, Nunavut.

Michelle Paon (issue 57) is a reference librarian at Dalhousie University in Halifax, Nova Scotia.

Wayne Paquet (issue 55) is a systems librarian in Truro, Nova Scotia.

Karen Parusel (issue 55) is with the Technology and Science Secretariat in Halifax, Nova Scotia.

Kathleen MacLeod Prentiss (issue 46) is the manager of cataloguing and processing at the Halifax Regional Library in Lower Sackville, Nova Scotia.

Nathalie Richard (issue 61) is a freelance editor.

Wendy Richardson (issue 46) is a teacher in Nova Scotia.

Joanie Sebastian (issue 64) is a librarian in Des Plaines, Illinois.

Denise Somers (issue 44) is an adult services librarian in Nova Scotia.

Patricia Stachiw (issue 62) is a librarian in Queens, New York.

Mary V. Thornton (issue 57) is a community librarian in Washington State.

Sue Watson (issue 56) is the project coordinator at the Ecology Action Centre in Halifax, Nova Scotia.

Ruby B. Weinshenker (issue 44) is a youth service librarian in Vancouver, British Columbia.

Tamara Weterings (issue 61) is a librarian at the National YMCA Office in Toronto, Ontario.

Carolyn Whalen (issue 62) lives in Calgary, Alberta.

Cory Williams (issue 59) is an assistant librarian in Sydney, Nova Scotia.

Muriel M. Zimmer (issue 44) is a teacher librarian at King's-Edgehill School in Windsor, Nova Scotia.